Hidden Champions in the Chinese Century

Hermann Simon

Hidden Champions in the Chinese Century

Ascent and Transformation

Hermann Simon
Founder and Honorary Chairman
Simon-Kucher and Partners
Bonn, Germany

ISBN 978-3-030-92596-3   ISBN 978-3-030-92597-0   (eBook)
https://doi.org/10.1007/978-3-030-92597-0

© The Editor(s) (if applicable) and The Author(s), under exclusive license to Springer Nature Switzerland AG 2022
This work is subject to copyright. All rights are solely and exclusively licensed by the Publisher, whether the whole or part of the material is concerned, specifically the rights of reprinting, reuse of illustrations, recitation, broadcasting, reproduction on microfilms or in any other physical way, and transmission or information storage and retrieval, electronic adaptation, computer software, or by similar or dissimilar methodology now known or hereafter developed.
The use of general descriptive names, registered names, trademarks, service marks, etc. in this publication does not imply, even in the absence of a specific statement, that such names are exempt from the relevant protective laws and regulations and therefore free for general use.
The publisher, the authors and the editors are safe to assume that the advice and information in this book are believed to be true and accurate at the date of publication. Neither the publisher nor the authors or the editors give a warranty, expressed or implied, with respect to the material contained herein or for any errors or omissions that may have been made. The publisher remains neutral with regard to jurisdictional claims in published maps and institutional affiliations.

This Springer imprint is published by the registered company Springer Nature Switzerland AG
The registered company address is: Gewerbestrasse 11, 6330 Cham, Switzerland

Contents

Part I   The Concept and Its Reception

1 A Brief History of the Hidden Champions — 3
Mittelstand — 4
The Discovery — 4
The Global Dimension — 5
Publications — 5
References — 6

2 Hidden Champions and Export Success — 7
Large Companies or SMEs? — 8
Hidden Champions and Germany's Image — 10
References — 11

3 Hidden Champions: The Definition — 13
Market Position — 13
Revenue — 14
Name Awareness — 14
Standard Definition — 15
Reference — 15

4 Why Are There Hidden Champions? — 17
Division of Labor — 18
Increasing Market Size — 18

v

Standardization of Markets ... 18
Deepening of the Value Chain ... 19
Product Diversity ... 20
Little Things ... 20
Communication and Logistics ... 21
References ... 22

5 Reception of the Hidden Champions Concept ... 23
Politics ... 23
Business ... 24
Press and Literature ... 25
Education ... 26
Academic Research ... 26
References ... 27

Part II The Ascent of the Hidden Champions

6 Hidden Champions Worldwide ... 31
Hidden Champions by Country ... 31
Structures ... 33
Emerging Countries ... 33
The Question of Global Validity ... 35
References ... 35

7 German Hidden Champions ... 37
Market Position ... 37
Revenue ... 38
Employment ... 39
Age ... 40
Regional Distribution ... 41
References ... 43

8 Austrian and Swiss Hidden Champions ... 45
Austrian Hidden Champions ... 45
Regional Distribution ... 46
Swiss Hidden Champions ... 47
Regional Distribution ... 47

	Reference	49
9	**Decades of Ascent**	**51**
	From Hidden Champion to Fortune Global 500	51
	Beyond €5 billion	52
	Approaching the €1-billion Threshold	53
	From Dwarf to Hidden Champion	54
	What Drives This Ascent?	54
10	**Why Are There So Many Hidden Champions in Germany?**	**57**
	No Nation State	57
	Decentralization	58
	Dual Vocational Training	58
	Manufacturing Base	59
	Productivity	59
	Regional Ecosystems	60
	Central Location	60
	Mental Internationalization	60
	Made in Germany	61
	References	61

Part III   The New Game of Globalization

11	**On Rough Roads to Globalia**	**65**
	Global Per Capita Exports	65
	Global Exports since 1990	66
	Global Service Exports	68
	Foreign Direct Investments	70
	References	71
12	**Quo Vadis Globalia: Population and Economy**	**73**
	Population Dynamics	74
	Economic Power and Growth	75
	The Population-Economy-Divide	77
	References	78

13 Quo Vadis Globalia: Dynamic Framework — 79
Winners of Globalization — 79
More Globalization? — 81
Transforming Globalization — 82
Declining Transport Costs — 84
Dematerialization — 85
Location-Competence Assimilation — 85
Travel or Zoom? — 87
References — 88

14 Target Market America — 91
America vs. China — 91
Transatlantica: A Failed Dream? — 92
Challenge USA — 93
Higher Priority for the US Market — 94
Overcoming Barriers — 95
Capital Market USA — 96
References — 97

15 Target Market China — 99
Pioneers in the Chinese Market — 100
German Hidden Champions in China — 100
Where China Is Tops — 101
Innovation from China — 102
China as Test Market — 102
Chinese Hidden Champions — 104
Chinese Hidden Champions in Germany — 107
Greenfield Plants — 109
Entrepreneurial Cooperation — 110
The Political Dimension — 110
References — 111

Part IV The New Game of Transformative Forces

16 Business Ecosystems — 115
Industry Clusters as Business Ecosystems — 116
The Tuttlingen Medical Technology Ecosystem — 117

Contents   ix

    The Jena Photonics Ecosystem   120
    Regional Importance of Ecosystems   120
    Entrepreneurial Business Ecosystems   121
    The ASML-Trumpf-Zeiss SMT Ecosystem   122
    The MK Technology Ecosystem   123
    On the Future of Business Ecosystems   124
    References   125

17 Digitalization   127
    Radical or Incremental?   127
    B2C vs. B2B   128
    Digital Products   129
    Digital Industrial Processes   131
    Digital Services   133
    Digital Ecosystems   135
    Monetization   136
    Conclusion   137
    References   138

18 Sustainability   141
    Sustainability as a Major Transformation   142
    The Role of Consumers   142
    Drivers of Sustainability   143
    Investors as Drivers   143
    ESG Ratings   144
    Sustainability and the Long Term   144
    Sustainable Products and Processes   145
    Social Sustainability   148
    References   149

19 Innovation   151
    Patents   151
    World-Class Patents   152
    Patents in Germany   153
    The Gartner Hype Cycle   154
    Incremental Innovations   155
    Breakthrough Innovations   155
    KSB Additive Manufacturing   156

x   Contents

Volocopter 156
Lilium 156
Torqeedo 157
Hydrogen Train iLint 157
Ottobock Orthobionics 157
Disinfection with UV-C LED 158
Va-Q-Tec Thermoboxes 158
Graforce 158
Magnetically Levitated Train TSB 159
Vectoflow 159
Twaice Battery Analytics 159
Combustion Chambers for SpaceX Rockets 160
Flying Dogs, Smart Birds, and Chameleons 160
Quantum Sensor 161
Innovation Processes 161
References 162

Part V The New Game of Strategy

20 Ambition 167
Market Leadership 168
Will 169
Competence 170
Opportunities 171
The New Game: Ambition 171
References 171

21 Focus 173
Product Focus 174
Customer Focus 174
Focus and Investors 175
Multidimensional Focus 175
Loss of Focus 176
The New Game: Focus 177
References 177

22 Depth — 179
- Depth of the Value Chain — 179
- Non-core Competencies — 180
- Uniqueness — 181
- Know-How Protection — 181
- Depth and Growth — 181
- Depth as a Millstone — 182
- New Competencies — 182
- Technology and Depth — 183
- The New Game: Depth — 184
- References — 184

23 Customers — 185
- Top Performance — 186
- Service — 187
- Systems Integration — 187
- Brand — 187
- Price — 188
- Focus on Top Customers — 188
- Customers as a Source of Innovation — 189
- No "No" Without the Boss — 190
- Employee–Customers — 191
- In-House Customers — 191
- Customers and Digitalization — 192
- The New Game: Customers — 193
- References — 193

24 Competition — 195
- Competitive Goals — 196
- Dynamics of Market Structures — 197
- Intensity of Competition — 198
- Soft Competitive Advantages — 198
- Price as a Competitive Disadvantage — 199
- New Pricing Models — 200
- Secondary Brands and LEAs — 200
- Competition and Ecosystems — 201
- Lighthouse Projects — 202
- The New Game: Competition — 203
- References — 204

Contents

25	**Organization**	205
	Functional Organization	205
	Multifunctionality	206
	Foreign Assignments	207
	Decentralization	207
	New Work Organization	208
	Divisional Organization	209
	The New Game: Organization	211
	References	211
26	**Profit and Finance**	213
	Profit	213
	Profit Stars	214
	Financing	216
	Initial Public Offering (IPO)	216
	Private Equity	217
	Strategic Investors	218
	The New Game: Profit and Finance	218
	References	219
27	**Employees and Leaders**	221
	Motivation	221
	Qualification	223
	Talent War	224
	Diversity and Inclusion	226
	The Leaders	227
	Leadership Continuity	227
	Young CEOs	228
	Female CEOs	229
	Internationalization of Management	229
	Leadership Styles	230
	The New Game: Employees and Leaders	231
	References	232
28	**The Future of the Hidden Champions**	233
	Sunset Industries	234
	Sunrise Industries	235
	Preserving Strengths	238

Specialization	238
Choice of Location	239
Capital	240
Global Citizens	240
Money or Fame	241
The New Game	242
References	243

Part I

The Concept and Its Reception

1

A Brief History of the Hidden Champions

"Why are German companies so successful at exporting?"

Harvard Professor Theodore Levitt asked me that question at a meeting in Dusseldorf in 1987. The previous year, Germany had become the world export champion for the first time, a spectacular success that he wanted to understand. He was very interested in the competitiveness of countries and companies and had recently popularized the term "globalization" through a highly regarded article in the *Harvard Business Review* [1].

The quest to answer his question evolved into a decades-long wave of research that led to the coining of another popular management term: Hidden Champions. If you search "Hidden Champions" on Google you get 1.75 million results [2].

The term did not exist in 1987 when Levitt asked me about the reasons behind Germany's export success. At that time, most people associated the German export performance primarily with large corporations such as Bayer, Siemens, Daimler, Volkswagen, Bosch, or E. Merck. These giants were already very successful exporters in the twentieth century. Like many other large German companies, they had been building international distribution networks since the nineteenth century. Bayer had entered the US market as early as 1864, and Bosch achieved more than half of its sales abroad before World War I. Siemens has been active in China since 1872. By comparison, small- and medium-sized enterprises (SMEs) were only beginning to internationalize in the 1980s.

Mittelstand

It is interesting to look at Professor Levitt's assessment of the prospects for the *Mittelstand* (the German phrase to describe the SMEs). At the conference in 1987, journalist Peter Hanser from the magazine *Absatzwirtschaft* interviewed Levitt and me and asked: "One problem of German industry is the large number of mid-sized companies with a high export share. Is global marketing a strategy for these companies?"

Levitt replied: "All companies started small. It is primarily the larger ones that have survived. The smaller family businesses, on the other hand, are struggling to survive" [3]. He was skeptical about the globalization opportunities for SMEs and saw large companies as the clear winners in the intensifying worldwide competition. Some 80% of all German companies belong to the Mittelstand, including craftsmen or the bakery on the corner. Most of them do not export. At the time, no one was thinking about the phenomenon of Hidden Champions.

The Discovery

While wrestling with Levitt's question, I noticed that a considerable number of Mittelstand companies were rapidly growing world market leaders whose contribution to German exports was steadily increasing. Could these SME market leaders explain Germany's extraordinary export performance? How many of these market leaders existed in Germany? How crucial were they to Germany's export success? And what were their strategies?

With questions like this in mind, I invited Daniel Klapper to write a master's thesis on the topic in 1989 [4]. He was a student at the University of Bielefeld and is now a professor at Humboldt University in Berlin. I tasked him with tracking down mid-sized world market leaders and collecting basic data on them.

Klapper identified 39 of these global market leaders. The results surprised me and inspired further research. These mid-sized companies were growing strong, had numerous international subsidiaries, and were successful even in a challenging market like Japan. Trumpf, the current global leader in laser machines, had expanded into the Japanese market in 1964. Karl Mayer, world market leader for warp knitting machines with a global market share of 75 percent, sold more of its products in Japan than in Germany. Lenze, a manufacturer of small gearboxes, had been cooperating closely with a Japanese company for many years. Such companies were real champions, but apart from a few specialists nobody knew them.

What would be a good name for these mid-sized global market leaders? The term "Hidden Champions" turned out to be a stroke of luck, not least because of the inherent contradiction of the two words. Champions are usually well-known. You don't expect them to be concealed or "hidden." The term generated curiosity and interest after I used it for the first time in a publication in September 1990 entitled "Hidden Champions—Spearheading the German Economy" [5] and shortly thereafter in an article in the *Harvard Business Review* [6]. In these early publications, it was still unclear how much these companies contributed to German exports as a whole and how many Hidden Champions there were in Germany.

Fast forward 30 years to 2021, and the roster of German Hidden Champions now contains 1573 companies that is 46.2% of all Hidden Champions identified in the world. Search for global market leaders in specific US cities on Google and you will almost always find more results for German companies than for American ones. This attests to the German Hidden Champions' impressive global presence. All these mid-sized German companies had an office, a branch, or a factory in the American cities we looked at.

The Global Dimension

The Hidden Champions concept has transcended its German origins to become a globally accepted strategy and management concept. I have identified thousands of them around the world and have personally met hundreds of the entrepreneurs behind them. The most astonishing insight for me has been that these hidden champions share remarkable similarities across national and cultural boundaries. This is true for their ambitions, their strategies, their leaders, and their corporate cultures.

Publications

Harvard Business School Press published my first book on the subject in 1996 under the title *Hidden Champions—Lessons from 500 of the World's Best Unknown Companies* [7]. Twelve years later, I published the second, completely rewritten, edition called *Hidden Champions of the 21st Century* [8]. The third edition from 2012—*Hidden Champions–Departure towards Globalia*—analyzed not only Hidden Champions from Germany but also from Austria and Switzerland [9]. In the meantime, my Hidden Champions books have been published in 26 countries. More than one million Hidden Champions books have been sold in China alone.

This is one of many indications that we are living in the Chinese century, a period in which China develops into an economic powerhouse. Beyond the continually strong growth rates for more than a generation, Chinese companies are now shoring up their historic relative weaknesses in areas such as quality, branding, marketing, and breakthrough innovations. I will cite many examples on how Chinese companies are making a concerted effort to implement the Hidden Champions concept. Some have already achieved impressive successes through shifts in strategy, organic growth, and key acquisitions.

References

1. Levitt, T. (1983, May/June). The globalization of markets. *Harvard Business Review*, pp. 92–102. The term "globalization" first appeared in 1917, but did not become common until 1983.
2. www.google.com, accessed on 5 April, 2021.
3. Hanser, P. (1987). ASW discussion with Theodore Levitt and Hermann Simon. *Absatzwirtschaft, 8*, 20–22.
4. Klapper, D. (1989). *Internationale Erfolgsstrategien mittlerer Unternehmen.* Dissertation, University of Bielefeld.
5. Simon, H. (1990). Hidden Champions—Speerspitze der deutschen Wirtschaft. *Zeitschrift für Betriebswirtschaft, 60*(9), 875–890.
6. Simon, H. (1992). Lessons from Germany's midsize giants. *Harvard Business Review, 70*, 115–123.
7. Simon, H. (1996). *Hidden champions–Lessons from 500 of the world's best unknown companies*, Boston: Harvard Business School Press.
8. Simon, H. (2009). *Hidden Champions of the 21st century*, New York: Springer; German edition: Simon, H. (2007). *Hidden Champions des 21. Jahrhunderts–Die Erfolgsstrategien unbekannter Weltmarktführer*, Frankfurt: Campus.
9. Simon, H. (2012). *Hidden Champions—Aufbruch nach Globalia.* Frankfurt: Campus.

2

Hidden Champions and Export Success

Ted Levitt's question about the roots of the spectacular German export success was not easy to answer. But one fact is indisputable: Germany has sustained its exceptional export performance for more than three decades since he posed his question. Figure 2.1 shows the total exports of the 10 largest exporting countries for the period 2010–2019.[1]

China succeeded Germany as the world's export champion in 2009 and has held the top position ever since. The United States is likewise ahead of Germany in terms of absolute exports. However, the economies of those two countries are many times larger than Germany's. The dominant export performance of German companies clearly stands out in the per capita comparison shown in Fig. 2.2.

In terms of per capita exports, Germany is an extreme outlier among major countries, particularly compared with its European neighbors. One would expect that France, Italy, the UK, and Spain would have higher per capita exports than Germany, because countries with smaller populations typically have higher per capita exports than larger countries. In Germany's case, the opposite is true. German per capita exports tend to be at least twice as high of those of its large European neighbors, even though they are all roughly the same geographical distance away from important markets such as the USA or China. What explains these enormous discrepancies? There is no simple explanation, but the number of Hidden Champions in a country may well play an important role.

---

[1] I deliberately chose the 10 years up to 2019 as the 2020 numbers are heavily distorted by COVID-19.

© The Author(s), under exclusive license to Springer Nature Switzerland AG 2022
H. Simon, *Hidden Champions in the Chinese Century*,
https://doi.org/10.1007/978-3-030-92597-0_2

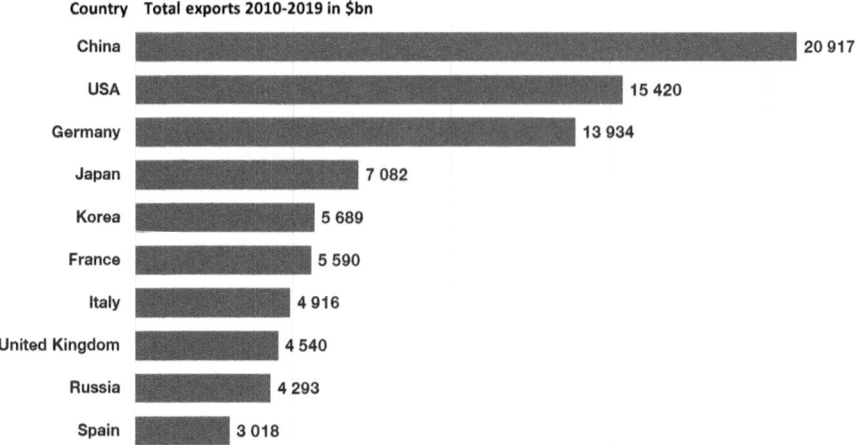

Fig. 2.1 Total exports of the largest exporting countries, 2010–2019

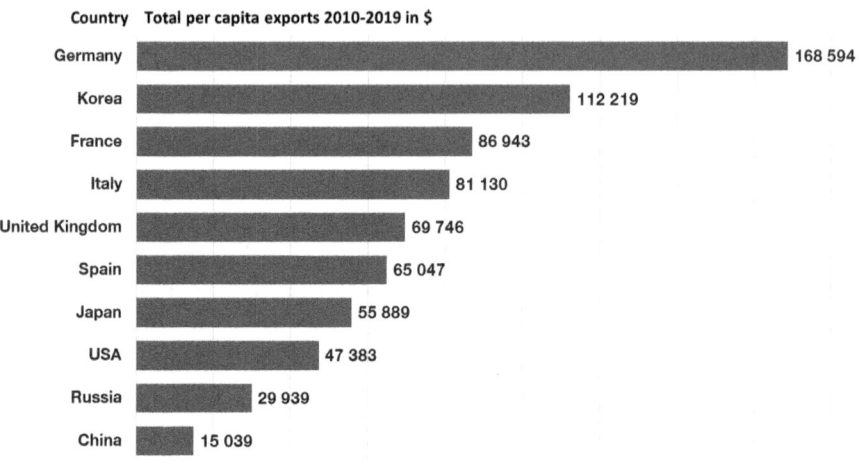

Fig. 2.2 Per capita exports of the largest exporting countries, 2010–2019

Large Companies or SMEs?

We can thank Harvard professor Marc Melitz for the rather obvious insight that national export statistics are an artifact [1]. Companies—not countries—are the real exporters, and, according to Melitz, "only the best can handle business with foreign countries" [2]. Only the best are able to produce internationally competitive products and sell them at profitable prices. As Levitt's answer in the 1987 interview revealed, the large, globally active corporations

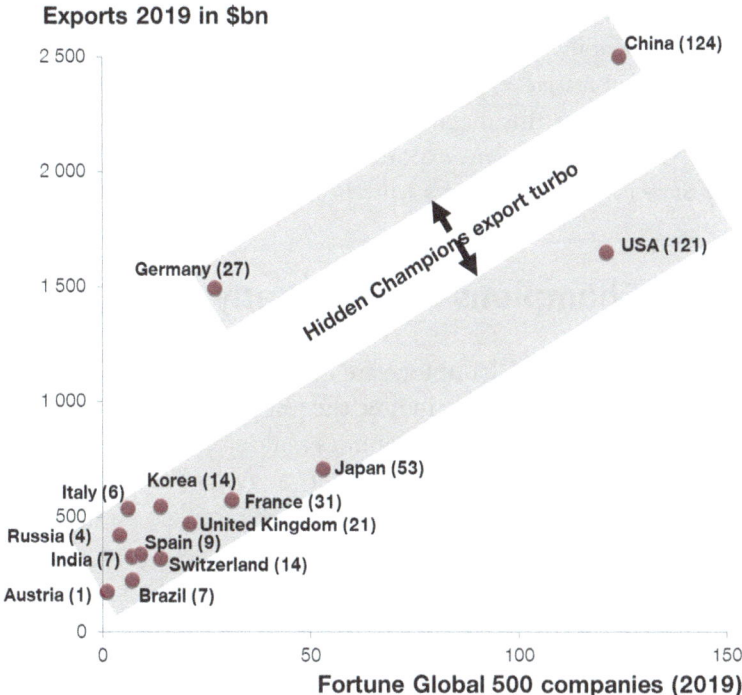

Fig. 2.3 Number of Fortune Global 500 companies and exports, by country

like those in the Fortune Global 500 are more likely than mid-sized companies to have these abilities. Does this mean that the number of large firms in a country can explain its export performance?

Figure 2.3 attempts to answer this question. The horizontal axis shows the number of Fortune Global 500 companies in each country.[2] These are the 500 largest firms in the world. The vertical axis shows the respective country's exports.

The hypothesis that large companies determine a country's export performance is true for most countries. There is an almost linear relationship between the number of large corporations and export performance for the USA, Japan, France, Korea, the UK, Italy, and Spain. Only China and Germany deviate from this pattern—precisely the two countries that are number one in absolute and in per capita exports, respectively. China and Germany are very different in so many ways, so what do they have in common? In China, about two-thirds of all exports come from mid-sized companies, and the export share

---

[2] Cf. *Fortune*, August–September 2020, S. F1-F22. Number of companies and export figures for 2019.

of SMEs in Germany is similar.[3] Not every SME exports, which means there is a high probability that the Hidden Champions are a major driver behind Germany's impressive export success. The Hidden Champions Fund from Singapore supports this diagnosis: "The Hidden Champions form the backbone of Germany's resilient export-driven economy. They have their roots in the *esprit de corps* of Germany's Mittelstand" [3].

Hidden Champions and Germany's Image

Although the Hidden Champions are not well-known individually, they play an important role collectively in how the rest of the world perceives Germany. In international business and economics rankings, Germany is usually among the top 10 in the world. A study by *U.S. News and World Report* ranked Germany fourth [4]. The Wharton School even ranked Germany as the "best country in the world." Still more surprisingly, when it came to entrepreneurship, the study's author, Professor David Reibstein, saw Germany at the top: "The top nation for entrepreneurs isn't the United States. It's Germany" [5].

In recent books by foreign authors, Germany is increasingly portrayed in a positive light. They explicitly mention and recognize the Mittelstand and especially the Hidden Champions. The British author John Kampfer writes: "Most of all, it is the smaller firms that set Germany apart. Hermann Simon has coined the term Hidden Champions. These are success stories of globalization and free trade. Half of them come from Germany. The USA, Japan, and China follow, a long way behind. Other European countries are nowhere in sight" [6].

Germans' own perception of their country tends to be more skeptical, but even very critical authors emphasize the positive role of small- and mid-sized enterprises and the Hidden Champions. Gabor Steingart, a well-known journalist, writes: "With inventiveness and tenacity, courage and modesty, the Hidden Champions work the global markets" [7]. The Hidden Champions make a decisive contribution to Germany's image and reputation. They are "the secret force of Germany."

---

[3] The Economist reported already in 2009 that 68% of Chinese exports come from companies with less than 2000 employees (cf. 2009. "Small Fish in a Big Pond," *The Economist*, September 10). Our estimate is that this share remains unchanged if you look at companies with less 4000 employees.

References

1. Melitz, M., Mayer, T., & Ottaviano, G. (2014). Market size, competition, and the product mix of exporters. *American Economic Review, 104*(2), 495–536.
2. N.A. (2104, May 5). Nur die stärksten Unternehmen exportieren. *Frankfurter Allgemeine Zeitung*, p. 18.
3. Retrieved 1 May, 2020, from https://hiddenchampionsfund.com/.
4. Retrieved from https://www.usnews.com/media/best-countries/overall-rankings-2020.pdf.
5. Retrieved 15 May, 2016, from https://knowledge.wharton.upenn.edu/article/entrepreneurial-country-world/.
6. Kampfner, J. (2020). *Why the Germans do it better: Notes from a grown-up country*, London: Atlantic Books, p. 84. See also Neiman, S. (2019). *Learning from the Germans*, New York: MacMillan.
7. Steingart, G. (2020). *Die unbequeme Wahrheit—Rede zur Lage unserer Nation* (p. 84). Munich: Penguin Verlag.

3

Hidden Champions: The Definition

To be classified as a Hidden Champion, a company must meet three criteria:

1. It must be among the top 3 in the world in its market, or number 1 on its continent.
2. Its revenue must be less than €5 billion.
3. It must have a low level of awareness among the general public.

With the exception of the revenue ceiling, I have applied these criteria consistently since the 1990s.

Market Position

The market position of Hidden Champions is usually defined by market share, which in most cases is based on the companies' own assessments. It is impossible to verify data on market positions for thousands of companies. In addition, market positions and market shares depend on the definition of the market, which is necessarily subjective and open to debate. In fragmented markets, one cannot always quantify market shares precisely. It is often easier to estimate relative market positions, i.e., whether a company ranks first, second, or third. Some Hidden Champions describe themselves as "one of the market leaders" without being able to express their market share or market position in exact numbers. I have personally checked the data for all German Hidden Champions covered in my study. Nonetheless, some subjective assessments are inevitable.

Revenue

The revenue criterion is the only one that has changed. In the first Hidden Champions book, the revenue ceiling was $1 billion (the € did not exist in 1996). In 2007, I raised the upper limit to €3 billion and finally to €5 billion in 2012. These caps reflect the strong growth of Hidden Champions in recent decades. For this book, I had considered raising the upper limit to €10 billion, but ultimately refrained from doing so, because only a few companies from my original list exceed the €5 billion limit. Now, €5 billion of revenue may seem high as an upper limit for a mid-sized company. This figure must be seen in a global context, especially in comparison with the largest corporations. The Fortune Global 500 averaged $66.6 billion in revenue in 2019, and even the smallest of them generated $25.4 billion.[1] The maximum revenue of Hidden Champions is therefore less than one-tenth of the average of the Fortune Global 500, or one-fifth of the smallest company. By global standards, a company with €2 or €3 billion in sales is a mid-sized company, not a large one. The average revenue of the German Hidden Champions is €467 million. I do not set a lower revenue limit because in the age of modern communication and logistics even small enterprises can serve customers all over the world and achieve globally leading market positions. That's a fundamental difference from the times when worldwide marketing was rare and not very realistic for small companies. However, companies with sales of less than €10 million account for only 2% of the German Hidden Champions.

Name Awareness

The third criterion is a low level of awareness among the general public. I refrained from quantifying this criterion in precise numbers. I excluded some companies which fulfill the first two criteria, but have a high brand awareness. Examples are Haribo (gummi bears), Jägermeister (liqueurs), and Melitta (coffee filters). I am sure that almost all of the Hidden Champions in my list are not known to the general public on a global scale.

---

[1] *Fortune*, August/September 2020.

Standard Definition

The definition with a global or continental market-leading position, the upper revenue limit of €5 billion, and the low level of name awareness have become established in the literature. A survey of 94 academic articles on the Hidden Champions, the most comprehensive of its kind to date, states: "Simon's definition has become firmly established in the research field. 88 of the 94 publications follow Simon's definition of Hidden Champions" [1]. If more than 90% of academic researchers dealing with the subject adopt the definition, one can justifiably call it a standard.

Reference

1. Julian Schenkenhofer, J. (2020). Hidden champions: A review of the literature and future research avenues. *Working Paper Series 06-20*, Chair of Management and Organization, University of Augsburg, p. 9.

4

Why Are There Hidden Champions?

In light of the fact that we have tracked down several thousand Hidden Champions around the world, it seems odd to ask why Hidden Champions even exist at all. If we look back 200 years, there were essentially no mid-sized companies that were also global market leaders. A typical mid-sized company in those days was limited to its home country or, at best, neighboring small states.

The rare exceptions included trading companies such as the Fugger dynasty, which was already doing business throughout Europe in the fifteenth century and was Europe's number one in copper. Fugger would have qualified as a Hidden Champion according to our definition. Later, companies such Estado da India (Portugal), Dutch East India Company (Holland), and the East India Company (England) expanded their businesses to Asia. England's East India Company accounted for half of world trade, making it the world market leader. Of course, these companies were not only economic, but also political heavyweights and hardly "hidden." The East India Company at times had 260,000 soldiers under contract, twice as many as the British army.

Why is this fundamentally different today? What has contributed to the emergence of the large number of mid-sized, little-known global market leaders? Not surprisingly, this development does not have a single origin, but rather a mix of several causes.

Division of Labor

Adam Smith first recognized and popularized the advantages of the division of labor in his famous work, "An Inquiry into the Nature and Causes of the Wealth of Nations," published in 1776 [1]. Increasing division of labor means that generalists who manufacture an entire product give way to specialists who manufacture only individual components, which are then assembled by a final product manufacturer, a so-called OEM (original equipment manufacturer). Huge productivity gains result from specializing in making individual components. However, division of labor and specialization only work if a market is sufficiently large. According to Adam Smith, "The division of labor is limited by the size of the market" [2]. That explains why small towns only have general grocers with a limited assortment, while big cities will have specialty stores.

Increasing Market Size

To take advantage of the opportunities offered by the division of labor, one must enlarge the market areas served by specialists. This enlargement can occur in a variety of ways. For example, previously separate markets can merge and remove barriers to trade. Examples include the formation of the German Empire from many small states in the nineteenth century, the European Union and its predecessors, and the abolition of tariffs through free trade agreements. Market expansion can also emerge after peace agreements, such as the transformation of the Franco-German "hereditary enmity" into a friendship between the two countries, or the fall of the Iron Curtain, which freed the Austrian economy from its border location. In larger markets, a specialist serving only a small niche can grow to considerable size. This is precisely the strategy of Hidden Champions when they expand the limited market potential of the local or national niche through internationalization to the point of globalization.

Standardization of Markets

The standardization or homogenization of markets is not the same as enlargement. The difference between the United States and the European Union demonstrates this. Both markets are similar in size, but while the USA forms one largely homogeneous market, the EU still comprises 27 individual markets. The disparity between the EU countries derives from numerous factors such as language, currency (only 15 countries have the euro), standards, trade structures, and consumer habits. This has grave consequences for business expansion.

Uber tested its system in San Francisco for a few years and was then able to roll it out in New York and other major American cities without major modifications. In Europe, a similar expansion requires overcoming language, cultural, and bureaucratic barriers. This increases both costs and the time required. Modern, so-called "born global" markets such as smartphones, software, and the Internet are standardized from the outset so that internationalization costs less, can proceed faster, and thus promotes the emergence of Hidden Champions. One important component is the standardization of language. With English, it is now possible to do business virtually anywhere in the world, although mastery of English still varies greatly from region to region. Adjusting to consumers' habits is still necessary in many markets.

Deepening of the Value Chain

Modern value chains are characterized by tremendous depth, an aspect closely related to specialization and the division of labor. Numerous suppliers contribute to a product as simple as a T-shirt, e.g., the sewing shop in Bangladesh, chemical manufacturers, cotton growers, machine builders, logistics companies, retailers, and other service providers. The supply chains are much more complex for car manufacturers, who directly or indirectly use parts and services from several thousand suppliers, who in turn obtain parts from subvendors. The supply chains in the electronics industry are similarly complex. Apple has 767 suppliers in Germany alone [3]. The individual parts of cars, computers, or smartphones come from many countries. Global value chains typically comprise numerous stages. It is doubtful whether so-called Supply Chain Acts, meant to sanction companies for supplier misconduct, take this enormous complexity into account. Michael Stietz, head of purchasing at the Körber Group, which includes several Hidden Champions, says: "If we are to be held accountable for the entire supply chain, including the suppliers of our suppliers, then we quickly arrive at a six-digit number, i.e., more than 100,000 different companies scattered all over the world, about which we have to collect and evaluate data" [4]. That is clearly an unmanageable burden, especially for mid-sized companies and globally active Hidden Champions.

Product Diversity

If you ask people on the street what "the economy" is, they usually name large industries and companies whose products and services they know from their own experience, such as the automotive industry, telecommunications, retailers, banks, and Internet companies like Google or Facebook. These visible industries and companies are only parts of the economy. No one knows exactly how many discrete markets there are in the world, but the number is certainly very high. Amazon alone carries 229 million items [5]. Perhaps only 2% of all markets are large markets, and the remaining 98% are medium, small, and niche markets. Many of these markets have traditionally been local, and many will remain so, but the number of globalizing markets is growing all the time. Sectors such as fast food, cafés, drugstores, catering, and scientific publishing are already well advanced in this respect. Sectors that are still highly regulated today, such as transport or pharmacies, are likely to follow a similar path in the future.

Little Things

There are countless small everyday things that people take for granted without thinking about the fact that someone has to produce and distribute them. Each of these markets of "little things" offers the opportunity to build up a Hidden Champion position. The market potential becomes attractive and relevant for mid-sized companies when they can operate such businesses worldwide. There are numerous Hidden Champions that produce such tiny everyday things. Most of the companies listed in Table 4.1 are global market leaders.
While the value of the individual item is low, the unit volumes are enormous. M + C Schiffer produces 1.3 million toothbrushes per day. Lined up in a row, the annual production would cover a distance of 760,000 km, or 19 times the circumference of the earth. At Schott, the unit prices for pharmaceutical packaging made of glass are between 3 and 10 cents, and the average price is 5 cents. However, 11 billion units for this product category alone add up to a remarkable €550 million in sales [6]. The world is full of business opportunities, even with little things. Hidden Champions have often seized these opportunities as pioneers and achieved leading market positions worldwide.

Table 4.1 Hidden Champions in markets with small products but large unit volumes

Hidden Champion	Product	Number of units
Kalle	Sausage casings	850 million/year
Heitkamp & Thumann	Battery cans	10 billion/year
Anton Häring	Precision turned parts	2.5 million/day
Spies Kunststoffe	1-substance packaging	1.2 billion/year
Schott	Pharmaceutical packaging	11 billion/year
OKE Group	Profile extrusion	80,000 km/year
Sanner	Desiccants for packaging	2 billion/year
Reline Europe	Sewer rehabilitation	700,000 m/year
Gottschalk	Staples	12 million/day
Lübke & Vogt	Molded rubber parts	1.5 billion/year
Rohi	Fabric covers for aircraft seats	7,000,000 m/year
Alupak	Nespresso capsules	9 billion/year
Bericap	Closures for beverage bottles	86 billion/year
Ludo Fact	Board games	70,000/day
Utsch	License plates	Hundreds of millions/year
BHS Tabletop	Hotel China	40 million/year
Job	Thermo bulbs/sprinkler triggers	1.2 billion/year
LTS Lohmann	Transdermal therapy	770 million/year
Rhenoflex	Caps for shoes	1 billion/year
Aenova	Tablets, capsules	28 billion/year
M+C Schiffer	Toothbrushes	1.3 million/day
Hello Fresh	Cooking boxes	280 million/year
Prym	Snap fasteners	15 million/day

Communication and Logistics

Exploiting the opportunities of expanded markets requires the ability to communicate with business partners in the whole world and to get one's goods to them easily and cost-effectively. Modern information technology and globally functioning logistics systems are very recent developments that play an important role in the emergence of Hidden Champions. Some 22% of German Hidden Champions have annual sales of less than €50 million. In the past, this was not a revenue category with which to be globally active, but today these small Hidden Champions sell their products and services all over the world. The "global village" predicted by Canadian communications scientist Marshal McLuhan has become a reality [7].

Logistics in this context refers not only to the transportation of goods, but also to the people who are constantly traveling around the world to keep their global businesses running. They include salespeople, planning engineers, service technicians, and assemblers. A small company like Klais, based in Bonn, Germany, has only 65 employees, but builds top-quality pipe organs in New

Zealand, Japan, China, the United States, Argentina, Israel, and other countries. This is only possible with state-of-the-art communications and efficient logistics systems for products and personnel.

References

1. Smith, A. (1993). *An inquiry into the nature and causes of the wealth of nations.* Hackett Publishing.
2. Smith, A. (2012). *Untersuchung über Wesen und Ursachen des Reichtums der Völker* (p. 101). Mohr Siebeck.
3. Retrieved from https://www.tagesspiegel.de/wirtschaft/zulieferfirmen-so-viel-deutschland-steckt-im-iphone/24057266.html#:~:text=Bosch,f%C3%BCr%20das%20iPhone%208%20herstellt.
4. Giersberg, G. (2020, August 12). Interview with Michael Stietz, *Frankfurter Allgemeine Zeitung*, p. 22.
5. Retrieved from https://de.statista.com/infografik/7849/bei-amazon-deutschland-gelistete-produkte/#:~:text=Rund%20229%20Millionen%20Produkte%20bietet,gegen%C3%BCber%202014%20mehr%20als%20verdoppelt.
6. Freytag, B. (2020, June 30). Impfstoffampullen für die Welt. *Frankfurter Allgemeine Zeitung*, p. 22.
7. McLuhan, M. (1962). *The Gutenberg galaxy: The making of typographic man.* University of Toronto Press.

5

Reception of the Hidden Champions Concept

From the beginning, the Hidden Champions concept has experienced broad and sustained interest in politics, business, the press, education, and academic research. The huge number of 1.75 million "Hidden Champions" entries in Google shows that this strong reception is worldwide and not confined to German-speaking countries.[1]

Politics

In 2017, the concept made it into the contract of the grand coalition that formed the German government: "Many small and mid-sized enterprises are innovation leaders worldwide. This is demonstrated by the German 'Hidden Champions' with their top position in certain technology fields" [1]. The Internet portal of North Rhine-Westphalia, the largest state in Germany, says: "Hidden Champions are extremely successful and make a major contribution to NRW's good image abroad. One in four German world market leaders is based in North Rhine-Westphalia!" [2, 3].

Numerous regional business initiatives and chambers of industry and commerce publish brochures with portraits of Hidden Champions from their region [4]. The German state Hesse offers a Hidden Champions Award for leading SMEs. In 2019, the Association of German Hidden Champions was

---

[1] Accessed on February 16, 2021. This number varies from day to day.

established.[2] Several large-scale Hidden Champions competitions have been held in Taiwan [5].

The Hidden Champions concept draws its strongest interest in China. At the beginning of 2021, the Chinese government launched an ambitious program to create 1000 Hidden Champions and acknowledged that the concept was first proposed by "the German management mastermind Hermann Simon" [6, 7]. It has allocated a budget of $1.3 billion for this program and formulated a detailed implementation plan [8]. Only three weeks after the official launch, a contact in Shandong province informed me that detailed directives had arrived at the local level. The China International Investment Promotion Agency (CIIPA) has organized dozens of Hidden Champions conferences in China.

Business

The Berlin-based company Avesco Financial Services operates a Sustainable Hidden Champions Equity Fund [9]. Singapore also has a Hidden Champions Fund that invests in mid-sized market leaders in the Asia–Pacific region [10]. In Zurich, James Breiding has launched a Hidden Champions Fund that focuses on eight small countries. He calls these countries the "S8" and has published a book on their outstanding performance [11]. The Zurich-based private bank Vontobel distributes a Hidden Champions Europe Ex-UK Ex-CH Share Basket, which contains a broad European selection of 36 Hidden Champions, including 12 from Germany.

Throughout the world, numerous companies have applied the Hidden Champions strategy. The example of one textile machinery manufacturer, who does not wish to be named, is typical: "With the help of the Hidden Champions strategy, we have become the world market leader. Today, our world market share is 70 percent, up from 40 percent ten years ago." The Chinese entrepreneur Yang Shuren learned about the concept in 2002 and applied it rigorously by radically trimming his sprawling product portfolio and globalizing his activities. His company, Shandong Moris Technologies, Ltd., is now the global market leader in three specialty chemicals.

---

[2] Initiators of the "Verband Deutscher Hidden Champions e.V." (VDHC), as the association is called in German, are Dieter Boening, Dieter Beste and Georg Türk.

Press and Literature

The Hidden Champions concept has enjoyed an enduring global presence in the media. The number of articles in newspapers and magazines runs into the thousands.

In the United States, *Business Week* devoted a cover story to the Hidden Champions in January 2004. Figure 5.1 shows Nerio Alessandri, CEO of the

Fig. 5.1 Hidden Champions on the cover of Business Week

Italian Hidden Champion Technogym.[3] Then, in 2019, *Forbes* ran a feature entitled "The Leadership Secrets of the Hidden Champions" [12].

The German TV station n-tv awards Hidden Champions prizes annually. A Hidden Champions lecture broadcast by Chinese state television CCTV and Tencent on various channels reached 20 million viewers [13]. Amazon lists more than 20 books (not counting my own) from various countries that have the term Hidden Champions in the title [14–16]. Recent books on Germany regularly portray Hidden Champions as pillars not only of the German economy, but of society as a whole. This applies equally to foreign and domestic authors [14, 15, 17–19].

Education

The European School of Management and Technology (ESMT) in Berlin has established the world's first Hidden Champions Institute (HCI) [20]. South Korea, meanwhile, boasts a Hidden Champions Management Institute [21]. In 2021, Zhejiang University in Hangzhou established the International Research Center for Hidden Champions and invited me to be an honorary director.[4] A new business school established in Shouguang, Shandong province, is dedicated to training according to the Hidden Champions concept. Figure 5.2 shows the building of the new school, which is named after me.

Academic Research

Over the years, I have received countless inquiries from undergraduate and graduate students who are working on topics related to Hidden Champions. Julian Schenkenhofer from the University of Augsburg writes, "I have been working on Hidden Champions for four years and have now assigned and supervised hundreds of seminar papers, bachelor's and master's theses on the subject. The students are crazy about this topic!"[5]

The research focus on Hidden Champions has increased sharply in recent years and I expect the trend to continue. Schenkenhofer presented a comprehensive and in-depth survey of academic Hidden Champions articles [22]. He analyzed 94 scientific publications and assigned them to four research

---

[3] *Business Week*, January 26, 2004.
[4] Invitation by the Dean, Faculty of Social Sciences, Zhejiang University, February 27, 2021.
[5] Personal E-Mail from Julian Schenkenhofer, July 30, 2020.

Fig. 5.2 Hermann Simon Business School in Shouguang, China

directions: internationalization, research and development/innovation, global distribution of Hidden Champions, and others. Over 80% of these research articles were written after 2010. The academic research has largely confirmed my own findings, most of which stem from my personal experience. One example is from Schenkenhofer's analysis: "Employees in Hidden Champions are more involved in the innovation process than in other companies, creating an organizational climate that particularly encourages innovation" [22].

References

1. N.A. (2018, February 7). *Ein neuer Aufbruch für Europa—Eine neue Dynamik für Deutschland—Ein neuer Zusammenhalt für unser Land*, coalition contract between the three parties in the German parliament that formed the government, Berlin, lines 2804–06.
2. Retrieved from https://www.land.nrw/ru/node/10564
3. IHK Schleswig-Holstein. (2019). *Made in Schleswig-Holstein, Weltmarkt- und Technologieführer im Portrait*. IHK Schleswig-Holstein.
4. IHK Südwestfalen (Ed.). (2018). *Directory of industrial global market leaders from Southern Westphalia* (5th ed.). IHK Südwestfalen.
5. Retrieved from https://english.ey.gov.tw/Page/61BF20C3E89B856/9543ee48-8e64-4d61-a413-b6c214efa32d

6. N.A. (2021, February 16). *China Market Insider*.
7. Ministry of Finance and the Ministry of Industry and Information Technology. (2021, January 23). *Notice on Supporting the High-quality Development of 'Specialized, New SMEs'*, Beijing.
8. The Ministry of Finance and the Ministry of Industry and Information Technology. (2021, January 23). *Notice on supporting the high-quality development of 'Specialized, new SME'*. Beijing. 财政部、工信部印发《关于支持"专精特新"中小企业高质量发展的通知》.
9. Retrieved from http://sustainable-hidden-champions.de/.
10. Retrieved from https://hiddenchampionsfund.com/.
11. Breiding, J. (2019). *Too Small to Fail: Why Some Small Nations Outperform Larger Ones and How They Are Reshaping the World*. New York: Harper Business. The eight countries are Switzerland, Israel, Singapore, Netherlands, Denmark, Finland, Ireland, Sweden.
12. https://www.forbes.com/sites/rainerzitelmann/2019/07/15/the-leadership-secrets-of-the-hidden-champions/#7e5f03a26952
13. Retrieved from https://v.qq.com/x/page/b31199dk8bo.html
14. Büchler, J.-P. (2017). *Fallstudienkompendium Hidden Champions: Innovationen für den Weltmarkt*. Wiesbaden: Springer Gabler.
15. Greeven, M. J., Yip, G. S., & Wei, W. (2019). *Pioneers, hidden champions, change-makers, and underdogs: lessons from China's innovators*. MIT.
16. Braček, A., & Purg, D. (Eds.). (2020). *Hidden champions in dynamically changing societies*. New York: Springer Nature.
17. Braček, A., & Purg, D. (Eds.). (2021). *Hidden champions in dynamically changing societies*. New York: Springer Nature.
18. Kampfner, J. (2020). *Why the Germans do it better: Notes from a Grown-Up Country*. London: Atlantic Books.
19. Steingart, G. (2020). *Die unbequeme Wahrheit—Rede zur Lage unserer Nation* (p. 84). Munich: Penguin Verlag.
20. Retrieved from https://execed.esmt.berlin/de/hci
21. Retrieved from www.hcmi.kr, homepage in Korean.
22. Julian Schenkenhofer, J. (2020). Hidden champions: A review of the literature and future research avenues. *Working Paper Series 06-20*, Chair of Management and Organization, University of Augsburg, p. 15.

Part II

The Ascent of the Hidden Champions

6

Hidden Champions Worldwide

I have been collecting the names of Hidden Champions worldwide since 1989. In some countries, local researchers have systematically recorded and researched these mid-sized market leaders.[1] There are also cross-national studies in which numerous researchers have participated [1, 2]. In other countries, however, the coverage is incomplete because the collection has been less systematic.

Hidden Champions by Country

Research has so far identified 3406 Hidden Champions that meet the three criteria mentioned in Chap. 3. These firms come from 59 countries. Table 6.1 shows the numbers of Hidden Champions—in absolute terms and per million inhabitants—for countries with at least 20 Hidden Champions.

The numbers clearly show that Hidden Champions are primarily a phenomenon of German-speaking countries. Germany, Austria, and Switzerland are the only countries in which these mid-sized global market leaders exist in large numbers on a per capita basis, with each having roughly 18 per million inhabitants. The next closest are the Scandinavian countries, the Netherlands, and Japan. In all other countries, Hidden Champions are rare relative to population size. This is true for the large European countries and even more so for large economies such as the USA and China.

---

[1] In Japan Stefan Lippert, in China Deng Di and Jan Yang, in Korea Pil H. Yoo, in Poland Marek Dietl, in Italy Danilo Zatta, in France Stephan Guinchard, in the Netherlands Onno Oldeman.

Table 6.1 Hidden Champions by country—absolute and per million inhabitants

Country	Number of Hidden Champions	Population	Hidden Champions/million inhabitants
Germany	1573	83,166,711	18.91
USA	350	330,104,197	1.06
Japan	283	125,960,000	2.25
Austria	171	8,910,696	19.19
Switzerland	171	8,619,259	19.84
France	111	67,098,000	1.65
Italy	102	60,244,639	1.69
China	97	1,403,917,760	0.07
UK	74	66,796,807	1.11
Netherlands	38	17,496,531	2.17
Poland	37	38,356,000	0.96
Russia	29	146,748,590	0.20
Finland	28	5,498,827	5.09
Sweden	24	10,348,730	2.32
Canada	23	38,131,154	0.60
South Korea	22	51,780,579	0.42
Belgium	20	11,528,375	1.73
Denmark	20	5,824,857	3.43
Spain	20	47,329,981	0.42

The reasons for the low numbers are numerous. In America, only 20% of all companies' export. Among these, the largest 10% account for more than 90% of American exports [3]. American SMEs confine themselves mostly to their huge domestic market. Some authors criticize that "the U.S. is leaving midsize companies behind" [4]. In France, large companies dominate, while small- and mid-sized enterprises play only a minor role. In Chap. 2, we said that about two-thirds of all Chinese exports come from mid-sized companies. The number of Chinese mid-sized exporters is high, but only few of them are Hidden Champions. While low in absolute terms, the number of Chinese Hidden Champions has grown strongly in recent years. I expect this trend to continue, yielding a significantly higher number of Chinese Hidden Champions in 10–20 years. Nevertheless, the per capita density in China is likely to remain small due to the large population.

The 19 countries with at least 20 companies account for 93.7% of all Hidden Champions I have found. The German-speaking region accounts for the largest share of this, at 56.2%. If Luxembourg and Liechtenstein are included, 56.9% of all Hidden Champions come from German-speaking countries.

Structures

The structures of Hidden Champions differ by country. The American Hidden Champions are broadly diversified in terms of sectors, with the proportion of Internet-related companies increasing sharply in recent years. This is another trend that is likely to continue. The Hidden Champions in Japan often do not have their own global presence, but achieve their global market leadership indirectly as suppliers to large corporations. They are predominantly suppliers to major Japanese companies in the electronics sector, which are themselves world market leaders in their markets. Italian Hidden Champions come almost exclusively from northern Italy and have a similar industry structure to their German-speaking counterparts. Sectors such as machinery, engineering, infrastructure, and construction technology play a major role. Italy as well as France also has concentrations of suppliers to the fashion and luxury goods industries. Some other French Hidden Champions belong to the high-tech sectors, such as Dassault Systèmes, the world market leader in computer-aided design (CAD). The UK has many technology and research-intensive Hidden Champions, such as ARM, the world market leader in RISC processors used in most smartphones and tablet computers. In the Netherlands, service providers, plant breeders, and related suppliers play an important role.

Emerging Countries

It is interesting to ask whether Hidden Champions are found in emerging countries, and if so, in which industries. Not surprisingly, their overall numbers in these countries are small. Most Hidden Champions there exist in sectors in which the respective country has competitive advantages or special resources. These include citrus fruits in the case of Brazil, natural rubber in Malaysia, jute in Bangladesh, and mango in Egypt. Two typical examples of Hidden Champions in a raw materials sector are the Egyptian company Nakhla, the world market leader in shisha tobacco, and the Russian company VSMPO-AVISMA, the world market leader in titanium.

Emerging countries and their companies would be well advised not to limit themselves to the production and export of raw materials and primary goods. Rather, they should deepen their value chains, process the raw materials, and sell them as semi-finished or finished products at higher prices. Malaysia provides an example of such an extension of the value chain. The country is the third largest producer of natural rubber, but has become the most important supplier of disposable gloves [5]. Around 70% of all rubber gloves come from

Fig. 6.1 Internationalization of a Hidden Champion from emerging countries: Employees of the Malaysian global market leader Top Glove at a trade show in China

Malaysia [5, 6]. The world market leader is Top Glove with a global market share of 25%, and several other manufacturers are active worldwide and have established global brands. Figure 6.1 shows three employees of Top Glove at a trade fair in China.

In Brazil, Hidden Champions such as the Fischer Group (world leader in fruit concentrates), Cutrale (world leader in citrus fruits), or Sadia (world leader in frozen meat) prove that deepening the value chain is a feasible path to world market leadership. In a similar manner, Middle Eastern countries are acquiring petrochemical processing firms to gain a larger share of the oil-based value chain.

Ultimately, companies in these countries should have bolder and broader ambitions in terms of becoming world-class manufacturers. Countries such as Taiwan and South Korea have gone through this process and achieved spectacular successes. Brazil provides convincing evidence of this strategy with Hidden Champions such as Embraer, the world's leading manufacturer of regional aircraft, and Embraco, a leading producer of compressors. The same applies to India with Hidden Champions such as Essel Propack, the world market leader for toothpaste tubes, or the Serum Institute of India, the world's largest manufacturer of vaccines. These examples show that SMEs from emerging markets can become globally competitive not only in commodity-related upstream markets, but also in downstream markets with higher added value.

The Question of Global Validity

The fact that more than half (56%) of the identified Hidden Champions come from German-speaking countries raises several important questions. First, can the concept claim global validity, or is it limited to a specific region that offers particularly favorable conditions? Second, can companies from other regions learn from the successes of German-speaking Hidden Champions? Finally, do insights derived largely from the Germans have relevance for SMEs in other countries?

The answer to all three questions—in my view—is a resounding "yes."

I have personally met hundreds of Hidden Champions in countries on all continents and have always been amazed at their pronounced similarities to the German pioneers. Hidden Champions can emerge in any country, and they do indeed exist in almost all countries. All my findings suggest that the key success factors of German-speaking Hidden Champions apply in some way to other countries and continents.

In this book, I aim to provide lessons for ambitious SMEs from all over the world. While these lessons rely predominantly on success strategies of German-speaking Hidden Champions, I am convinced that the Hidden Champions concept can claim a high degree of global validity.

References

1. McKiernan, P., & Purg, D. (Eds.). (2019). *Hidden champions in CEE and Turkey: Carving out a global niche*. Berlin/Heidelberg: Springer.
2. Braček Lalić, A., & Purg, D. (Eds.). (2021). *Hidden champions in dynamically changing societies*. Cham: Springer Nature.
3. Armbruster, A. (2014, May 5). Nur die stärksten Unternehmen exportieren. *Frankfurter Allgemeine Zeitung*.
4. Govindarajan, V., Srivastava, A., & Enache, L. (2021, February 18). The U.S. Economy is Leaving Midsize Companies Behind. *Harvard Business Review Online*.
5. Retrieved 2 November 2020, from https://www.everprogloves.com/glove-manufacturers-malaysia/.
6. N.A. (2020, November 17). Corona bremst Top Glove aus. *Frankfurter Allgemeine Zeitung*, p. 18.

7

German Hidden Champions

The current list of German Hidden Champions contains 1573 companies that meet the criteria presented in Chap. 3. Figure 7.1 shows the number of German Hidden Champions identified and recorded in the various surveys since research began in 1989.

It should be noted that Fig. 7.1 does not express the increase of the actual number of Hidden Champions; it merely shows those recorded in the surveys. The increase can be explained by both broader and more systematic research and the emergence of new or previously undiscovered Hidden Champions. On the other hand, some companies lost their Hidden Champion status due to declines in market share, insolvencies, mergers, or takeovers. Of the 1307 Hidden Champions in 2012, around 70 no longer meet the criteria and have disappeared from the list. I estimate that, over the long term, about 1% of Hidden Champions lose their status each year.

Market Position

A good third of German Hidden Champions (35.2%) claim to be the global number one in their market, while 41.7% say they are one of the world market leaders, and 23.1% that they are number 1 in the European market. Precise market shares are only available for a selection of the German Hidden Champions. On average, the median market share for the respective market (world or Europe) is 40%, but this figure should be considered indicative, not

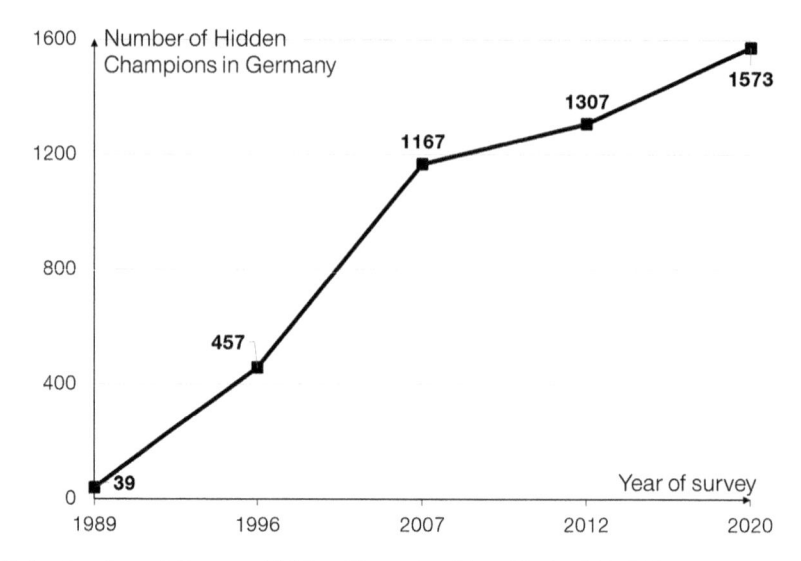

Fig. 7.1 Number of German Hidden Champion identified, 1989–2020

representative.[1] It does correspond with a large-scale study that found a mean market share of 34% for the Hidden Champions [1].

Revenue

The average revenue (arithmetic mean) of the 1573 German Hidden Champions is €467 million.[2] The smallest Hidden Champion has a revenue of €1 million, while the largest generates €4.966 billion. Figure 7.2 shows the distribution of revenues of the German Hidden Champions.

The median, which removes the influence of outliers, is more meaningful than the arithmetic mean with respect to the typical size of Hidden Champions. The median revenue is €150 million, meaning that half of them have sales above that level and the other half below it.

Today, the average German Hidden Champion's revenue is around five times larger today than it was 25 years ago, when the 1995 survey revealed an average revenue of €95 million across 457 Hidden Champions. This factor

---

[1] On the one hand, some companies do not report their market shares; on the other hand, companies with "impressive" market shares may be more likely to report them than companies with less strong positions.
[2] Revenue figures are available for about 90.8% of the German Hidden Champions, mostly for 2018/19, in some cases for other years. Smaller companies and partnerships are not required to publish their revenues.

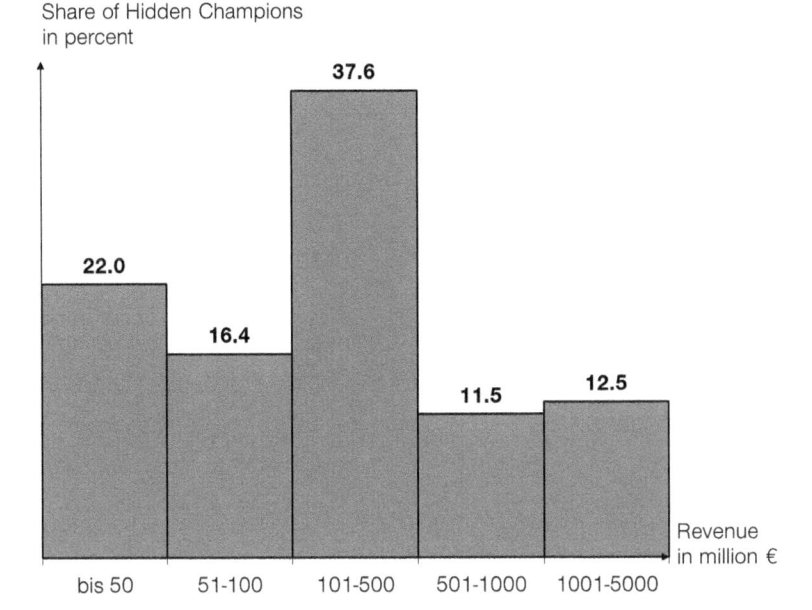

Fig. 7.2 Distribution of revenues of German Hidden Champions

Share of Hidden Champions in percent:
- bis 50: 22.0
- 51-100: 16.4
- 101-500: 37.6
- 501-1000: 11.5
- 1001-5000: 12.5

(Revenue in million €)

corresponds to an annual growth rate of just under 7%, which is quite spectacular for such a long period of time. The German Hidden Champions can look back on a quarter of a century of unbridled growth, an era of ascent characterized by continuity rather than erratic leaps and shifts. We will explore this aspect in greater depth later for individual companies and discuss whether companies can expect similar growth patterns in the future.

Employment

The German Hidden Champions have an average workforce of 2252 employees.[3] The smallest company in the survey has 16 employees, the largest 79,000. Note that the German Hidden Champions have more employees abroad than in their home market. Figure 7.3 presents the distribution of employee numbers of German Hidden Champions.

The 457 Hidden Champions in the 1995 survey had 735 employees on average. Since then, the average number of employees has grown by a factor of 3.1, corresponding to an annual growth rate of just under 5%. The Hidden

---
[3] Employee figures are available for 93.2% of the Hidden Champions in the study, mostly for 2018/19, in some cases for other years.

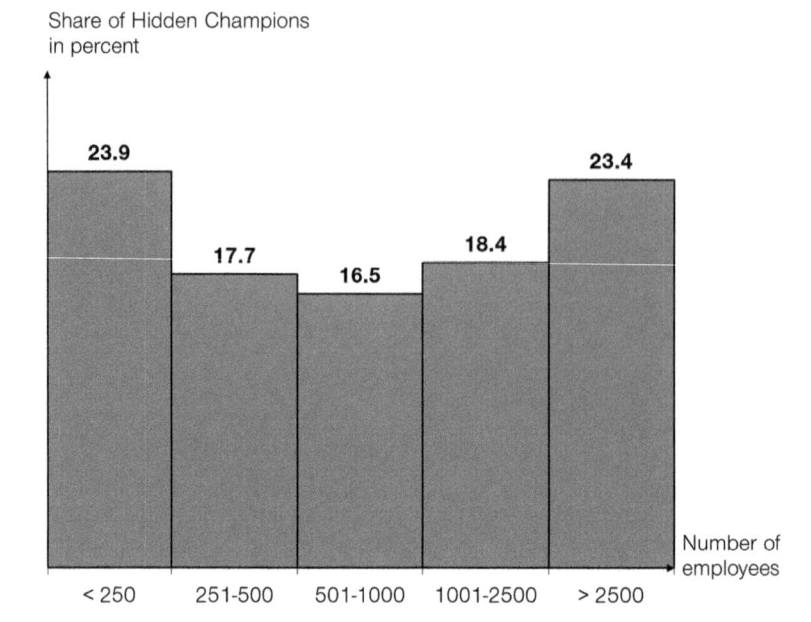

Fig. 7.3 Distribution of employee numbers of German Hidden Champions

Champions have created a large number of new jobs. The 457 Hidden Champions of 1995 employed a total of 335,895 people; the 1573 companies on the current list have 3.55 million employees. I estimate that 1.5–2 million new jobs were created in these 25 years, about one-third in German locations and two-thirds outside Germany.

Revenue per employee has increased by almost 30% in the last 10 years, to €207,371 from €160,039 in 2010.[4] This corresponds to annual productivity growth of 2.9%. An assessment by Harvard professors—that Hidden Champions are "obsessed with productivity"—seems to reflect reality.[5]

Age

Hidden Champions are not young companies. The median age is 71 years.[6] One in nine Hidden Champions is even older than 100 years. In 1995, the average age was 67. The fact that 25 years have passed since then, yet the

---

[4] Not taking into account inflation, which was low in those years.
[5] Personal communication from Professor Nitin Nohria, Dean of Harvard Business School, April 3, 2019. See Chap. 8 for more details.
[6] In this case, the median is a valid measure to exclude the influence of some very old companies.

average age has only risen by 12 years, is explained by the inclusion of younger and new Hidden Champions.

The age structure demonstrates the high survival rate of the Hidden Champions. They probably even outshine large companies in this respect. In 2018, General Electric was the last company to disappear from the original Dow Jones Index, which was founded in 1897.[7] In the German DAX index of 30 companies, which was founded on July 1, 1988, only 12 companies are left from the original list [2].

Since I only cover the survivors, it is unclear how many of the Hidden Champions that existed 100 years ago have disappeared. The period from 1915 to 1945 constitutes three lost decades for the development of international trade and the world economy, due to two world wars and the Great Depression. Extremely few new companies were founded in that period. The great era of German Hidden Champions came after World War II, during the so-called German economic miracle, when German entrepreneurs laid the foundations for the ongoing success of globalization. Four decades passed between the end of World War II and Germany's emergence as the world's leading exporter in 1986.

The rise of a company to Hidden Champion status is not a short-term project. Around half of today's German Hidden Champions were created in that era after World War II. Young Hidden Champions, on the other hand, are rare. Only around 5% are younger than 25 years, and those companies are primarily from the digital sector. This low figure is a sign of Germany's relatively weak presence in new markets.

Regional Distribution

The Hidden Champions are not only little known *per se*; their locations are also not generally well known. Table 7.1 shows the numbers of German Hidden Champions by federal state, ranked by absolute number.

North Rhine-Westphalia has the most Hidden Champions, closely followed by Baden-Wuerttemberg, and Bavaria follows in third place. More than two-thirds (68.7%) of all German Hidden Champions are based in these three states. The East German states have the lowest numbers, with a total of 54 Hidden Champions. This figure can be interpreted as a great success if you consider that in my first survey in 1995, shortly after the reunification of Germany, I found only three Hidden Champions in the former communist

---

[7] GE Drops Out of the Dow after More than a Century, The Wall Street Journal, June 19, 2018.

Table 7.1 German Hidden Champions by federal state: absolute numbers, number per million inhabitants, and shares

Federal state	Hidden Champions		
	Number	By million inhabitants	Share in %
North Rhine-Westphalia	410	22.8	26.1
Baden-Wuerttemberg	367	33.1	23.3
Bavaria	303	23.1	19.3
Hesse	126	20.0	8.1
Lower Saxony	87	10.9	5.5
Rhineland-Palatinate	76	18.6	4.8
Schleswig-Holstein	47	16.2	3.0
Hamburg	39	21.1	2.5
Berlin	37	10.1	2.4
Saxony	23	5.6	1.5
Bremen	17	25.0	1.1
Thuringia	15	7.0	1.0
Saarland	10	10.1	0.6
Brandenburg	6	2.4	0.4
Mecklenburg-Western Pomerania	5	3.1	0.3
Saxony-Anhalt	5	2.3	0.3

East Germany. Per million inhabitants, Baden-Wuerttemberg is in first place with 33.1 Hidden Champions. The city state of Bremen is second in the per capita figure. Most Western German states have around 20 Hidden Champions per million inhabitants. The East German states still lag well behind in terms of Hidden Champion density.

In Fig. 7.4, the locations of the 1573 German Hidden Champions are illustrated by dots.

This figure provides important insights. First of all, it shows that Hidden Champions are scattered throughout Germany. These mid-sized market leaders are virtually everywhere. The Hidden Champions are a constituent element of Germany's decentralized structure. Nevertheless, there are strong concentrations, especially in Baden-Wuerttemberg, Bavaria, and North Rhine-Westphalia. This contrasts with regions in which there are comparatively few Hidden Champions. These include not only the East German states, but also areas in the west. In Chap. 16 "Business ecosystems," we will analyze further regional aspects.

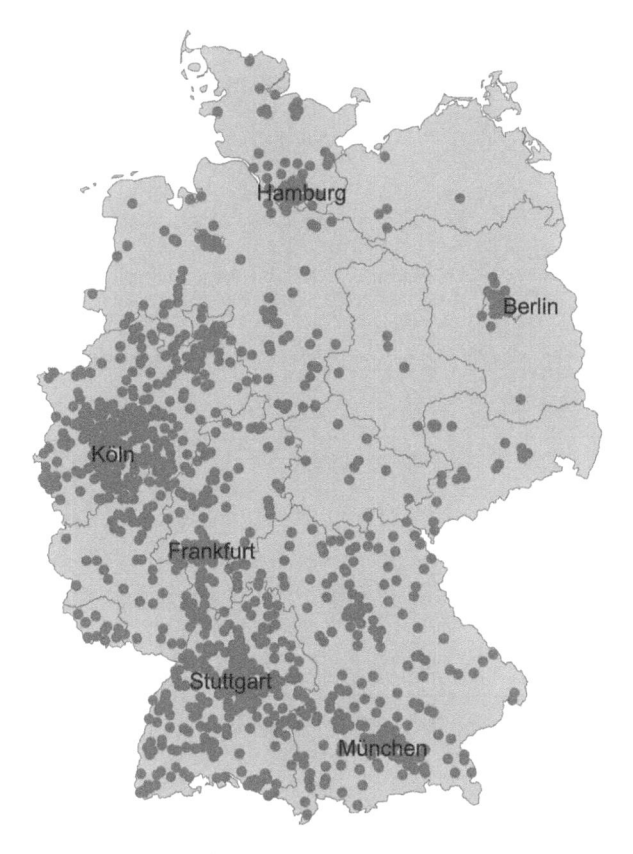

Fig. 7.4 Regional distribution of Hidden Champions in Germany

References

1. Rammer, C., & Spielkamp, A. (2015). *Hidden Champions—Driven by Innovation, Empirische Befunde auf Basis des Mannheimer Innovationspanels*. Mannheim: ZEW.
2. Retrieved from https://de.wikipedia.org/wiki/DAX.

8

Austrian and Swiss Hidden Champions

As we learned in Chap. 6, Germany, Austria, and Switzerland have very similar per capita figures of Hidden Champions. The number per million inhabitants is around 19 in all three countries.

Austrian Hidden Champions

There are currently 171 Austrian companies in the list of Hidden Champions, an increase of 47% since 2012, which outpaced the growth in the number of German Hidden Champions. One reason for the sharp increase is that the earlier research in Austria was less complete than in Germany. Of course, there are also Austrian companies that did not meet the Hidden Champion criteria in 2012, but do so now. A good two-thirds (69%) of Austrian Hidden Champions claim global market leadership, a significantly higher percentage than in Germany and Switzerland. Austrian Hidden Champions have an average revenue of €372 million, 21% less than Germany's. The median, on the other hand, is slightly higher at €163 million. The average number of employees is 2036, resulting in an average revenue per employee of €182,711.

Table 8.1 summarizes the most important data of the Austrian Hidden Champions.

Overall, the structures of Austrian and German Hidden Champions are very similar. Austrian Hidden Champions are on average somewhat smaller in terms of revenue, but not in terms of employees.

Table 8.1 Data on the Austrian Hidden Champions

Average revenue	€372 million
Median revenue	€163 million
Average number of employees	2036
Median number of employees	900
Revenue <€50 million	21%
Revenue €51–100 million	15%
Revenue €101–500 million	43%
Revenue €501–1000 million	11%
Revenue >€1000 million	10%

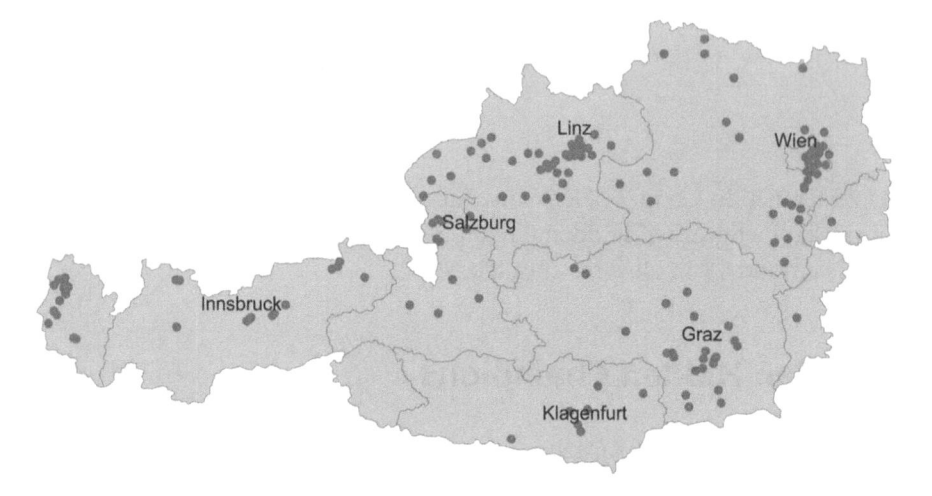

Fig. 8.1 Regional distribution of Hidden Champions in Austria

Regional Distribution

The regional distribution of Austrian Hidden Champions is shown in Fig. 8.1.

Austrian Hidden Champions are as unevenly distributed as the German ones. We observe strong concentrations around Vienna, Graz, Linz, and Bregenz. In contrast, large parts of the country are without Hidden Champions. Table 8.2 details the picture for the Austrian states.

Four of the nine federal states—Upper Austria, Styria, Vienna, and Lower Austria—account for almost three quarters of all Austrian Hidden Champions. Vorarlberg has three times as many Hidden Champions per million inhabitants as Carinthia and Burgenland.

Table 8.2 Austrian Hidden Champions by federal state—absolute number and per million inhabitants

Region	Hidden Champions	Million inhabitants	Hidden Champions per one million inhabitants
Vorarlberg	13	0.39	33.0
Upper Austria	43	1.48	29.1
Salzburg	11	0.56	19.8
Styria	24	1.24	19.3
Vienna	32	1.90	16.9
Lower Austria	27	1.68	16.1
Tyrol	12	0.75	15.9
Carinthia	6	0.56	10.7
Burgenland	3	0.29	10.2

Table 8.3 Data on the Swiss Hidden Champions

Average revenue	€933 million
Median revenue	€389 million
Average number of employees	3765
Median number of employees	1304
Revenue <50 million €	14%
Revenue 51–100 million €	11%
Revenue 101–500 million €	32%
Revenue 501–1000 million €	13%
Revenue >1000 million €	30%

Swiss Hidden Champions

The Swiss list includes 171 Hidden Champions, an increase of 55% from 110 companies in 2012. Some 44% of the Swiss Hidden Champions are number 1 in their global market. With average revenue of €933 million, they are significantly larger than their German and Austrian counterparts. They employ an average of 3765 people. These figures translate into revenue of €247,808 per employee. Revenues per employee differ considerably between Switzerland, Germany (€207,371), and Austria (€182,711). Table 8.3 summarizes the most important structural data of the Swiss Hidden Champions:

Regional Distribution

The regional distribution of the Swiss Hidden Champions is shown in Fig. 8.2.

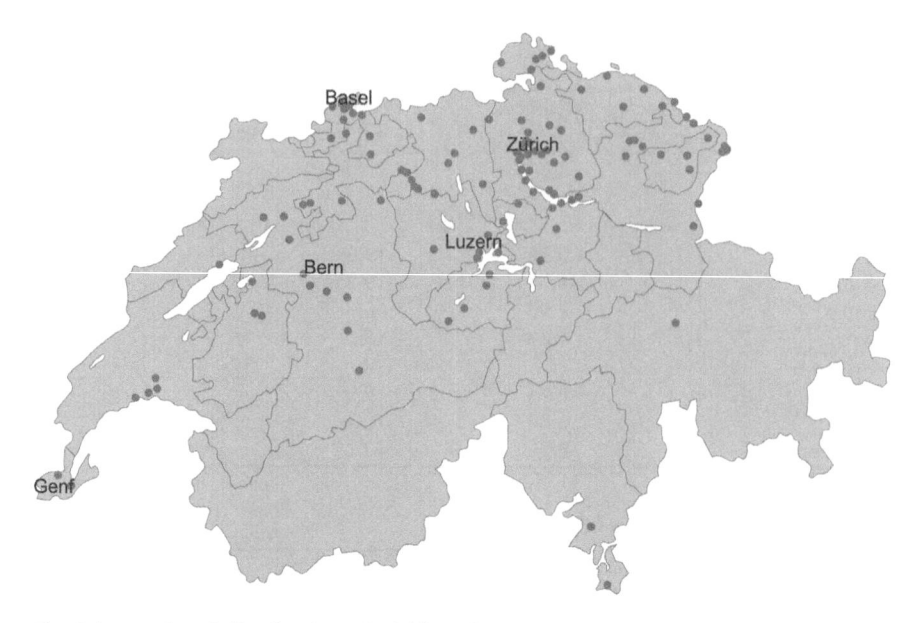

Fig. 8.2 Regional distribution of Hidden Champions in Switzerland

Table 8.4 Five Swiss cantons with the highest Hidden Champion density

Region	Hidden Champions	Million inhabitants	Hidden Champions per one million inhabitants
Basel District	10	0.29	33.0
St. Gallen	14	0.51	28.3
Zürich	38	1.54	19.8
Bern	16	1.04	19.3
Aargau	10	0.69	16.9

The figure shows a very uneven regional distribution. Similar to Germany's and Austria's, the Swiss Hidden Champions are concentrated in a small number of regional clusters. The differences become even more striking when viewed at the level of the 26 Swiss cantons. Four Swiss cantons have no Hidden Champions, while five cantons have more than ten Hidden Champions (see Table 8.4).

Noteworthy is that all five cantons are located in the German-speaking part of Switzerland, and they account for 53% of the Swiss Hidden Champions. It is also interesting to note that across the three countries, the adjacent regions of Basel District (33), Vorarlberg (33), and Baden-Wuerttemberg (32.7) have almost identical per capita numbers of Hidden Champions. The outstanding performance of Swiss hidden champions is acknowledged in the book

Masterpieces of Swiss Entrepreneurship: Swiss SMEs Competing in Global Markets, which examines 36 Swiss companies, including numerous hidden champions, in depth [1].

Reference

1. Jeannet, J.-P., Thierry Volery, T., Bergmann, H., & Amstutz, C. (2021). *Masterpieces of Swiss entrepreneurship: Swiss SMEs competing in global markets*. Cham: Springer.

9

Decades of Ascent

We will now explore how the Hidden Champions in the three largest German-speaking countries achieved their status and success. It is instructive to look at the growth of specific firms rather than a region or country as a whole. This chapter will describe four case studies for companies of different size categories.

From Hidden Champion to Fortune Global 500

Figure 9.1 shows the growth of three companies who ascended from Hidden Champion status (revenues between €1 and €5 billion) to Fortune Global 500 prominence in the period from 1995 to 2019. The revenue of Fresenius grew by a factor of 40, while SAP's grew by a factor of 20 and ZF Group's by more than 10. Hearing about such growth factors regularly causes great astonishment among my listeners both at home and at abroad. This kind of spectacular growth is expected from companies in Silicon Valley or China, but not from stuffy German firms.

These cases help to explain the emergence of large and mega-companies. The "big champions" simply emerge from mid-sized companies that grow continuously over long periods of time. However, in all three cases, the current size was not achieved exclusively through organic growth. Acquisitions also played a significant role.

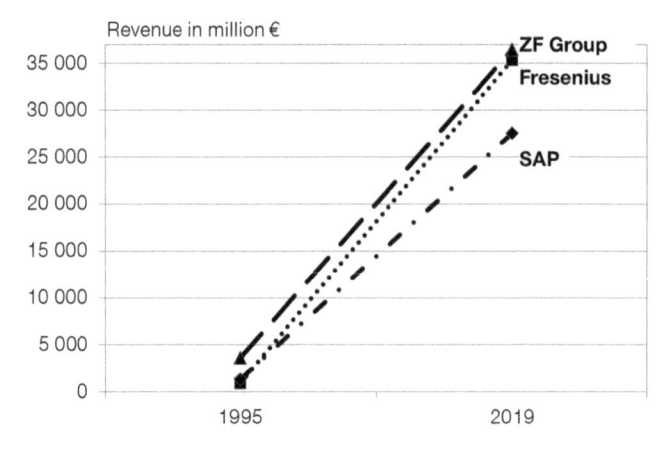

Fig. 9.1 Ascent of former Hidden Champions to the Fortune Global 500

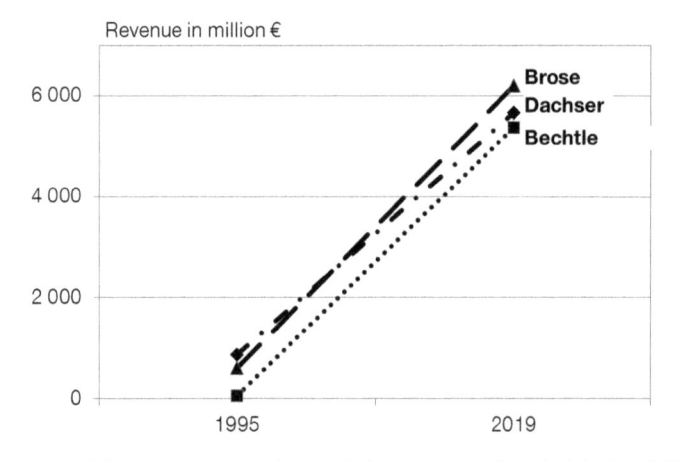

Fig. 9.2 Former Hidden Champions beyond the revenue threshold of €5 billion

Beyond €5 billion

Figure 9.2 shows the growth of three former Hidden Champions whose revenues now exceed the €5 billion threshold. All three had revenues of less than €1 billion 25 years ago.

Brose is the world market leader for automotive door and window systems. Dachser is number 1 in Europe for systems logistics. Bechtle is one of Europe's leading IT services providers. Numerous other Hidden Champions have achieved similar growth multiples since 1995. These include Enercon in wind turbines with a multiple of 29, Leoni in automotive cable systems with a multiple of 16, Exyte[1] in cleanroom systems with a multiple of 12, and Trumpf in laser machines with a growth multiple of 8.

My list contains 190 German Hidden Champions with revenues between €1 and €5 billion. Their aggregate revenue is €399 billion, or €2.10 billion on average. Austria has 18 Hidden Champions with revenues of more than €1 billion, and they average €2.06 billion. In Switzerland, 37 Hidden Champions exceed 1 billion Swiss francs in revenue and achieve an average revenue of 2.43 billion Swiss francs.

Approaching the €1-billion Threshold

Many smaller Hidden Champions have achieved similarly strong growth. Figure 9.3 shows three companies that had revenues of less than €100 million in 1995, but are now approaching the revenue threshold of €1 billion.

Rational is the world market leader in professional appliances for commercial kitchens, with a global market share of more than 50%. Igus is the world's number 1 supplier of plastic bearings and also holds a high market share in so-called energy chains. Birkenstock has become a generic term for comfortable shoes for health-conscious consumers. Birkenstocks are just as well known in the USA as they are in Germany, so "hidden" only applies to a limited extent.[2]

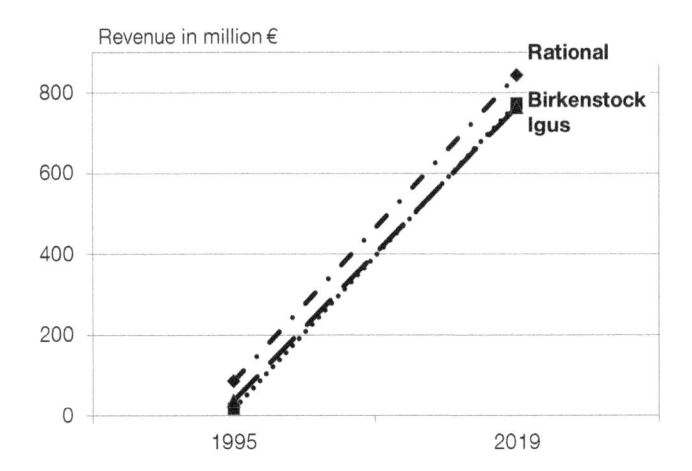

Fig. 9.3 Formerly small companies, today close to the €1 billion mark

---

[1] Former name was M+W Zander.
[2] In 2021, Birkenstock was acquired by Bernard Arnault, majority owner of the French luxury goods group LVMH.

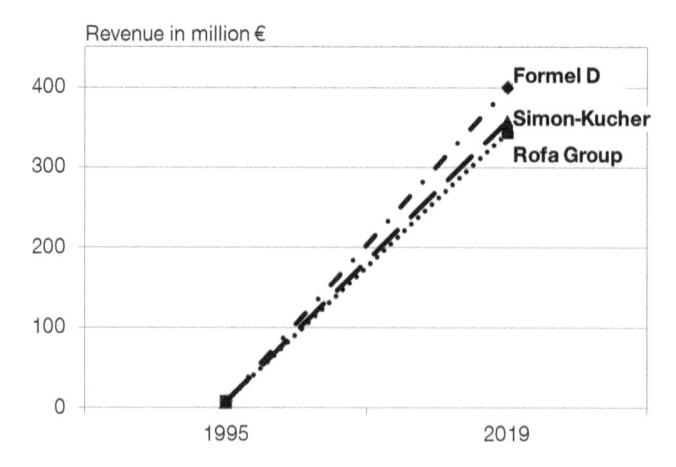

From Dwarf to Hidden Champion

Finally, we find numerous companies that have gone from dwarves to Hidden Champions. Figure 9.4 shows three such cases.

Formel D is a global market leader in specialized automotive services. Simon-Kucher is the global number one in price consulting. The Rofa Group is the European leader in industrial automation.

In 1995, the revenues of each of these companies were less than €10 million, but over the last 25 years, their revenues have increased at least 41-fold, a tremendous rise turning these "dwarfs" into successful Hidden Champions. A large proportion of the 527 Hidden Champions in the revenue range of €100 to €500 million show similar growth performances.

What Drives This Ascent?

The first and foremost driver is globalization. In a sample of larger Hidden Champions, the average number of foreign subsidiaries has more than doubled in the last decade, from 40 to 84. Acquisitions also play a significant role, especially for Hidden Champions that have grown faster than average. Innovations and product range extensions, deeper value chains, and expanded services are further growth drivers. Diversification, in contrast, has been less important for their growth.

Overall, the Hidden Champions have experienced spectacular decades of ascent since the 1990s. Many of them—regardless of size—have seen their

Fig. 9.4 From Dwarf to Hidden Champion

sales grow by more than tenfold. The question is whether the Hidden Champions of German-speaking countries will succeed in maintaining those high growth rates in the coming decades. I have no conclusive answer, but I can say that if the Hidden Champions want to continue their growth trajectory, they need to undergo a transformation that takes into account the numerous emerging growth opportunities as well as the barriers to growth. Fulfilling unmet basic needs—clean water, hygiene, transportation, or health—create vast opportunities in emerging countries. At the same time, factors such as the environment, climate, energy consumption, consumer attitudes, trade frictions, and political tensions may create new barriers to growth.

10

Why Are There So Many Hidden Champions in Germany?

The Hidden Champions are the phenomenon that most clearly sets apart Germany and the German-speaking region from the rest of the world. The German "world market share" is higher for Hidden Champions than in any other field—be it art, science, or sports—as Table 10.1 shows.

Comparisons to other countries lead to the question: "why is Germany home to so many Hidden Champions?" The prevalence of Hidden Champions in Germany results from a complex bundle of interacting causes and cannot be traced back to a single root. Many of these causes are difficult for other countries to imitate, because they are deeply anchored in history, traditions, and value systems. A number of these contributing factors also apply to Austria and Switzerland.

No Nation State

Countries like France or Japan formed into nation states relatively early in the modern era. The German-speaking areas of Europe, meanwhile, continued much longer as a patchwork of hundreds of small states. Germany did not become a nation state until the end of the nineteenth century. Today, it is still organized decentrally, as are Austria and Switzerland. In past centuries, entrepreneurs from the German-speaking regions who wanted their businesses to grow had to expand their activities beyond the narrow boundaries of their tiny states. They were forced to start internationalizing earlier than entrepreneurs in other countries and over time the urge to operate outside the borders of their home country has become part of the DNA of German-speaking entrepreneurs.

Table 10.1 German "global market shares" in various fields of society

Area	Criterion	German "global market share" in percent
Mittelstand	Number of Hidden Champions	46.2%
Artists	Fame barometer of the top 100	29.0%
Formula 1	World champions	16.1%
Soccer	World champions	15.8%
Science	Nobel Prizes	12.5%
Universities	Times University Ranking 2018 (top 100)	10.0%
Sports	Olympic gold medals 1896–2016	9.3%
Large corporations	Number of Fortune Global 500 companies 2019	5.4%
Tennis	World rankings, men	5.5%
Wikipedia	Entries (2.5 million out of 53.9 million)	4.6%
Society	Time: 100 most influential personalities 2009–2011	3.3%
Population	Population	1.2%
Land area	Square kilometers	0.2%

Decentralization

In most countries, knowledge and creativity are concentrated in one place, which is usually the capital. This applies to Paris, London, Tokyo, and Seoul. Few countries have such decentralized structures as Germany, Austria, or Switzerland, where world-class companies can be found throughout the country. As far as the development of an entrepreneurial spirit is concerned, the regional dispersion of knowledge and creativity represents an enormous advantage over centrally organized countries. One example is East Germany, where 54 Hidden Champions have emerged since the centralized Communist system ended 30 years ago.

Dual Vocational Training

One pillar of Germany's competitive strength is its unique dual vocational training system. Dual vocational training means that the programs combine practical and theoretical training. The apprentices work in a company 3 days a week and attend a vocational training school for 2 days. While other countries have higher rates of college and university graduates, the German dual vocational training system produces the best-qualified skilled workers in the world. Some countries are trying to establish dual vocational education systems, but it turns out to be a complicated and lengthy process.

Manufacturing Base

Unlike the UK or the USA, Germany has not abandoned its manufacturing base. That may make the structure of the German economy look old-fashioned, but it is the basis for the country's successful performance. The correlation between a country's manufacturing base and its trade balance, i.e., the difference between exports and imports,[1] is close to 80%. This underscores the historical importance of manufacturing. Today, about a quarter of Germany's gross domestic product (GDP) still comes from the manufacturing sector, whereas in other highly developed countries, this share has fallen to less than 15%.

Germany has often been criticized for failing to manage the transition from an industrial to a service society, especially before the Great Recession of 2008. Since then, this view has changed. Countries with service-dominated economies such as the USA, the UK, or France are making great efforts to rebuild their manufacturing base. During the COVID-19 crisis, Germany faced criticism for its strong dependence on exports, but I feel that criticism is misguided. An economy that diversifies its markets instead of depending unilaterally on domestic demand actually enjoys an advantage, especially in times of crisis. The industries affected by the COVID-19 pandemic would probably have suffered even greater sales declines if their only focus had been on German customers.

Productivity

Not too long ago, a group of professors from the Harvard Business School came to Europe to visit German Hidden Champions. The professors unanimously gave me the feedback that these companies are "obsessed with productivity." Steadily increasing productivity leads to lower unit labor costs, from which the Hidden Champions benefit, especially relative to their European neighbors. The Harvard professors also observed that "the Hidden Champions try to do something better every day." Michael Porter pointed out the close relationship between fierce internal competition and sustained international competitiveness [1]. One-third of the Hidden Champions say that their fiercest competitors are in Germany, often in regional proximity. This close

---

[1] The trade balance is the difference between exports and imports. The more a country produces internally, the more it can export, and the less it needs to import.

competition drives productivity and contributes to the export and competitive strength of the German Hidden Champions.

Regional Ecosystems

Many German regions have centuries-old competencies that still endure and even thrive in today's markets. In today's management parlance, they are industrial or business ecosystems. Clocks have always been made in the Black Forest, and clockmaking is considered "the key machine of the modern industrial age" [2]. This tradition has given rise to more than 500 medical technology companies in the Black Forest region.

Or take the university town of Goettingen in northern Germany. Why does this small town have 39 manufacturers of measurement technology? The explanation lies in the university's department of mathematics, which has been world class for centuries. Most of the 39 companies in Goettingen trace their roots to principles discovered by Carl Friedrich Gauss and other famous mathematicians. Former Siemens board member Edward Krubasik noted that "Germany is using the technology base that goes back to the Middle Ages to succeed in the 21st century."

Central Location

Even in a globalized world, distances and time zones retain their importance. Under geostrategic aspects, the German-speaking countries have an ideal location. Communication with Japan and California is possible within normal office hours, and travel times to the world's most important business centers are shorter than those that Asians or Americans have to live with. Even within Europe, the German-speaking region is centrally located. These are enormous advantages in a globalized world.

Mental Internationalization

International business requires a wide cultural horizon. This starts with language. "The best language is the language of the customer," said Anton Fugger in the late Middle Ages. In the English Proficiency Index, which covers 100 countries, the Netherlands ranks first, followed by other small countries such as Sweden and Singapore [3]. Among the countries with a population of more than 50 million, Germany is leading with an overall rank of 10, far ahead of France (rank 31), Spain (35), Italy (36), Russia (48), and Japan (53) [3].

The "Global Connectedness Index" compiled by DHL confirms this picture. The Netherlands, Singapore, and Switzerland occupy the top three places. Among the major countries, only the United Kingdom, in ninth place, is ahead of Germany in tenth place, with France (15th), Spain (21st), and Italy (26th) falling well behind [4]. Hidden Champions are "mentally global." Rational, the world market leader for commercial kitchen machines, presents its information in 59 languages.

Made in Germany

The label "Made in Germany" has become a first-class seal of quality that has massively helped German Hidden Champions in their globalization process. "Made in Switzerland" or "Swiss Made" has practically the same value [5].

Yet few people know the origins of the phrase "Made in Germany." The British originally imposed it in 1887 as a sign of *inferior* quality of German products!

Almost 150 years later, "Made in Germany" leads the international Made-in ranking with 100 points, closely followed by "Made in Switzerland" with 99 points. "Made in Austria" at 72 points still has some improvement potential [5].

References

1. Porter, M. (1990). *The competitive advantage of nations*. London: Palgrave Macmillan.
2. Mumford, L. (1934). *Technics and Civilization*. New York: Harcourt, Brace & Co.
3. Retrieved from https://www.ef.de/__/~/media/centralefcom/epi/downloads/full-reports/v9/ef-epi-2019-german.pdf.
4. Altman, S. A., Ghemawat, P., & Bastian, P. (2018). *DHL global connectedness index 2018—The state of globalization in a fragile world*. Deutsche Post DHL Group.
5. Breiding, J. (2013). Swiss made: *The untold story behind Switzerland's success*. London: Profile Books.

Part III

The New Game of Globalization

11

On Rough Roads to Globalia

The title of my 2012 book is *Hidden Champions—Departure towards Globalia*. What has happened to Globalia since then? Since the end of the Great Recession in 2010, globalization has not progressed as smoothly as in the decades before. Fundamental changes left globalization "on rough roads" and the COVID-19 crisis has made those roads even bumpier.

In this chapter, I look at the development of globalization in the recent past. Whether these trends and changes will remain permanent or even intensify is the subject of the following chapter, "Quo Vadis Globalia?"

Global Per Capita Exports

World trade and exports are generally considered the most relevant indicators of globalization. Figure 11.1 displays a very long-term view of global per capita exports.

This long-term retrospective illustrates the breathtaking dynamics of the global economy. The trends since the beginning of the twentieth century suggest extremely favorable expectations for globalization.

In 1900, per capita exports were close to zero, at $6. Due to the two world wars, it took 50 years for that figure to rise to a modest $23. Over the next 30 years, per capita exports increased 20-fold to $437. Despite the higher level, they then more than doubled from 1980 to 2000 and more than doubled again until 2019. One should remember that these are per capita figures. In 1900, the world had a population of 1.6 billion; today the global

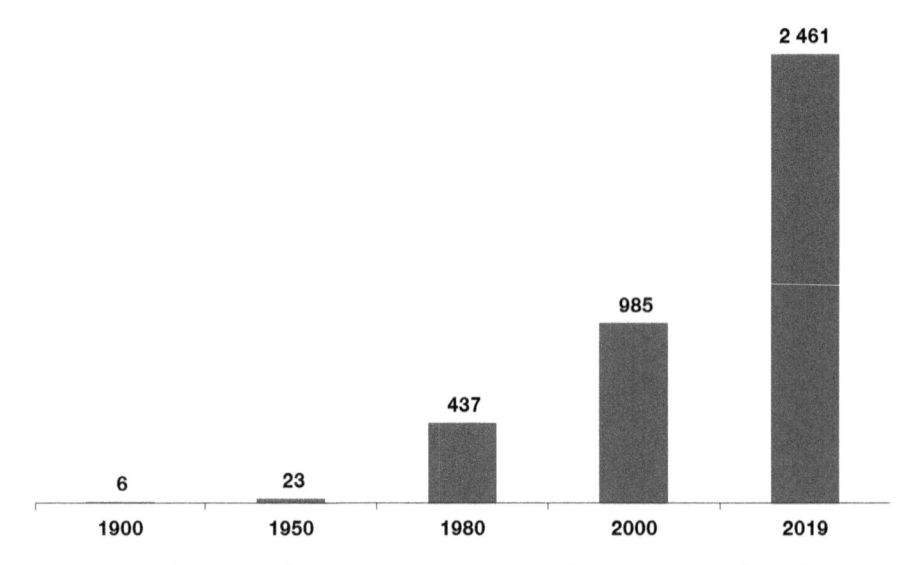

Fig. 11.1 Development of global per capita exports since 1900 (in US dollars)

population is 7.8 billion. In absolute dollar terms, global exports today are nearly 2000 times what they were just over a century ago.[1]

Global Exports since 1990

Figure 11.2 provides a shorter-term view, which shows global exports since 1990 [1].

Exports have grown by a factor of 5.4 over the three decades since 1990. This corresponds to an annual growth rate of 6.0%. Figure 11.2 reveals two clearly distinguishable phases: From 1990 to 2008, the year in which the Great Recession began, the annual growth rate stood at a robust 9.4%. In the 11 years from 2008 to 2019, total growth was only 17%, which corresponds to an annual growth rate of merely 1.6%. In the eight years between 2011 and 2019, annual export growth came close to a virtual standstill, with an annual growth rate of 0.4%.

Complementing this picture, Fig. 11.3 shows how the growth rates of global exports evolved relative to the growth rates of global GDP. The ratio of two percentages—in this case, the two growth rates—is called an elasticity.

---

[1] Exactly 1974 times as high as in 1900.

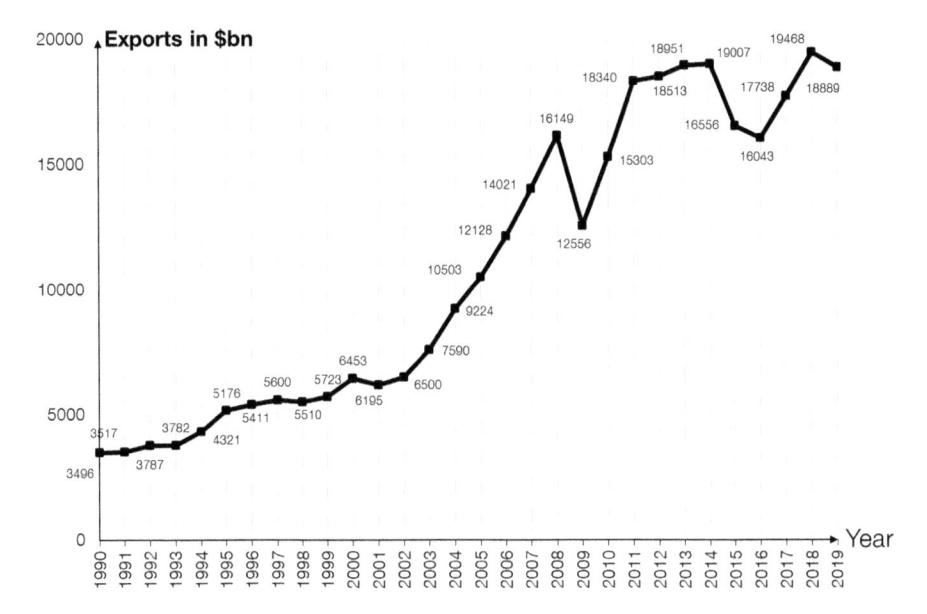

Fig. 11.2 Development of global exports since 1990

Figure 11.3 shows the trade elasticity, which is the change in global exports relative to the change in global GDP.[2]

Looking at the average values of the trade elasticity is very illuminating. From 1990 to 1999, the trade elasticity exceeded 2, meaning that exports grew more than twice as fast as GDP. From 2000 to 2009, the trade elasticity fell to around 1.5, meaning that world trade grew 50% faster than world GDP. The development in the years 1990 to 2010 is aptly described as "hyperglobalization" [2]. Since 2010, however, the growth rates of the two variables have been roughly equal. Since 2014, the trade elasticity has even remained well below 1.

The bottom line is that the globalization engine has stalled. Global exports have been growing at a slower rate than global GDP for several years. Although we cannot speak of deglobalization in absolute terms, we can certainly speak of "relative deglobalization." This is a dramatic development, especially for strongly export-oriented countries such as Germany, Austria, and Switzerland, as well as the Hidden Champions. It is a development that started several years before Trump, Brexit, tariff increases, tightened sanctions, and the collapse of global supply chains due to COVID-19.

---

[2] German Federal Ministry for Economic Affairs and Energy (2019). "**Weltwirtschaft im Wandel**—Wie die Digitalisierung, Handelskonflikte und Chinas Aufstieg globale Handelsverflechtungen verändern," online version, December 5.

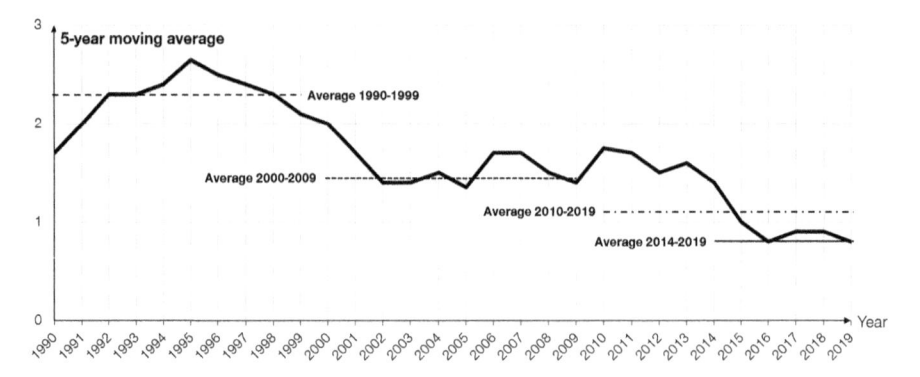

Fig. 11.3 Ratio of global export growth to global GDP growth (trade elasticity)

If these or similar trends continue, they will hamper world trade and may cause growth rates to remain permanently below the rates seen in the hyper-globalization phase. They could even lead to shrinking trade volumes.

The framework of international trade is highly dynamic and difficult to predict. It seems advisable to speak of "framework processes" and not of a fixed framework. Hidden Champions must align their global strategies with these rapidly changing framework processes and undergo a transformation. In Chap. 13, we will discuss how these framework processes will shape future exports.

Global Service Exports

The picture of globalization remains incomplete if we look only at exports of goods. In 2018, the United States led the way in service exports with €549 billion, followed by the United Kingdom with €312 billion. Germany was third with €245 billion, followed by China with €147 billion [3]. Figure 11.4 shows the development of global service exports since 1990 [4].

Since 1990, global service exports have increased by a factor of 6.91. The annual growth rate of 6.9% exceeds the rate for goods exports by about 1% point. In 1990, service exports accounted for 25.6% of total exports; by 2019, this percentage had risen to 32.5%. The value of exported goods is thus still more than double that of exported services.

The share of service exports relative to the GDP has almost doubled since 1990, from 7.7 to 13.3% in 2019. It has also increased over the past decade, rising from 11.6 to 13.3%. For the period of 1990 to 2019, the elasticity of service exports growth relative to GDP growth was 1.5, which means that the

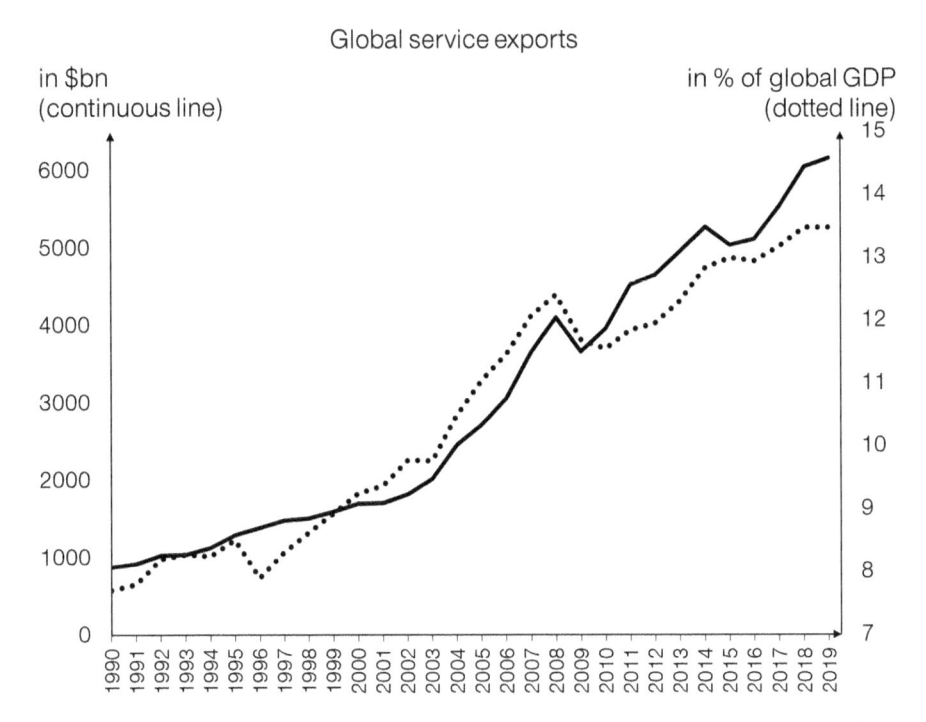

Fig. 11.4 Global service exports in absolute terms and as a percentage of the global GDP

growth rate of service exports was 50% higher than the growth rate of the GDP during this period. Also, for the last 5 years the trade elasticity of service exports—unlike that of goods exports—is 1.67, significantly greater than 1. This means that service exports are growing faster than goods exports and GDPs.

It should be noted that service exports cannot be viewed as fully independent of goods exports. On the one hand, goods exports include considerable service components such as planning, assembly, transport, insurance, or training. The German Ministry of Economics puts the share at 39.3% [3]. In addition, exports of goods trigger demand for exports of services. According to Eurostat, the percentage is between 25 and 30% and trending upward [5]. In the case of Hidden Champions, the share is likely to be even higher due to the extent of the know-how embedded in their products. In addition, many of these market leaders aim to enrich their offerings with services. Digitalization supports these efforts.

Foreign Direct Investments

A third, increasingly important route of globalization is foreign direct investment (FDI). Figure 11.5 shows the development of global FDI since 1990 [6].

FDI was an enormously important driver of globalization in the 17 years from 1990 to 2007. At its peak in 2007, the value of global FDI had increased 10.8-fold to $3.197 trillion from $278 billion in 1990. This represents an annual growth rate of 16.0%, which far exceeds the growth rates of goods and service exports. The elasticity of direct investment relative to GDP during this period was 2.56, meaning that direct investment grew about 2.5 times as fast as GDP.

Since the onset of the Great Recession in 2008, FDI has exhibited an erratic, downward sloping trajectory. After two maxima in 2011 and 2015 of around $2.2 trillion each, FDI fell back to $1.1 trillion in 2019. From 2007 to 2019, the investment elasticity was -2.47, meaning that for every percent GDP growth, FDI growth has declined by 2.47%, a dramatic negative trend. We can indeed speak of deglobalization during this period. However, we should not forget that annual direct investment is a flow variable that increases the respective FDI stock. This stock almost doubled between 2007 from $18.6 trillion to $34.6 trillion in 2019 [7]. This observation, which is

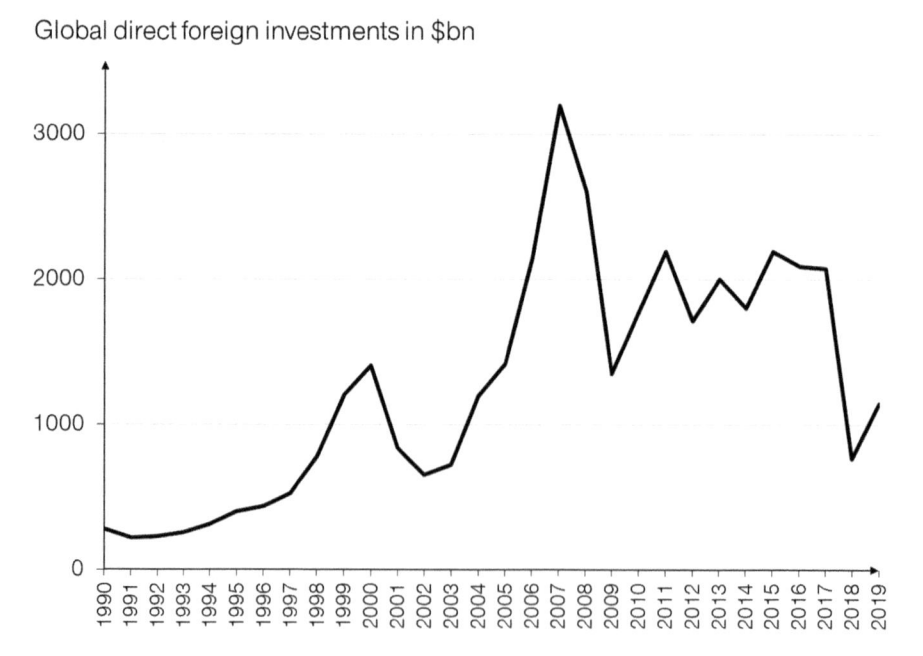

Fig. 11.5 Global Foreign Direct Investments since 1990

ultimately more relevant than annual figures, suggests that globalization has made considerable progress in terms of direct investment. However, this progress is running along rough roads. In Chap. 13, we will return to the question of the role that direct investment can play for the future of globalization and the Hidden Champions.

References

1. Retrieved from https://de.statista.com/statistik/daten/studie/37143/umfrage/weltweites-exportvolumen-im-handel-seit-1950/.
2. Rodrik, D. (2020, May 4). *The future of globalization after the Covid crisis*. Webinar, Princeton Bentheim Center for Finance.
3. Berlin. (2019). Retrieved from https://www.bmwi.de/Redaktion/EN/Publikationen/facts-about-german-foreign-trade.pdf?__blob=publicationFile&v=8.
4. Retrieved from https://data.worldbank.org/indicator/BX.GSR.NFSV.CD.
5. Luxemburg. (2019). Retrieved from https://ec.europa.eu/eurostat/statistics-explained/index.php/International_trade_in_services_by_type_of_service#International_trade_in_services_.E2.80.94_focus_on_selected_service_categories.
6. Retrieved from https://data.worldbank.org/indicator/BM.KLT.DINV.CD.WD?end=2019&start=1990.
7. Retrieved from https://unctad.org/en/Pages/DIAE/World%20Investment%20Report/Annex-Tables.aspx.

12

Quo Vadis Globalia: Population and Economy

In the previous chapter, we looked back to analyze where Globalia stands at the beginning of the 2020s and how it got to that point. We now turn to the future in order to try to understand how the global population and economy will develop in the coming decades.

I say "try" because there are no certain answers to the question, "Quo vadis Globalia?" Despite countless publications, no one can say how the aftereffects of COVID-19 will play out. Extreme scenarios are conceivable. In a worst-case scenario, there are multiple waves as the virus mutates further and plunges the global economy into years of depression. In the optimistic scenario, there are no further waves of infection, the vaccination campaigns have a lasting effect, and the virus is contained. With this outcome, the COVID-19 crisis could prove to be a temporary blip without any longer-term impact on the global economy.

This chapter looks at the longer-term demographic (population) and economic trends. While COVID-19 may have accelerated, amplified, or weakened these trends, I doubt that they will have been fundamentally altered by the pandemic in the long run. Globalia continues to grow strongly in terms of both population and economic power. The important insight and the essence of this chapter are that there will be large discrepancies between population growth and economic growth.

Population Dynamics

Population dynamics have significant effects on the economic growth and strength of a region or country. At present, the world population is growing by 83 million a year. According to UN forecasts, there will be 8.6 billion people on earth in 2030 and 9.7 billion in 2050. This corresponds to an annual growth rate of 0.75%. Figure 12.1 shows the latest UN projection of population numbers by 2050 for selected regions and countries.[1]

In 2050, 55% of all people will live in Asia–Pacific and 26% in Africa. You have to let that sink in. More than four-fifths of humanity will be living in Asia–Pacific and Africa. Europe will account for only 7.3% of the world's population, and North and South America together will account for 12.2%. India will be the most populous country with 1.6 billion people, surpassing China by 242 million or 17%. Africa will experience by far the strongest growth, with its population almost doubling from the current 1.34 billion to 2.49 billion in 2050. Other regions will grow more moderately or shrink in

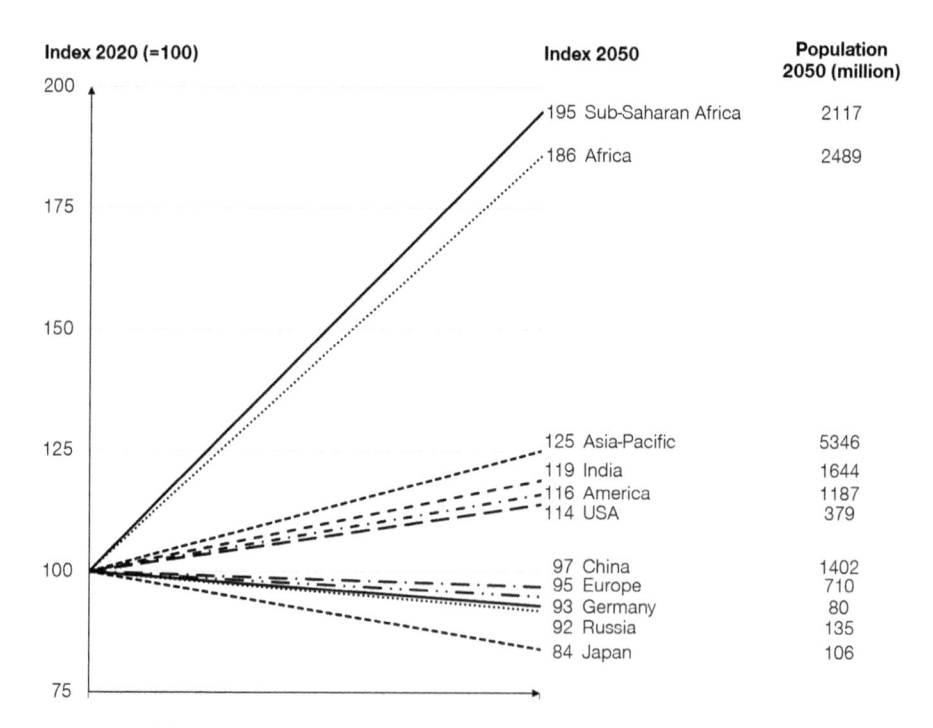

Index 2050	Population 2050 (million)
195 Sub-Saharan Africa	2117
186 Africa	2489
125 Asia-Pacific	5346
119 India	1644
116 America	1187
114 USA	379
97 China	1402
95 Europe	710
93 Germany	80
92 Russia	135
84 Japan	106

Fig. 12.1 Global population by 2050

---

[1] United Nations World Population Prospects 2019.

comparison. Japan is expected to experience the steepest decline of 20 million or 16%. The UN forecast presented in Fig. 12.1 is the so-called "medium variant," which UN experts consider the most likely. These figures are an important planning basis for politicians, business, and individual companies, including of course the Hidden Champions.

Although population forecasts are considered to be relatively reliable, some experts are increasingly skeptical of the UN projections. In their book *Empty planet—The shock of global population decline*, authors Bicker and Ibbitson consider a low variant scenario to be much more likely [1]. Charles Goodhart and Monaj Pradhan argue along the same lines in their book *The great demographic reversal: Ageing societies, waning inequality, and an inflation revival* [2]. The reasoning in these books that urbanization and better education of women lead to massive reductions in births per woman sounds convincing to me. The low variant scenario assumes that women have 0.5 fewer children than in the medium variant forecast. This means that in 2050 the world population would reach 8.5 billion rather than 9.7 billion and then decline. In China, this decline is likely to be dramatic. Bicker and Ibbitson state: "The Chinese population will fall to around 754 million by 2100. China's population could decline by almost half this century" [3]. I also question the UN forecast for Germany. In my opinion, Germany will have 93 million people in 2050, not the 80 million projected by the UN. Since 2014, the population has increased by two million. If the annual increase continues at 300,000 due to immigration, Germany will end up with 93 million people in 2050 [4].

In any case, the world population will grow and the center of gravity will continue to shift toward Africa and Asia. Individual regions and countries will develop very differently. The strategies of the Hidden Champions must adapt to these changes.

Economic Power and Growth

Population growth does not automatically mean increased economic power. A 30-year forecast of economic growth and GDP levels based solely on population predictions would be extremely speculative. We limit our economic projection to the next 10 years, i.e., up to 2030, which is also a realistic planning horizon for many companies. Figure 12.2 shows the World Bank's GDP projections for selected regions and countries in 2030.[2] The GDP values for

---

[2] Sources: World Bank World Development Indicators, International Financial Statistics of the International Monetary Fund (IMF), IHS Global Insight, and Oxford Economic Forecasting, as well as

Gross domestic product 2030 in $bn

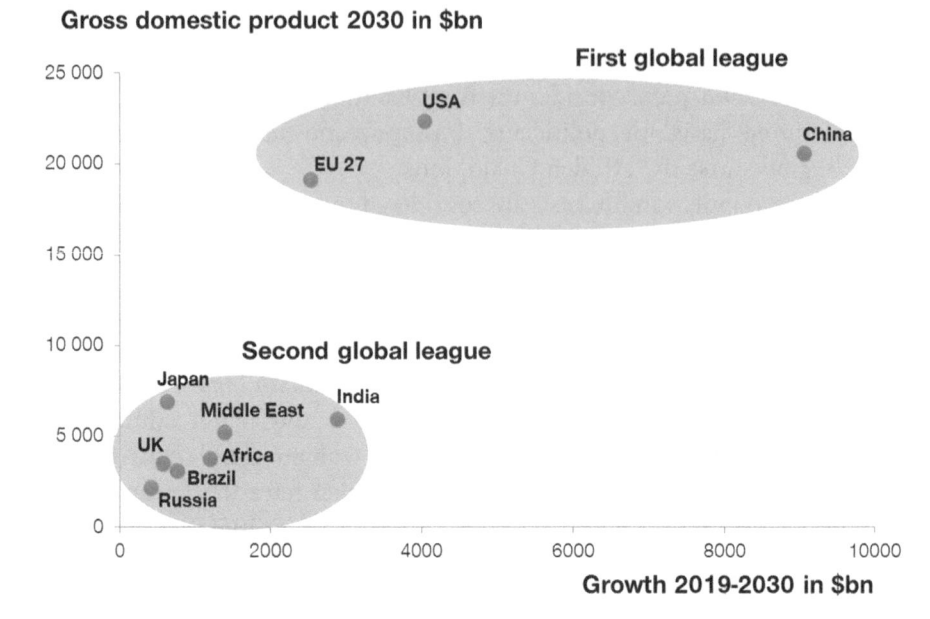

[Chart showing GDP 2030 vs Growth 2019-2030. First global league: USA (~22,500), China (~20,500), EU 27 (~19,000). Second global league: Japan, Middle East, India, UK, Africa, Brazil, Russia (all between 0-5,000 range).]

Fig. 12.2 GDPs and their growth by 2030

2030 are shown on the vertical axis, and absolute GDP growth from 2019 to 2030 is on the horizontal axis.

World GDP grows by 34.7% from $84.0 trillion in 2019 to $113.2 trillion in 2030. That growth of $29.2 trillion in absolute terms means that the global economy expands by the equivalent of one and a half USAs over the next decade. The USA will continue to be number 1 in GDP in 2030, while China will lead in growth by a wide margin. Economic power and growth will continue to be concentrated in a few regions. The "first global league," which includes the United States, China, and the European Union, will generate 54.4% of the world GDP in 2030. The first league's share of the growth is almost identical at 53.5%, with more than half of that coming from China.[3]

In 2030, the "second global league"—which includes the UK, Japan, Brazil, India, Russia, Africa, and the Middle East (Iran, Iraq, Saudi Arabia, and Turkey)—will account for 26.9% of the global GDP. Its share in world GDP growth is almost identical at 27.0%. The growth of the second league is not as high as expected for a variety of reasons. Japan and the UK start from a high GDP level, but have low growth. The remaining countries have higher growth

---

estimated and projected values developed by USDA, Economic Research Service all converted to a 2010 base year. The data were updated on March 20, 2020.

[3] If you include the UK and Switzerland in Europe, it is even 58.4%.

rates, but the starting level is low. Russia has the weakest growth in absolute terms with $415 billion (+23.7%). Africa is growing by 47.5%, but in absolute terms the growth is only $1.201 trillion due to the low starting base. This is a mere 13% of the growth of China or 29.7% of the growth of the United States.

The Population-Economy-Divide

So what is the answer to the question "Quo vadis Globalia?" in terms of population and economy? Whether population size or purchasing power is more important for a company depends on the product(s) it sells. If a company sells low-priced smartphones, it can be guided by population size. Even in poorer countries, virtually every consumer buys a cell phone. If, on the other hand, GDP is more likely to be the relevant indicator of market attractiveness if a company operates a business with sophisticated medical technology. Ultimately, the business and growth opportunities offered by a country arise from the size and the growth of its GDP, not from the sheer size of its population. Although Africa's population will almost double by 2050, its share of global GDP will increase only minimally from 3.0 to 3.3% over the next 10 years. Economic power will remain concentrated in the first global league, both in terms of level and—from a social perspective—unfortunately also in terms of growth.

COVID-19 may exacerbate this discrepancy. In a survey of economists in the United States, 62% believe the pandemic will be detrimental to developing countries [5]. Whether you like it or not, the battlefield for global market leadership, which for many Hidden Champions is part of their identity, will be the first global league: the USA, China, and the EU. One does not become or remain a Hidden Champion without a strong market position in the first global league. It is difficult for success in the second league to offset weakness in the first-league markets. The first aim of Hidden Champions, or companies that want to become one, must therefore be to shine in the first global league. Staying in this first division poses major challenges for Hidden Champions in terms of global organization, market presence, innovation, and, last but not least, digitalization. The need for transformation is obvious.

References

1. Bricker, D., & Ibbitson, J. (2019). *Empty planet—The shock of global population decline*. London: Little, Brown Book Group.
2. Goodhart, C., & Pradhan, M. (2020). *The great demographic reversal: Ageing societies, waning inequality, and an inflation revival*. London: Palgrave Macmillan.
3. Bricker, D., & Ibbitson, J. (2019). *Empty planet—The shock of global population decline*. London: Little, Brown Book Group, quote: Kindle position 2504.
4. Simon, H. (2016, February 25). 93 Millionen werden wir sein. *Die Zeit*.
5. Rodrik, D. (2020, May 4). *The future of globalization after the Covid crisis*. Webinar, Princeton Bentheim Center for Finance.

13

Quo Vadis Globalia: Dynamic Framework

While the previous chapter described the broad lines of population and economic development in Globalia, we now take a more detailed look at the political, legal, and cultural frameworks that directly affect business. In the next ten years, global businesses will be operating under constantly changing conditions, leading to greater uncertainty and volatility. In this context, a natural strength of the Hidden Champions—agility—will become even more relevant.

Winners of Globalization

There is no doubt that globalization has brought massive prosperity to the world, but the benefits are very unevenly distributed. The Globalization Report 2020 quantifies the wealth gains resulting from globalization in the years from 1990 to 2018 for 45 countries [1]. Table 13.1 shows the cumulative income gains for the twelve countries that have benefited most from globalization, led by Japan with a cumulative per capita income gain of €50,044.

Table 13.2 shows the other side of the coin, the countries with the smallest benefits from globalization.

Let us look at the third column first. The fact that the USA is not among the primary beneficiaries of globalization is less surprising than China's seemingly weak performance. However, with China, as with India, one must keep in mind that these numbers are per capita. Because of their large populations, these countries regularly show low values in per capita comparisons (for example, in exports and patents). The fourth column, however, shows that in

Table 13.1 Cumulative per capita income gains from increasing globalization from 1990 to 2018

Rank	Country	Cumulative income gain per capita since 1990 in €
1	Japan	50,044
2	Ireland	45,060
3	Switzerland	44,329
4	Finland	37,618
5	Israel	35,711
6	Netherlands	32,684
7	Germany	31,133
8	Denmark	29,988
9	Slovenia	27,685
10	South Korea	25,039
11	Greece	24,365
12	Austria	24,356

Table 13.2 Countries that have benefited less per capita from globalization

Rank	Country	Cumulative income gain per capita since 1990 in €	Cumulative income gain as a percentage of GDP per capita 1990
26	USA	12,650	52
39	Brazil	3,806	85
41	Russia	3,213	92
42	China	2,658	835
45	India	671	174

relative terms China is an outstanding winner of globalization. The cumulative income gain from globalization is 8.35 times China's per capita gross domestic product of 1990,[1] compared with only 1.74 times in India. This relative measure also shows that the USA has indeed benefited the least from globalization. This may explain the critical attitude of many Americans toward global trade.

Despite the massive prosperity gain, globalization currently faces increasing skepticism. In a recent study among economists, 86% believe it is necessary to rethink globalization. One author speaks of a "retreat from hyper-globalization" [2]. A study by one bank states: "Globalization has come to an end" [3].

Hastily drawn under the impression of the COVID-19 crisis, such conclusions seem premature. One expert on historical crises states: "The fact that the world will no longer be the same after 2020, as is often claimed, represents a factual simplification which is due to a perception hardly clear from a

---

[1] For the development of gross national products, see: https://de.wikipedia.org/wiki/Liste_der_L%C3%A4nder_nach_historischer_Entwicklung_des_Bruttoinlandsprodukts_pro_Kopf.

scientific point of view" [4]. Based on an evaluation of several studies, the *Financial Times* comes to a more succinct conclusion, "Reports of globalization's death are greatly exaggerated" [5].

The future of globalization is by no means clear. It is an open question whether the conflict between the USA and China, which has led to massive tariff increases and trade conflicts, will intensify further or be mitigated by new treaties. The same applies to sanctions against countries such as Russia and Iran. Some plans for free trade agreements have failed entirely (e.g., the agreement between the EU and the USA) or partially (the Trans-Pacific Agreement after the withdrawal of the USA). However, the latter agreement, called the Regional Comprehensive Economic Partnership (RCEP), was completed between 15 Pacific Rim countries. There have been free trade agreements between the EU and Canada, the EU and Japan, and the UK and Japan. Even during President Trump's term, Chinese government bonds were included in the FTSE Russell and other major global indices by JP Morgan and Bloomberg Barclays. An influx of $140 billion is expected in the coming years [6]. One of the first acts of President Biden was to reverse his predecessor's withdrawal of the USA from the World Trade Organization (WTO).

Trade barriers are among the many reasons why it may become more advantageous for global companies to have regional production capabilities. The following examples show how trade barriers sometimes lead to absurd consequences. A Hidden Champion with factories in Europe and China used its Chinese plant to supply the Chinese and American markets. When the higher tariffs, initiated by President Trump, made exports from China to the USA unprofitable, the company had no choice but to supply the USA from Europe and to fill the resulting supply gaps in Europe with imports from China. Because this led to a massive increase in logistics costs, the company is now setting up long overdue manufacturing capacity in the USA. Another example: After the outbreak of African swine fever in Germany, China banned imports of pork and gelatin of German origin. Gelita, the world leader in gelatin, responded by shipping goods from its U.S. plants to China.

More Globalization?

The more sensible solution in the current situation is more globalization, not less. Two numerical examples support this position. German per capita exports in 2019 were $18,018, compared with $1,797 in China and $240 per capita in India. In other words, China's per capita exports are only 10% of Germany's, and India's are a mere 1.3%. What does this comparison mean? India needs to export far more in order to acquire the purchasing power for the infrastructure goods, machinery, aircraft, etc., it needs from industrialized countries to "get on its feet." The same is true for Africa. In 2019, German companies exported goods worth €24.9 billion to Sweden. In the same year, the sum of German exports to all countries in Africa reached a value of €23.7 billion, and German imports from Africa were at a similar level of €24.4 billion. Africa has 120 times as many inhabitants as Sweden, whose population stands at 10.2 million. It is obvious that Africa must export much more in order to be able to import more from Germany in order to "get on its feet."

Leading economists share the observation that the world needs more globalization. Lars Feld, chairman of the German Council of Economic Experts, says: "In my view, we need more rather than less globalization in order to have a cushion against future crises" [7]. Policymakers should work to develop the framework necessary to foster further globalization and to prevent the continuation of the decoupling tendencies of recent years. It is important that freedom of trade is flanked by social measures. As Harvard economist Dani Rodrik states: "The expansion of the welfare state enabled the political support of the population for economic openness" [8]. The Hidden Champions need free global trade to realize their full potential. Their relatively small size might actually be an advantage. Large companies are in the public and political spotlight, while Hidden Champions can operate below the radar of public attention due to their low profile. In this vein, globalization expert Pankaj Ghemawat surmises: "The backlash against globalization is a backlash against big business" [9].

Transforming Globalization

Despite my plea for freedom of trade, I expect a transformation of globalization in the sense that the exports of goods will increasingly be replaced by exports of services and by direct investments. As reported in the previous chapter, service exports have already grown faster than goods exports in recent years. Foreign direct investments, however, have followed a more erratic trend, strongly influenced by the capital markets. In the short term, the COVID-19 crisis has caused a strong outflow of capital from developing countries [2]. The influence of the capital markets on foreign direct investments will not disappear, but it will also not prevent their growth in the long term. As a result, the share of exports in the sales of Hidden Champions, which is currently at 60%, will tend to decline and the share of sales generated within foreign countries will rise accordingly [10]. The German Hidden Champions have already been employing more workers abroad than in Germany since 2010.

Today, many Hidden Champions derive more than 90% of their sales from exports [11]. I do not believe that this will remain the case. There are many arguments in favor of substituting direct investment for some exports. Increasing customs duties and trade barriers are the most obvious reason. The COVID-19 crisis has exposed the considerable risks of complex global supply chains. Driven primarily by opportunities for lower cost and greater efficiency, companies may have underestimated the risks induced by supply chain complexity. As the head of a German Hidden Champion asked: "Does it actually make sense to have 200 components manufactured in China, transport them to Germany and then assemble the final product here?"

Increased inventories can mitigate the risks of such a supply chain, but they generate higher costs and are not a universal cure in times of prolonged crises. It may make more sense to move final assembly to China, to manufacture more components in Germany, or to buy more inputs locally. One expert notes: "Globalization is partly turning into regionalization; the complete flow of goods is then organized within one market" [12]. Harvard professor Willy C. Shih formulates the challenge as follows: "The challenge for companies will be to make their supply chain more resilient without weakening their competitiveness" [13].

Environmental concerns are becoming increasingly important in this context. Why do so many products need to be transported around the world in such quantities? Evian water from France can be found in the minibars of better hotels all over the world. I was served Gerolsteiner, Germany's leading brand of sparkling water, on a ship in Halong Bay in northern Vietnam. The prices of these international brands can easily exceed the prices of local mineral waters by a factor of 10. I sincerely doubt anyone would be able to tell them apart blindfolded. So why does this phenomenon exist? The explanation is simple: Marketing and branding create an added value that is higher than the transport costs. However, it is doubtful whether transportation costs fully capture environmental damage, the so-called externalities.

The COVID-19 crisis has shown the dangerous risks in the global value chain for health and safety products. India accounts for a very high global share of production for some pharmaceutical substances. The world's largest vaccine manufacturer is the Serum Institute of India, a Hidden Champion. Around 80% of antibiotic components are produced in China. The reluctance to deal with Chinese telecommunications providers Huawei and ZTE highlights the limits of globalization. Global cooperation is likely to be scaled back in areas where systemic risks exist.

The COVID-19 crisis does not mean the end of globalization. An increase of inbound investments may actually strengthen the USA and Europe [14]. According to one survey, two-thirds of top European managers expect COVID-19 to benefit Europe as a manufacturing location [15]. The same is likely to apply to the USA.

Declining Transport Costs

The steady decline of transport costs can hardly be overestimated as a driver of globalization. As Fig. 13.1 shows, the real costs of shipping cargo, passenger flights, and international telephony have fallen to small fractions of their former values [16]. These costs have hit rock bottom and cannot fall much further. In fact, the costs of shipping and air transportation are more likely to rise

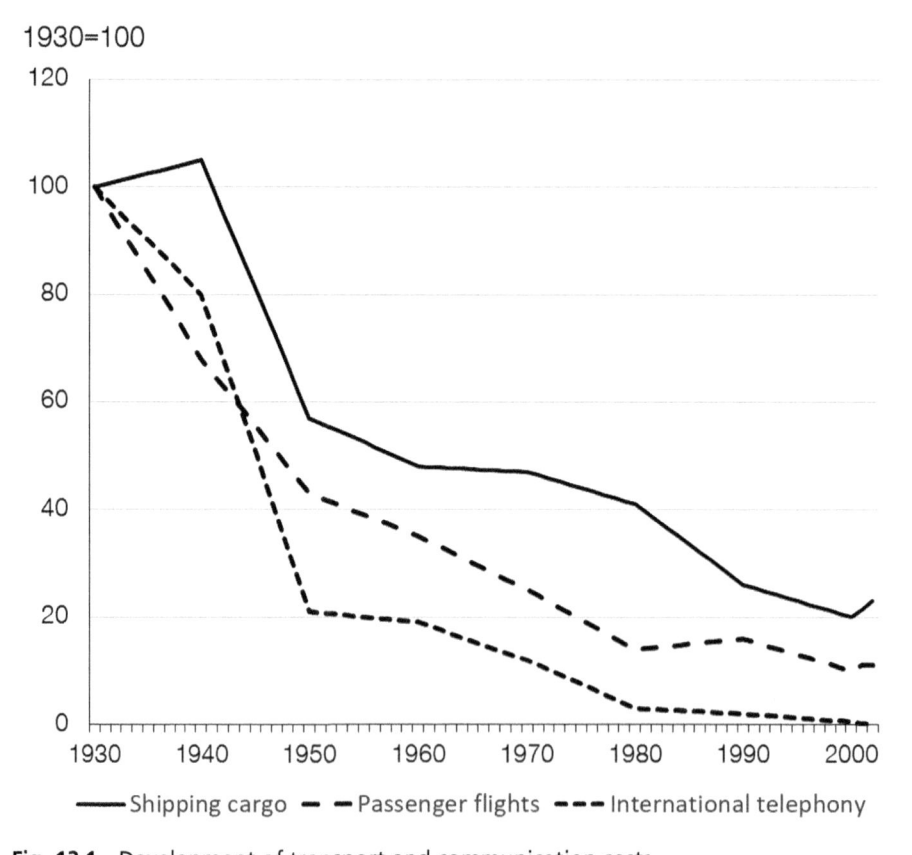

Fig. 13.1 Development of transport and communication costs

again, meaning that the globalization stimulus from falling logistics costs will no longer hold, at least as far as material goods are concerned.

Dematerialization

Dematerialization is another reason why the physical volumes of exports are likely to grow less quickly in the future. In the past, a transatlantic cable required 120,000 tons of copper. Today, a few hundred kilograms of the metal are enough to achieve the same performance via satellite. Smartphones weighing less than seven ounces replace a whole range of products such as cameras, computers, radios, and navigation devices. 3D printing will have a similar effect. Instead of manufacturing products in one country and exporting them to the target market, companies will send the data to the target market and use additive manufacturing processes to make the finished goods. MIT researcher Andrew McAfee provides a comprehensive analysis of dematerialization in his book *More from Less* [17]. In the USA, consumption of almost all raw materials has been declining or stagnating for years, even though the economy continues to grow. McAfee sees digitalization and capitalism as the key drivers of dematerialization. The role of digitalization is obvious. Capitalist competition also plays a central role because it requires constant cost-cutting and material savings. The most effective way to do this is to replace physical raw materials or their transport with bits.

Location-Competence Assimilation

Companies tend to be rooted in locations, countries, and cultures where they originate. Such ties are weaker in some multinational corporations than in traditional, less internationalized companies. One advantage of abandoning national ties is the freedom to carry out certain activities in locations where the conditions for those activities are optimal. I call this location-competence assimilation. Siemens CEO Roland Busch speaks of "glocalization" in a similar sense [18]. The necessity to carry out any activity where that activity can be done best is by no means confined to large multinationals. Any company exposed to global competition must apply location-competence assimilation. Hidden Champions must not close their minds to this necessity.

The trend is clearly toward serving a market from the respective region. Many German Hidden Champions already practice this. Webasto, the global market leader in sunroofs for cars, produces "in the market for the market"

[19]. Günter Frölich, CEO of Tristone Flowtech Group, a Hidden Champion for fluid applications, said: "We produce in China only for the Chinese market, we supply the European market only from European factories, and we supply the North American market only from factories in Mexico and the USA" [20].

Of course, each individual case must take the relationship between economies of scale and transport costs into account. Christian Diemer, CEO of Heitkamp & Thumann, global market leader in battery cans, remarks: "It is insanely cheap to transport a container from one end of the world to the other. Ideally, the external costs of the environmental impact of ocean shipping would have to be added on to the container freight. Since this is a global business, the question is: 'Who is going to do it?' There is no world government. Therefore, these shipments are likely to continue at these prices. The business question is how much value of goods can fit into a container, and thus how high the transport costs are as a percentage of the product's value. For simple steel, transport is expensive relative to value. An example is our battery cans. They are difficult to transport, so the cost of logistics is high, making local production more economical, but we make similar cans for asthma sprays. They have a higher value because of the special materials we use and the requirements of the pharmaceutical industry. A lot more value fits in a container than with battery cans, and economies of scale tip the balance in favor of manufacturing in Europe".[2]

The logic for decisions on locations must extend further. If China—for whatever reasons, and not just its market—offers the best conditions for manufacturing a product or for a research and development activity, then a globally active company is well advised to carry out this activity there. If, on the other hand, you see more favorable conditions in Silicon Valley or India, then you should become active there. In this sense, Westerners must become Asians and Asians must become Westerners. Or, as Stefan Oschmann, CEO of E. Merck, Germany puts it, "We should become more Asian" [21]. The reverse is also true. If Germany offers optimal conditions, then the Chinese, Americans, or Indians should locate their operations in Germany. This is exactly what the Chinese are doing with car design centers and what Tesla is doing at the gigafactory in Grünheide, close to Berlin. At a meeting of 100 Chinese auto suppliers, many expressed the intention to invest and produce in Germany in order to supply German automakers. I expect a strong increase in foreign direct investment in all directions in the coming years. This process

---

[2] Personal communication with Christian Diener, September 21, 2020.

will take various forms such as greenfield plants, acquisitions, and joint ventures.

Travel or Zoom?

Travel, especially international air travel, came to a virtual standstill during the COVID-19 crisis. Yet surprisingly, global business did not totally collapse. International trade in goods continued, albeit at reduced levels, even though planners, engineers, salespeople, consultants, and service technicians could no longer travel and communicate with their customers personally.

Communication is communication, and businesspeople will always find a way. Virtual communication quickly replaced in-person communication. Zoom and similar software experienced a boom that would have previously been unimaginable. At Simon-Kucher alone, we had 415,000 Zoom sessions in 2020.

Does this mean that the "Zoom globalization" will supplant "travel globalization?" There are many reasons for at least a partial but permanent shift: time savings, reduction of physical and mental stress, and last but not least, the environmental aspects. Is it reasonable to fly from Germany to Shanghai or Beijing for a short lecture, as I often have? Such a trip pollutes the air with two tons of CO_2. You are underway for at least 48 h and come back exhausted. During the COVID-19 crisis, I did such lectures from the comfort of my home via Zoom. If the lecture needed to be more professional, a camera team came to record my presentation. Time, costs, and the environment are only one side of the coin. The other side concerns the impact or, more generally, the benefit or value of communication. First, there is a quantitative benefit. In-person conferences in China reach a maximum of a few thousand listeners, whereas one of my virtual speeches reached 20 million people there. A digital interview in India reached 14,000. Expressing the qualitative dimension defies such straightforward quantification. What is the value of communication with a physical presence versus one with only a virtual presence? How does this difference change the value of communication in consulting or sales conversations, in meetings, in conferences, or in lectures?

In a recent study, Harvard researchers concluded that 17% of global economic output is at risk if business travel is permanently eliminated [22]. Business travel is indispensable for the dissemination of knowledge and know-how. Complex knowledge can be transferred most effectively in personal trainings by experts onsite. According to the study, the most frequent destination for business trips is the company's own subsidiaries. The more often employees of a car manufacturer travel to foreign factories, the more productive those facilities subsequently become. The researchers were able to prove that this relationship is not only causal, but also endures for several years.

When it comes to the outflow or dissemination of know-how via business trips, Germany was ranked first, ahead of Canada, the USA, the UK, South Korea, France, and Japan. India was ranked 12th, Brazil 15th, and China only 17th. Austria, Ireland, Switzerland, Denmark, Belgium, Hong Kong, and Singapore benefited the most as recipients of that know-how. No developing country ranked in the top 25.

Ricardo Hausmann, the study's lead author, concludes: "Our research implies that the world will pay a significant price for the shutdown of business travel, which will become apparent through lower post-crisis productivity growth, employment, and output" [23]. This study suggests that only a portion of business travel and communication in Globalia should be replaced by digital communication. The progress of globalization will continue to depend critically on the international mobility and presence of people.

References

1. Prognos AG. (2020, June). *Globalisierungsreport 2020: Wer profitiert am stärksten von der Globalisierung?* im Auftrag der Bertelsmann Stiftung, Baseline.
2. Rodrik, D. (2020, May 4). *The future of globalization after the Covid crisis*. Webinar, Princeton Bentheim Center for Finance.
3. Bayern LB/Prognos. (2020, June 30). Die Globalisierung ist zu Ende: Deutschland muss sich neu erfinden—Study of Bayern LB and Prognos: Deutschland braucht dringend ein neues Geschäftsmodell, Berlin/Munich.
4. Näther, B. (2020, September 9). Schlimme Zeiten stehen uns bevor—Wie uns die Covid 19-Epidemie mit historischen Erfahrungen verbindet—und warum diese Verbindung trügerisch ist. *Frankfurter Allgemeine Zeitung*, p. N1.
5. Tett, G. (2020, December 3). Reports of globalisation's death are greatly exaggerated. *Financial Times*.
6. BNY Mellon. (2020, October 6). *New haven in Chinese bonds*. New York.
7. Heuser, H. (2020). Mehr statt weniger Globalisierung, Interview with Lars Feld, *Institutional Money*, 2, pp. 32–42, here p. 42.
8. Retrieved from https://drodrik.scholar.harvard.edu/files/dani-rodrik/files/wars_das_jetzt_mit_der_globalisierung.pdf.
9. Ghemawat, P. (2017). Globalization in the age of trump. *Harvard Business Review*, p. 123.

10. Rammer, C., & Spielkamp, A. (2019). *The distinct features of hidden champions in Germany: A dynamic capabilities view*, Mannheim: ZEW. The authors put the export share of the Hidden Champions they researched at 63 percent.
11. N.A. (2019, November 26). Diese 40 Top-Mittelständler machen über 90 Prozent Auslandsumsatz. *Die Deutsche Wirtschaft*.
12. N.A. (2020, November 2). Die Industrie ist nicht schlank, sondern magersüchtig. Interview, *Wirtschaftswoche*, special edition, pp. 34–35, here p. 35.
13. Shih, W. C. (2020). Global supply chains in a post-pandemic world. *Harvard Business Review*, p. 84.
14. Karabell, Z. (2020, March 20). Will the Corona-Virus bring the end of globalization? Don't count on it. *Wall Street Journal*.
15. Bastian, N. (2020, September 4). Unternehmenschefs sehen Wirtschaftsstandort Europa durch Corona gestärkt. *Handelsblatt*.
16. Retrieved from http://www.oecd.org/economy/outlook/38628438.pdf.
17. McAfee, A. (2020). *Mehr aus weniger: Die überraschende Geschichte, wie wir mit weniger Ressourcen zu mehr Wachstum und Wohlstand gekommen sind—Und wie wir jetzt unseren Planeten retten*. Munich: Deutsche Verlagsanstalt.
18. Meck, G., & Theurer, M. (2020, October 18). Was bleibt von Siemens, Herr Busch. Interview, *Frankfurter Allgemeine Sonntagszeitung*.
19. Frohn, P., Macho, A., & Salz, J. (2020, March 13). Wie viel Globalisierung ist gesund? *Wirtschaftswoche*, pp. 47–49, here p. 49.
20. Interview with Günter Frölich, Investment Plattform China/Deutschland, 2/2020, p. 8.
21. N.A. (2020, September 9). Merck-Chef Stefan Oschmann: Wir sollten asiatischer werden. *Handelsblatt*.
22. Coscia, M., Neffke, F., & Hausmann, R. (2020). Knowledge diffusion in the network of international business travel. *Nature Human Behavior*. https://doi.org/10.1038/s41562-020-0922-x
23. Hausmann, R. (2020, August 10). *Why zoom can't save the world*. Retrieved from project-syndicate.org.

14

Target Market America

Size and growth define the attractiveness of markets. For the Hidden Champions of German-speaking countries, this puts the USA and China at the top of their priority list, alongside their home market of Europe. A leading role in the global market requires a strong position in the home market. More than half of German exports (58.6%) go to the European Union. But the largest single national market for German companies is the USA, with 8.9% of German exports. If we include Canada and Mexico, North America accounts for 11%, while China accounts for 7.2% of German exports.

Size and growth will continue to make the USA and China extremely important target markets for Hidden Champions over the next decade. As mentioned in Chap. 12, the USA will still have the largest GDP in 2030. China, meanwhile, is the market with by far the biggest GDP growth through 2030.

America vs. China

Which future target market is more important for German companies and Hidden Champions: the USA or China? This is an interesting question with no easy answer. There is no doubt that Europeans feel politically, historically, and culturally closer to the USA than to China. This subjective proximity affects the perceived geographical distance. The USA seems closer in terms of travel time, but in reality, the proximity of both countries in terms of flight times is about the same. The flight time from Frankfurt to New York is 8 h and 40 min, while to Beijing it is 9 h and 15 min. The same applies to the more distant cities. The travel times to Los Angeles (11:35) and Hong Kong (11:30) are almost identical. Central Europe lies halfway between America and China, an ideal position for tapping into both giant markets.

So how successful are German companies and Hidden Champions in these target markets? In terms of German exports, the USA (€119 billion) is well ahead of China (€96 billion). But if we instead measure market penetration, i.e., the share of German exports relative to the GDP of the target market, German companies are stronger in China with a "market share" of 0.76% than in the USA with 0.62%.[1] This applies to an even greater extent to the German automotive industry. Volkswagen has a market share of around 15% in China, compared with only 3.8% in the USA.

For the German Hidden Champions, both markets are indispensable. German politics and business must do everything in their power to avoid getting caught between the millstones of a potential U.S.–China conflict. Deutsche Bank CEO Christian Sewing says that "in case of doubt, Atlantic Bridge must go before Silk Road" [1], but one can only hope that such a decision will never become necessary and that Germany and Europe will be able to continue their cooperation with both sides. The German government formulates this principle in its guidelines for the Indo-Pacific region: "No country should be forced—as during the Cold War—to make the choice between two sides" [2]. America and China are equally important to the Hidden Champions. Together with the European Union, they account for around 60% of future world market potential and 75% of Germany's exports. In order to become and remain a Hidden Champion, a company has to focus on these three regions.

Transatlantica: A Failed Dream?

The idea that America and Europe were growing into one economic unit was widespread in the 1990s. The most striking symbol was the DaimlerChrysler merger of November 17, 1998. As a member of the award jury of *Manager Magazin*, Germany's leading business monthly, I voted for Jürgen Schrempp, who forged that merger, as "Manager of the Year." The magazine wrote: "The experts praised Jürgen Schrempp for his courageous and visionary approach and drew attention to his spectacular Chrysler deal. Although still unfinished and by no means immune to failure, the merger was an exemplary

---

[1] This relative figure only serves as an indicator and does not make much sense in itself, as the gross domestic product is the sum of value creation, whereas exports are the sum of revenues.

forward-looking decision" [3]. I enthusiastically shared the vision of an American–European economic zone and coined the term "Transatlantica" [4]. A well-known supporter of this vision was John Kornblum, the U.S. ambassador to Germany at the time. He commented: "We must do more to adapt the best practices of the various regions in our community if our common organism, 'Transatlantica'—a term coined by management consultant Hermann Simon—is to prosper" [5].

Transatlantica turned out to be an illusion. Symptomatic of this was the selection of Jürgen Schrempp as "Worst Manager of the Year" by *Business Week* only a few years later [6] as well as the subsequent dissolution of DaimlerChrysler. Nevertheless, the vision of a future Transatlantica should not be abandoned.

Challenge USA

The American market was, is, and will remain a difficult challenge for German and European companies. This is true for large companies as well as for mid-sized enterprises, including the Hidden Champions. Large companies such as Deutsche Post DHL, Tengelmann, RWE, and Thyssen Krupp were unsuccessful in the American market and have partially or completely withdrawn. Adidas did not have much luck with its takeover of Reebok. For some companies, misguided U.S. commitments even brought about their demise. These include Hoechst AG, which was the world's largest pharmaceutical manufacturer in the 1980s, and the Gerling Group, a large insurer, which collapsed as a result of the hasty acquisition of the American reinsurer Constitution Re. Others are on a bumpy road, such as Bayer after its acquisition of Monsanto.

Nor did things always go well in the opposite direction. Walmart threw in the towel after just a few years in Germany. Following years of heavy losses, General Motors sold Opel to France's PSA, which is now Stellantis. In 2018, only three years after the acquisition of the German department store chain Galeria Kaufhof, the Canadian Hudson's Bay Company admitted defeat and handed the chain over to Signa Group.

Other German companies, however, are very successful in North America. Fresenius Medical Care AG generates 70% of its revenue there, and Deutsche Telekom generates half. The U.S./North American market accounts for 35% of Infineon's revenue and 33% of SAP's. The shares of revenue for German automakers in that market are 26% for Daimler, 19% for BMW, and 17% for Volkswagen.

Other German companies generate significant revenue in North America, but even more in Asia–Pacific. These include E. Merck (26% and 35%, respectively) and Adidas (23% and 34%). There are also large German companies that do little business in the USA. Allianz, the world's second largest insurance company, generates only 8.6% of its premium revenue in America. At Deutsche Bank, only 10.7% of receivables from lending business can be attributed to the USA. Other DAX companies such as Deutsche Börse or Vonovia, a large real estate company, are practically not active in the USA at all.

It is difficult to get an overall idea of the Hidden Champions' performance in North America, as many of them do not report regional sales. The U.S. share of sales at Karl Storz, global market leader in endoscopy, is 44%. Leanix, a provider of enterprise architecture software that was only founded in 2012, generates 39% of its sales in the United States. At laboratory equipment supplier Sartorius, the figure is 34%, at Simon-Kucher 27%.

The Freudenberg Group, which includes several Hidden Champions, generates 26% of its revenue in the USA. The specialty adhesives manufacturer Delo reports a significantly lower share of 11%. Some Hidden Champions achieve sales shares of less than 10% in the USA or have no significant business there. Others, for various reasons, deliberately decided against entering the U.S. market. These include the leading wind turbine manufacturer Enercon, which is only now planning to push ahead with its U.S. market entry [7]. Service providers have a harder time in the American market than product manufacturers, so their share of sales in the USA is low. TÜV Rheinland, one of the world's leading inspection and certification companies, generates only 8.6% of its sales in the U.S. market. German trade fair companies—which are global market leaders in many segments—attract just 3.1% of their millions of visitors in the USA.

Higher Priority for the US Market

The extreme importance of North America is by no means limited to exports. Operating in Transatlantica requires a European rather than a purely German perspective. In 2019, the USA imported $515 billion worth of goods from the EU, while the EU imported $337 billion from the USA.[2] This amounts to an American deficit of $178 billion in the trade of goods, but the situation is

---

[2] Source for this and the following figures: Hamilton, D. S. & Quinland, J. P. (2020). *The Transatlantic Economy 2020, Annual Survey of Jobs, Trade and Investment between the United States and Europe*, Baltimore: Johns Hopkins University, Paul H. Nitze School for Advanced International Studies.

reversed for services. EU exports of services to the USA were $236 billion, while $312 billion worth of services flowed from the USA to the European Union, leaving the USA a surplus of $76 billion. In total, the transatlantic exchange of services amounts to $548 billion. The corresponding figure for China is only $72.8 billion. This comparison shows that the transatlantic integration in services is far stronger than between Europe and China.

The transatlantic figures for direct investment are even more impressive. Some 61% of U.S. foreign investment flows to the European Union. Conversely, 50% of U.S. foreign investment comes from the EU. American companies employ 4.9 million people in Europe, while 4.7 million people work in the USA for European companies.

There has also been a strong uptick in acquisitions of American companies by German firms. Bertelsmann acquired publisher Simon & Schuster ($1.9 billion), Siemens Healthineers acquired rival Varian ($16 billion), Daimler acquired truck manufacturer Navistar ($3.7 billion), and Compugroup Medical acquired the Physician Information System ($240 million). "The United States is the most important target market for German companies in cross-border acquisitions," says Christian Kames, head of JP Morgan's German investment banking operations [8].

Digitalization puts additional pressure on transatlantic integration. The transatlantic data flow is 55% higher than the transpacific one. About three-quarters of the world's digital content is generated in Transatlantica, and transatlantic relations are particularly important as drivers of innovation. EU companies spend $44 billion a year on research and development in the USA, compared with $33 billion the other way around. A strong R&D presence in the USA is indispensable for companies that want to keep up in Globalia, because a large amount of global innovative thinking and research continues to originate in America. Despite the siren songs of deglobalization and decoupling, the USA and Europe will remain deeply intertwined. The U.S. market deserves a much higher priority from a German and European perspective. There is a need to catch up. This even applies to the Hidden Champions.

Overcoming Barriers

Why has the U.S. market been relatively neglected in the past? And what are the lessons for the future? One obvious answer is that for many companies, market development in China has consumed considerable resources over the past 20 years. It is usually easier to capture market share in a new, rapidly growing market than to penetrate an established market and take market share from competitors. Competition in the American market is extremely tough. The established players are mostly companies with strong financial power and market positions. The huge size of the U.S. market creates barriers to entry that can only be overcome with massive investments and great perseverance.

Companies often underestimate the differences between European and American consumers, because they assume that both belong to Western culture and thus want the same things. A German supplier of interior design products had major problems with the color preferences of American consumers. A manufacturer of components for air-conditioning systems found that the low noise level of its products was a disadvantage in America, because Americans want to "hear" their air-conditioning. The American retail market is even more concentrated in large chains than Europe's. If one wants to reach the end consumer, a listing in chains such as Walmart is a necessity. For little-known mid-sized companies like the Hidden Champions, these listings pose a high barrier.

The American legal system also acts as a deterrent, especially with regard to liability issues. Great care and caution are required here. As everywhere, products and services that are genuinely new to the US market have the best chances. Simon-Kucher, for example, succeeded in entering the market relatively quickly because price consulting was an innovation even in the USA.

Finally, a key success factor is the ability to attract qualified employees. The best graduates in the USA have essentially been pre-screened by the elite universities they attended. Competition for this elite is fierce. On the other hand, it is difficult to find skilled workers who meet German standards. Miele had great problems attracting technicians who could maintain and repair Miele machines. Often, the only solution in such cases is in-house training.

Capital Market USA

New York will continue to be the world's most important financial center for the foreseeable future. The valuations achieved on the New York stock exchanges, especially at NASDAQ, are inconceivable in Europe. A presence in New York is indispensable for companies with high capital requirements and for banks that want to play a global role. This is equally true for Hidden Champions in certain industries such as biotechnology and high-tech.

It is not surprising that the German companies BioNTech and Curevac, which attracted a great deal of attention with their COVID-19 vaccines, did not go public on the German stock exchange in Frankfurt, but rather on

NASDAQ in New York. BioNTech's IPO took place in October 2019. In early 2021, its market capitalization reached $25.7 billion. CureVac went public in August 2020, reaching a market capitalization of $18.3 billion half a year later. These valuations would have been unimaginable on the German stock exchange. Other German biotech companies such as Centogene and Immatics are also listed on NASDAQ.

The high importance and attractiveness of the US market will persist. The Hidden Champions will have to devote significantly greater resources to penetrating this market. They must not underestimate the barriers to entering this market and establishing a strong market position, but I know from my own experience with Simon-Kucher that the effort is worth it.

References

1. Sewing, C. (2020, September 4). Nur wer einig ist, der kann auch streiten. *Frankfurter Allgemeine Zeitung*, p. 11.
2. German government. (2020, September). Leitlinien zum Indo-Pazifik Deutschland—Europa—Asien, Das 21. Jahrhundert gemeinsam gestalten.
3. Retrieved from https://www.manager-magazin.de/unternehmen/karriere/a-167353.html.
4. Simon, H. (2000). Transatlantica: The New Atlantic century. *Harvard Business Review*, pp. 17–20.
5. Retrieved from https://de.usembassy.gov/de/globalisierung-und-die-new-economy-aus-personlicher-sicht/.
6. N.A. (2004, January 12). The worst managers: Jurgen Schrempp; DaimlerChrysler. *Business Week*, p. 72.
7. Retrieved from https://www.cleanthinking.de/windenergie-stuermische-zeiten-wie-geht-es-weiter/.
8. Smolka, K. M. (2020, December 5). Konzerne auf Jagd in Nordamerika. *Frankfurter Allgemeine Zeitung*, p. 25.

15

Target Market China

If a company wants to grow and remain competitive globally, it has to do business in China.

China has 18% of the world's population and generates 19% of global economic output. Its per capita income is currently slightly below the global average, but high growth rates will likely change this soon. By 2030, China alone will account for 31% of global economic growth. The global shares of China for individual products and services are even higher. China's share of global pork consumption, for example, is 54%. Growth has been China's main attraction over the last few decades and that will remain true for a long time to come.

In short, China, along with the United States, is vitally important for the Hidden Champions, both in terms of size and in terms of growth. While the political systems are fundamentally different in these two giant countries, the conditions for market development show some similarities. These include one national territory, one common national language (English and Mandarin), national regulations and standards, integrated transport and logistics systems, and national distribution systems. On the other hand, the sheer size of China's population poses massive challenges to companies of all sizes. Even Toyota needed 15 years to build up a nationwide dealer network there. For mid-sized companies, this task is much more difficult, especially with regard to the establishment of service networks.

Pioneers in the Chinese Market

Large German companies entered the Chinese market as early as the nineteenth century. Siemens has been active in China since 1872, and Bayer began selling dyes there in 1882. The Chinese city of Qingdao was part of the German Empire from 1898 to 1914 and the location of numerous Hanseatic trading companies.

Carl Zeiss established a Chinese branch in 1975, several years before China was opened by Deng Xiao Ping. After the opening, Liebherr entered into a cooperation with what was then the Qingdao Refrigerator Plant. The Chinese pronounce Liebherr as "Libo-haier." This gave rise to the name Haier—today the world's largest household appliance manufacturer [1].

Volkswagen took on a pioneering role by setting up production in Shanghai in 1984. In 2020, the German automotive groups Daimler, BMW, and Volkswagen sold a total of 5.41 million cars in China, 38.2% of their combined sales.[1] The Volkswagen investment attracted a convoy of medium-sized suppliers, among them many Hidden Champions. The largest concentration of German companies can be found in the city of Taicang, about an hour from Shanghai. The first German Hidden Champion to settle in Taicang in 1993 was Kern-Liebers, the global number one in seat belt springs with a world market share of 80%. Since then, this pioneer has been followed by more than 300 German companies, including 52 Hidden Champions. Taicang describes itself as the "second home" of the Germans and offers an ecosystem tailored to the needs of German SMEs, including schools, cultural centers, and service providers. Numerous other cities in China, including many newly established industrial parks, imitate this model and engage in attracting investments from German Hidden Champions. Simon-Kucher supported several industrial parks in these activities.

German Hidden Champions in China

Today, around 8500 German companies are active in China. They operate more than 2000 factories, most of which were established as greenfield projects. More than half of all German Hidden Champions (53%) have their own companies in China, and around 60% of these operate manufacturing plants there [2]. Sales and service companies account for the remaining 40% [2].

---

[1] *China Table*, January 25, 2021.

The number of employees underscores the importance of the Hidden Champions' subsidiaries in China. The global market leader in car lighting systems, the Hidden Champion Hella, has been in China since 1982 and employs 5200 people there, or 14% of its total workforce. Webasto, world market leader in sunroofs, has 3500 employees in China (25%), Carl Zeiss has 3200 (10%), Heraeus 2750 (18%), the measuring technology champion Jumo 450 (19%), and the textile machine manufacturer Karl Mayer 800 (25%). Arno Gärtner, CEO of the Karl Mayer Group, says that "Karl Mayer's success over the past 15 years has been largely determined by Karl Mayer China" [3].

These and similar pioneers benefited from their early market entry in two ways. First, China has become the most important sales market for many of these companies. Aixtron, the world leader in compound semiconductor manufacturing equipment, generates 46% of its sales in China, while Webasto's share of sales from China (35%) is almost double its share from the USA (18%). Secondly, as a major manufacturing location, China has contributed to the global market leadership of the Hidden Champions.

Where China Is Tops

As we said earlier, a company is well-advised to do things where they can be done best. So what are the things that can be done best in China? The question applies equally to mature industries and to the emerging industries of the future. An example of a mature industry is coal mining. In Germany, there has been no hard coal mining since 2018, and the era of lignite mining is coming to an end. If a mining supplier has no more customers in Germany, the location becomes problematic. But coal mining plays a very important role in China. Consequently, Schenck Process, a global market leader in the field of measurement and process technology for coal plants, has relocated its mining division to Beijing. SMT Scharf, the global number one in monorails for underground mining, was able to compensate for the decline of its European business with strong growth in China and is represented there by three companies.

What are the future industries in China where the Hidden Champions should do business as suppliers or cooperation partners? Oliver Hermes, Chairman & CEO of the Hidden Champion Wilo, global market leader in pumps, is convinced that Asia will lead the way in digital marketing. Consequently, Wilo has relocated its competence center for digital marketing to Shanghai. Another answer to this question is provided by the "Made in China 2025" initiative. It lists ten priority sectors in which China is striving to become the leader: (1) agricultural machinery, (2) shipbuilding and marine technology, (3) energy conservation and electromobility, (4) new-generation information and communication technologies, (5) high-end controlled machine tool systems and robotics technology, (6) electricity equipment, (7) aerospace equipment, (8) new materials, (9) advanced rail transportation equipment, and (10) biomedicine and high-performance medical equipment.

The USA and Europe have the strength and desire to defend their dominance in many of these sectors. Nonetheless, China is already a leader in some sectors. Half of all electric cars are driven in China, which produces 80% of all car batteries as well as 70% of all solar panels [4]. China is highly advanced in parts of information and communications technologies (e.g., artificial intelligence). The China Railway Corporation operates by far the largest and most modern high-speed system in the world. In aerospace, the process of catching up is ongoing.

Innovation from China

In China, more than one million patents are filed per year, including so-called utility patents. However, the Chinese patent standard is not comparable with that of highly developed industrialized countries, so a direct comparison of patent numbers makes little sense. More significant are the patent applications of Chinese origin in Europe and the USA, as shown in Figs. 15.1 and 15.2.

In both regions, the growth in Chinese patent applications has been spectacular. The Chinese are clearly making huge progress in terms of innovation. To participate in this enormous increase of expertise, companies must integrate themselves into the Chinese ecosystems. This requires not only production, but also research and development onsite in China, as well as cooperation with Chinese universities. It is the only way to remain world class.

China as Test Market

One feature of the Chinese market that has received too little attention to date is its role as a test market for innovations. Chinese consumers are considered to be particularly keen on innovation. They adopt new products more quickly than consumers in other countries. This is particularly true for digital services such as banking and e-commerce. An article in the Harvard Business Review says: "It's time to acknowledge that China's greatest asset in the

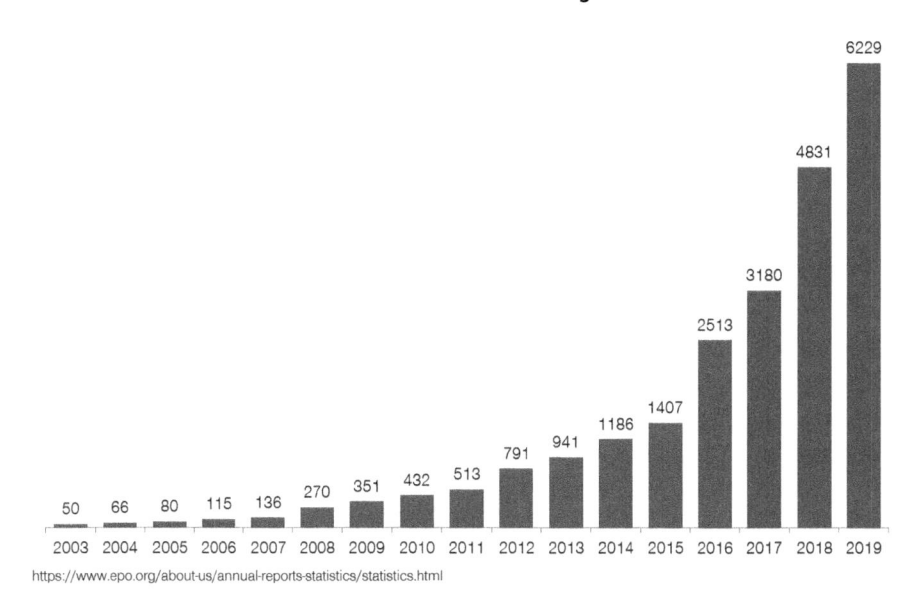

Fig. 15.1 Chinese patent applications in Europe

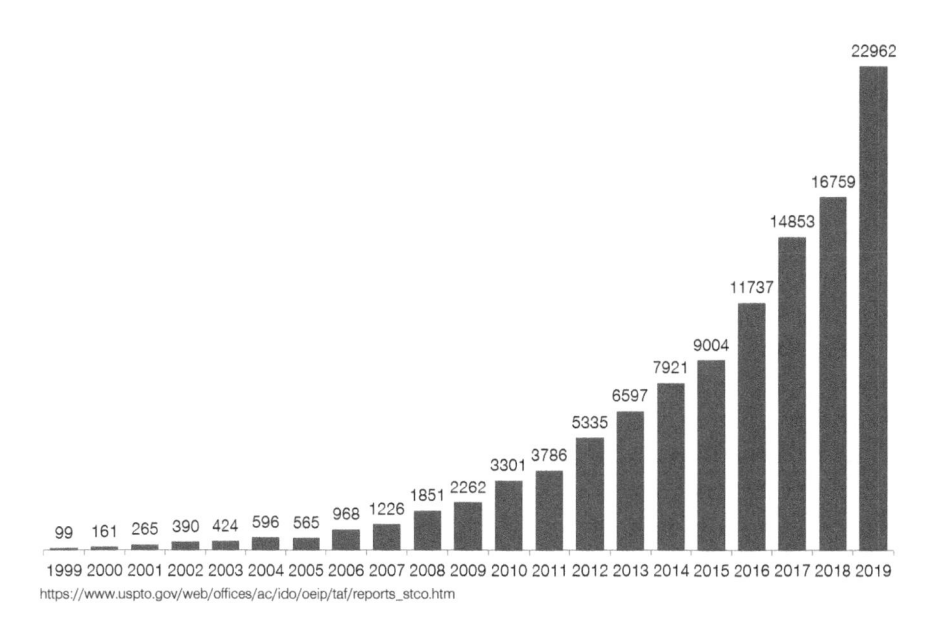

Fig. 15.2 Chinese patent applications in the USA since 1999

innovation arms race may be its uniquely adoptive and adaptive population. If the rest of us can recognize and learn from that, we can make China's new advantage our own" [5]. In line with our principle that a company should choose the best location in the world for any activity, this could mean introducing some innovations in China first so that one can quickly test how they are received by consumers. However, this approach could also entail the risk of rapid imitation by Chinese competitors.

Chinese Hidden Champions

Chinese companies are likely to become fierce competitors of the German Hidden Champions. Today, however, their number is still small. In our most recent survey, we were able to identify 94 Chinese Hidden Champions [6]. Examples include global market leaders such as DJI in drones, CIMC in containers, Bitmain in Bitcoin mining hardware, Jack in sewing machines, Soton in drinking straws, and Weixing in buttons. Among Chinese entrepreneurs, the ambition to become a Hidden Champion is very pronounced. When I ask entrepreneurs at presentations in China who would like to become a Hidden Champion, 50% usually raise their hand. In Germany, the figure is 5–10%. "Many Chinese entrepreneurs want to show the world how great and successful they are," a Chinese SME expert told me. When Chinese entrepreneurs internationalize, it raises their status in the peer group considerably.

In terms of strategy, I observe marked differences between German and Chinese Hidden Champions [7, 8]. The most striking features of each strategy are shown in Table 15.1.

Measured by the number of their own subsidiaries, the German Hidden Champions have a stronger global presence. Table 15.2 illustrates this with selected examples.

Typically, Chinese Hidden Champions have fewer than ten foreign subsidiaries, while German Hidden Champions have more than 50. These figures show that Chinese firms are at an early stage of globalization. The German Hidden Champions have also built global brands in their segments. This does not contradict the aspect "hidden," as these brands are only known in the respective target groups, but not by the general public. The Chinese Hidden

Table 15.1 Strategy differences between German and Chinese Hidden Champions

	German Hidden Champions	Chinese Hidden Champions
Global presence	High	Low
Global brands	Strong	Weak
Growth rate	Medium, gradual	High
IPO	Rather not	Very early
R&D employees	Few	Many

Table 15.2 International presence (number of subsidiaries) of selected German and Chinese Hidden Champions

German Hidden Champions			Chinese Hidden Champions		
Company	Product	Countries	Company	Product	Countries
Hillebrand	Logistics for alcoholic beverages	62	Goldwind	Wind energy	4
Kärcher	High-pressure cleaners	129	Hailide	Industrial resins	2
Germanischer Lloyd	Ship inspection	130	Han's Laser	Lasers	13
Krones	Bottling plants	90	Hikvision	Surveillance	28
Ottobock	Prosthetics	52	Lens	Electronics	3
Sartorius	Laboratory equipment	60	Mindray	Medical technology	42
Busch	Vacuum pumps	61	Ringpu	Veterinary medicine	only agents

Champions are only beginning to build global brands. Brand building not only requires resources, but also a lot of time.

The Chinese Hidden Champions are growing much faster than their German counterparts [9]. The size of the Chinese market promotes faster growth. Another key difference is financing. By going public early, the Chinese Hidden Champions raise large amounts of capital. German family-owned companies prefer financing from their own cash flow and shy away from going public.

Another consequence of better capitalization is that the Chinese Hidden Champions can afford larger research and development departments. Table 15.3 shows a comparison between selected German and Chinese Hidden Champions.

I estimate that Chinese Hidden Champions have about three to five times as many R&D employees as German ones. This ratio is a serious threat. Even the high level of training and competence of German engineers and researchers will not be able to compensate it in the long run. I recall a presentation by Huawei in New Delhi in 2010. At that time, Huawei employed 51,000 people, or 46% of its workforce, in research and development. I also remember a visit to Nokia in 2004, where Nokia executives expressed that they thought they were unbeatable with their huge R&D team of 19,000 employees. Everybody knows how that game ended.

The huge R&D capacities support the preference for diversification of many Chinese entrepreneurs. Encouraged by the multiple growth opportunities in their home market, successful entrepreneurs in China have a tendency

Table 15.3 R&D employee numbers of selected German and Chinese Hidden Champions

German Hidden Champions			Chinese Hidden Champions		
Company	Product	R&D-employees	Company	Product	R&D-employees
KWS	Seeds	2053	Goldwind	Wind energy	1200
Norma	Connectivity technology	365	Hailide	Industrial resins	270
DMG Mori	Mechanical cutting instruments	581	Han's Laser	Lasers	3000
ElringKlinger	Sealing technology	611	Hikvision	Security cameras	9300
Carl Zeiss	Optical products	3100	Lens	Electronics	8700
Trumpf	Industrial lasers	2087	Mindray	Medical technology	2000
Schott	Glass technology	800	Ringpu	Veterinary medicine	300

to enter new business areas [10]. In the process, they often lose the Hidden Champions' characteristic focus on a singular product or service. The R&D employees then research all sorts of things, even things that are only remotely related to the core business. This may generate growth, but often turns out to be unsustainable. One example is the failed entry of home appliance manufacturer Haier into mobile telephony.

I have personally convinced a few Chinese entrepreneurs to stay focused on their core competencies. One who remained focused is Yang Shuren, CEO of Moris Technologies, today the global market leader in three specialty chemicals. Entrepreneur Yongfu He, owner of Hangzhou Zhijiang Silicone Chemicals, also followed my advice to stay focused instead of entering other industries. Instead of diversifying the company internationalized and became a Hidden Champion.

It is high time to German Hidden Champions to reconsider some of their attitudes. They face very serious threats from Chinese companies, due to their faster growth, their greater financial power from going public, and their intensive R&D efforts. As indicated in earlier chapters, this involves the advice that "Germans must become Chinese." Activities that can best be done in China should be done there, as Schenck and SMT Scharf have demonstrated. It is obvious that this requires high investments not only in sales, but also in manufacturing and R&D capacities.

Chinese Hidden Champions in Germany

About 4,000 Chinese companies are active in Germany, most of them still with small sales and service offices. The locations with the most Chinese corporate presences are Frankfurt and Düsseldorf. The first acquisition of a German Hidden Champion occurred in 2005, when Shang Gong Group from Shanghai took over Dürkopp Adler, the global market leader for industrial sewing machines. Since then, Dürkopp Adler's revenue has increased from €128 million to €188 million, a remarkable performance in a mature industry. Impressive for a machine builder are the net returns on sales of 12.2% in 2017 and 6.8% in 2018 [11]. The automotive supplier Preh, which manufactures BMW's iDrive, was acquired by Ningbo-based Joyson Electronics in 2011. The Chinese Hidden Champion CIMC from Shenzhen, global market leader in containers and in passenger boarding bridges, bought the fire truck manufacturer Ziegler in 2014. All of these early takeovers can be considered successful.

As shown in Fig. 15.3, total Chinese direct investment in Germany remained at a very low level until 2010, but went up in the following years, reaching a peak of €11 billion in 2016.

The figure also shows German direct investments in China. With the exception of 2016, they are higher each year than the Chinese commitments in

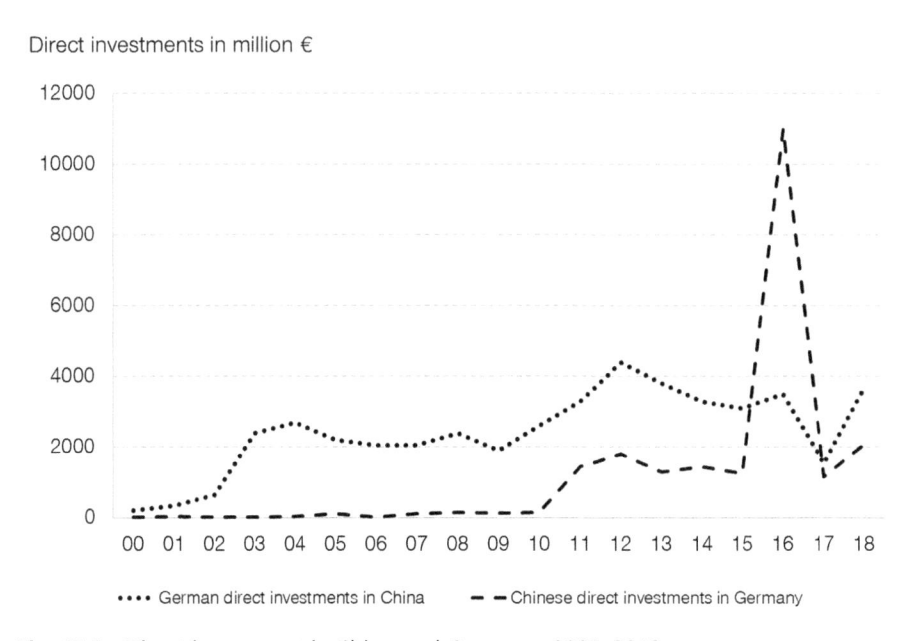

Fig. 15.3 Direct investment in China and Germany, 2000–2018

Germany. This makes it difficult to understand the agitation and the political moves to oppose Chinese takeovers in Germany since then. These reactions are likely due to the fact that some acquisitions have attracted a lot of attention. This is particularly true of the Chinese company Midea's acquisition of the robotics Hidden Champion Kuka. Other acquisitions have made the German public and politicians uneasy. These include the construction machinery manufacturer Sany's acquisition of Putzmeister, the global market leader in concrete pumps; Weichai Power's acquisition of Kion, the global No. 2 in forklifts; and Sinochem's purchase of Krauss-Maffei, the global market leader in plastics injection machinery. Political intervention has prevented Chinese companies from acquiring Aixtron, the global market leader in vacuum coating systems for chips, and Leifeld Metal Spinning, one of the market leaders in chipless metal forming. Surprisingly, Leifeld was acquired by the Japanese company Nihon Spindle Manufacturing in 2020 [12].

Figure 15.4 shows the number of acquisitions (M&A deals) in Germany with Chinese participation [13, 14].

A total of 300 acquisitions of German firms by Chinese companies took place in these seven years, compared with only about 60 acquisitions of Chinese firms by German companies in the same period. Based on my impression from numerous meetings and conversations with executives of acquired companies, Chinese-German acquisitions have mostly performed well, in

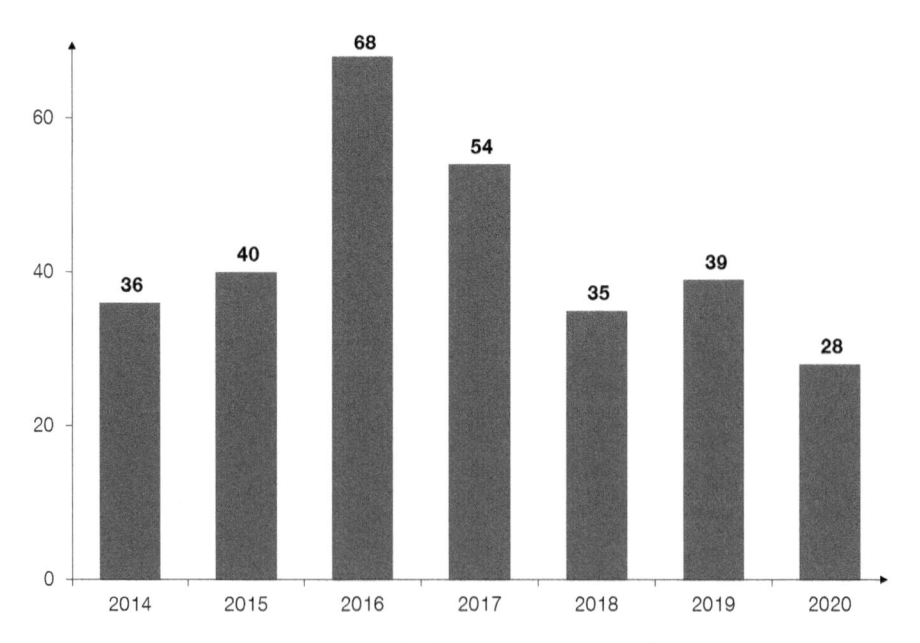

Fig. 15.4 M&A deals in Germany with Chinese participation from 2014 to 2020

many cases even better than takeovers of German companies by US companies. According to one study, three quarters of Chinese companies that have invested in Europe in the past five years say they are very satisfied or satisfied with their investment [15].

Chinese acquirers generally intervene less than American ones, at least as long as things are going satisfactorily. They are also more hesitant to impose their own corporate structure on the acquired company. Unlike typical American private equity investors, the Chinese inject their own money instead of burdening the companies with higher debt. In quite a few cases, having the new Chinese owner's support turned into a special advantage for mid-sized companies, because it helped them develop the Chinese market. This kind of support helped Preh, the Hidden Champion acquired by Joyson Electronics in 2011, increase its sales from €352 million in 2010 to €1.51 billion in 2019. Preh's number of employees rose from 2471 to 7162, though admittedly, Joyson integrated subsequent acquisitions (IMA Automation and Technisat) into Preh.

One study examines the motives of Chinese companies for their engagement in Germany. The results indicate that Chinese SMEs "not only pursue market- and strategic asset-seeking motives, but also efficiency- and resource-seeking goals" [16]. Integration in global value chains is another important motive, in line with our interpretation of the new game in globalization.

Greenfield Plants

While there are more than 2,000 German greenfield factories in China, the reverse development is just beginning. The first Chinese greenfield plant in Germany was built by the construction equipment manufacturer Sany in 2011, but it never went into operation. Sany took over Putzmeister at the beginning of 2012 and no longer needed the new capacity. Currently, only a few Chinese greenfield factories operate in Germany: Greatview Aseptic Packaging in the state of Saxony Anhalt, construction equipment manufacturer XCMG in North Rhine-Westphalia, and BM Bioscience Technology in Mecklenburg-Western Pomerania. The €1.87 billion investment by Chinese battery manufacturer CATL in Thuringia has a much larger dimension. On the Chinese side, there is considerable demand for more greenfield capacity, and I expect many more Chinese greenfield plants to be built in Germany in the next ten years. Chinese companies that want to become Hidden Champions must be strong in Europe. In addition to greenfield plants,

Chinese investments in German research and development centers already play an important role and will continue to do so.

Entrepreneurial Cooperation

The economic basis for long-term fruitful Chinese-German cooperation seems to be in place, because the two countries have commonalities that are conducive to cooperation. Like Germany, China has a decentralized structure, not with respect to the political system, but to the distribution of companies throughout the country. The 124 Chinese companies in the Fortune Global 500 are located in 35 different cities, while such large companies in countries like France or Japan are concentrated in the capital.[2] This distribution across the vast country is even more true for Chinese mid-sized companies.

In their attitude toward work, Chinese and Germans are considered industrious. I once told a British colleague somewhat flippantly that Germans actually work during working hours. With the typical British dry sense of humor, the colleague replied that it was precisely this behavior that constituted unfair competition and that the Chinese were probably imitating the Germans in this regard. Both China and Germany are also characterized by an "engineering culture." Despite all the other cultural differences, such commonalities contribute to the fact that the integration of acquired companies usually runs without much friction.

The Political Dimension

There is a striking difference between my discussions with Chinese and with non-Chinese. When talking about China with non-Chinese people, politics are almost always involved. Politics, on the other hand, is virtually non-existent in conversations with Chinese. I never initiate political discussions in encounters with Chinese individuals. Things are the way they are. China has a different system. The Communist party has the power and determines the rules of the game. Companies have the freedom to decide whether they want to do business in China. If they decide to do so, they cannot avoid accepting the rules of the Chinese market. I do not see any realistic chance of changing them, not for large companies, and certainly not for mid-sized enterprises.

---

[2] *Fortune*, August/September 2020, pp. F16–F17.

Inevitably, there are realities of the Chinese market that one does not like. Simon-Kucher itself was the victim of a copycat scam. A Chinese consultant copied our name, logo, and homepage and posed to German clients in China as the China office of Simon-Kucher. We had to go to court in Beijing to get the matter settled.

At dinners in China, I am often seated next to party secretaries. The local or regional party secretaries are the ones who have the last word, i.e., the power, and not the mayors or the provincial governors. The secretaries come across more as competent and educated managers than as politicians. When I asked one of them about his career, he said that he had studied religion for ten years. Now he is secretary general of the party in a city of eight million people.

In the realm of big politics, of course, everything must be done to achieve a "level playing field." There has been progress in this regard, most recently with the Comprehensive Agreement on Investment (CAI) between China and the European Union [17]. But tensions will remain. I conclude by quoting the President of Germany's leading economic institute, Professor Clemens Fuest: "The most important factor in avoiding blackmail is mutual dependence. For China, too, access to the European market is very important, and many important products are imported from Europe".[3] China is indispensable for European Hidden Champions, and Europe is just as indispensable for Chinese Hidden Champions. The same is true for the relationship between the USA and China. These three will remain the first global league for decades to come. Being a Hidden Champion demands strong performances in that league.

References

1. Gassmann, M. (2016, July 13). Chinas weißer Riese drängt in die deutschen Küchen. *Die Welt*.
2. Zhang-Lippert, C. (2020, September). *Success stories of German Champions in China—Best practice examples*. Friedrichshafen.
3. Retrieved from https://www.pressebox.de/inaktiv/karl-mayer-textilmaschinen-fabrik-gmbh/Wie-der-Markt-so-sein-Top-Player-staendig-in-Bewegung/boxid/990408.
4. Yergin, D. (2020). *The new map: Energy, climate, and the clash of nations*. London: Penguin.

---

[3] *Handelsblatt* Morning Briefing, September 2, 2020.

5. Dychtwald, Z. (2021). China's new innovation advantage. *Harvard Business Review*, pp. 55–63.
6. Simon, H., & Yang, J. (2019). *Hidden champions*. Beijing: HZ Books. (in Chinese).
7. Greeven, M. J., Yip, G. S., & Wie, W. (2019). *Pioneers, hidden champions, changemakers, and underdogs*. Cambridge, Mass.: MIT Press.
8. Greeven, M. J., Yip, G. S., & Wie, W. (2019). Understanding China's next wave of innovation. *MIT Sloan Management Review*, 75–80.
9. Lei, L. (2019). *The growth of hidden champions in China*. Retrieved from https://www.emerald.com/insight/1750-614X.htm.
10. Lei, L. (2020, April 20). Thinking like a Specialist or a Generalist? Evidence from Hidden Champions in China. *Asian Business Management*.
11. Yang, J. Y., Chen, L., & Tang, Z. (2019). *Chinese M&A in Germany*. Cham/Schweiz: Springer Nature. The authors provide in-depth case studies on Dürkopp Adler and two other companies acquired by the Chinese.
12. N.A. (2020, May 29). Nihon Spindle übernimmt. *Westfälische Nachrichten*.
13. Grummes, F. (2020). Stunde der chinesischen Käufer? *Investment Plattform China Deutschland, 2*, 10–15.
14. N.A. (2021, March 5). Chinesen übernehmen seltener. *Frankfurter Allgemeine Zeitung*, p. 21.
15. N.A. (2020, December 8). Chinesen sind auf der Suche. *Frankfurter Allgemeine Zeitung*, p. 22.
16. Hänle, F., Weil, S., & Cambré, C. (2021, June). Chinese SMEs in Germany: an exploratory study on OFDI motives and the role of China's institutional environment. *Multinational Business Review*. https://doi.org/10.1108/MBR-09-2020-0190.
17. Retrieved from https://ec.europa.eu/commission/presscorner/detail/en/ip_20_2541.

Part IV

The New Game of Transformative Forces

16

Business Ecosystems

Besides globalization, there are other important developments that determine the current transformation of the global economy. The four most important ones are ecosystems, digitalization, sustainability, and innovation. They are causing drastic and rapid changes in how to do business. In this and the next three chapters, we will try to understand how companies, especially the Hidden Champions, are affected by these developments and how they should adjust their strategies in order to remain successful.

Originating in biology, the term ecosystem was extended to business in 1993 by James F. Moore, who said that "[a] business ecosystem, like its biological counterpart, evolves from a random collection of elements into a more structured whole. Business ecosystems condense from the swirl of capital, customer needs and talent created by an innovation" [1, 2].

The term "business ecosystems" is one of the most commonly used terms in current strategy discussions. The book *Ecosystems Inc.—Understanding, Harnessing and Developing Organizational Ecosystems*, published by the Thinkers50 Initiative, provides an up-to-date and multifaceted overview with articles by 23 authors from various disciplines [3].

The Hidden Champion Celonis, global market leader in process mining systems, has appointed a Chief Ecosystem Officer, whose task it is to "accelerate Celonis' expansion and further develop the company's ecosystem strategy. In a modern, connected world, a strong and efficient partner and customer ecosystem is critical for growth" [4]. Companies bundle their capabilities in a business ecosystem for several reasons: to face other competitors, to bring new products to market, to better satisfy customer needs, and to accelerate innovations.

The term ecosystem spontaneously brings to mind the start-up scenes in the Silicon Valley, Shenzhen, Berlin, and Israel, or digital platforms like Apple, Amazon, or Alibaba. Ecosystem is a new term for what used to be called strategic alliances, cooperations, industry clusters, virtual organizations, or networks. Swedish researchers have been studying industrial networks for a long time and have classified them as essential characteristics of modern economies. They argue that marketing's classic two-dimensional supplier-customer view is too narrow and that modern business is much more dependent on complex network structures. Gummesson speaks of a "new dominant logic in the value-creating network economy" [5]. This view is very close to the concept of the business ecosystem or modern platform economies.

The question of whether certain activities should be done within a company or by external parties has occupied generations of economists. Ronald Coase determined as early as 1935 that the internal option has advantages when information asymmetry exists. Digitalization is rapidly transforming communication. It has made the exchange of information easier, faster, less costly, and more comprehensive. Blockchain technology will further accelerate these developments. As a result, we will see value creation shift more toward external contributions, which increases the importance of business ecosystems [6].

For Hidden Champions, business ecosystems are extremely important. Many of these companies have emerged from ecosystems and owe their continuing success to them. There can be little doubt that ecosystems will continue to gain in importance for several reasons. It is increasingly difficult for a single company to manage the growing complexity of products and services on its own. Examples include modern manufacturing systems, electromobility, and the transformation of the energy supply. In addition, change is occurring faster. There is not enough time to build up in-house capacities and competencies. This cause alone puts the traditional "do-it-yourself" culture of Hidden Champions to the test and will force a rethinking. Last but not least, digitalization facilitates the integration of value chains. It is increasingly necessary and at the same time increasingly uncomplicated for companies to cooperate in their efforts to remain globally competitive.

Industry Clusters as Business Ecosystems

Numerous industrial clusters with hundreds of Hidden Champions have existed for a long time in Germany and in German-speaking countries. Some of these traditional clusters have roots that are centuries old. These include cutlery in Solingen, roller bearings in Schweinfurt, locking technology around Düsseldorf, and the pencil cluster in the Nuremberg area. Others are of more recent origin, such as the fan cluster in Hohenlohe, the interface cluster in East Westphalia, the microelectronics cluster in the southwest, the wind energy cluster in northern Germany, and the e-commerce cluster in Berlin. After the reunification, clusters have "resurrected" from old traditions in the former East Germany. Examples are the optics cluster in Jena and the watch cluster in Glashütte. There are a large number of such concentrations of competencies and capacities all over the German-speaking countries.

Table 16.1 provides an overview of selected clusters, many of whose members are Hidden Champions. In modern terminology, these clusters can be called business ecosystems.

Some of the traditional clusters have survived into the twenty-first century. The knife–scissors–blades cluster comprises more than 150 companies in Solingen, which claims to be the world's only city whose name is trademarked, in the form of "Made in Solingen." Other traditional clusters have disappeared, such as the shoe cluster around Pirmasens or the textile cluster in Wuppertal. Still others have transferred their traditional competencies to new industries. These include the ecosystems for medical technology in the Tuttlingen area and for photonics in Jena.

The Tuttlingen Medical Technology Ecosystem

There are around 500 medical technology companies in and around Tuttlingen, a city of 35,000 in southwest Germany. The city alone is home to more than 400 of these companies. Among them are numerous Hidden Champions such as Aesculap (surgical instruments), Karl Storz (endoscopy), KLS Martin (operative surgery), Binder (simulation cabinets), or Hettich (laboratory centrifuges). One study concludes that "more than 100,000 different medical technology products are manufactured in Tuttlingen" [7]. The focus is on surgical instruments and implants. In some market segments, the Tuttlingen ecosystem achieves a global market share of 50% or more. But this ecosystem is not confined to manufacturers. The local university offers medical technology degree programs. The College of Engineering teaches surgical instrument and implant technology. Since most manufacturers have fewer than 20 employees, they cannot organize global marketing activities themselves. Gebrüder Martin bundles the worldwide marketing and distribution for numerous manufacturers. ACIG Medical features products from more than 100 companies in its showroom and organizes specialist conferences and

Table 16.1 Business ecosystems with many Hidden Champions

	Ecosystem/cluster	Region	Companies/Hidden Champions
Traditional	Pencils	Nuremberg	Faber Castell, Schwan-Stabilo, Staedtler-Mars, Lyra
	Locking systems	Velbert/Heiligenhaus	Kiekert, Huf Hülsbeck & Fürst, BKS, Witte Automotive, Jul. Niederdrenk
	Cutlery	Solingen	Zwilling Henckels, Pfeilring, Böker und 20 others
	Watch valley	Swiss Jura	Swatch, Rolex, Omega, Longines, Nivarox, Universo
	Rolling bearings	Schweinfurt/Franconia	SKF, Schaeffler, CSC + 20 companies
	Retail	Muelheim/Essen	Aldi, Tengelmann, Deichmann, Medion
	Chemical/pharmaceutical	Basel	Novartis, Hoffmann-La Roche, Syngenta, Clariant-Lonza
Mature	Chicken valley	Vechta/Lower Saxony	PHW, Big Dutchman, Deutsche Frühstücksei
	Sheet metal bending	Siegen/Haiger	Schäfer-Werke, Rittal, Siegenia-Aubi, Hailo
	Surgical instruments	Tuttlingen	Aesculap, Karl Storz +500 companies
	Plastics	Rhine-Sieg	Lemo, Reifenhäuser, Kuhne
	Medicinal plants	Luellingen/Geldern	approx. 1500 companies
	Compressors	Germany	Kaeser, Boge, Sauer, Bauer, MAN, and many more
	Packaging valley	Schwaebisch Hall	Optima, Schubert, Bausch & Ströbel, Groninger, Weiss, Syntegon
	Fan valley	Hohenlohe	EBM-Papst, Ziehl-Abegg, Nicotra-Gebhardt
	Materials valley	Rhine-Main	Heraeus, Schott, Merck, Umicore
	Measurement valley	Goettingen	39 companies/organizations

(continued)

Table 16.1 (continued)

	Ecosystem/cluster	Region	Companies/Hidden Champions
Young	Sensor technology	Southwest Germany	Pepperl & Fuchs, Sick, Endress & Hauser, Balluf, Testo
	Wind energy	North Germany, Denmark	Vestas, Enercon, Nordex, Siemens Wind Power
	Nanotechnology	Germany	Omicron, Nanogate, Nano-X, ItN Nanovation, Iontof
	Industrial vision	Germany	Basler, Vitronic, Geutebrück, Isra Vision
	Geothermal energy	Germany	Herrenknecht, Ochsner, Anger
	Energy from biomass	Germany	CropEnergies, Verbio, Loick, Envitec, Saria
	Laser	Germany	Trumpf, Rofin-Sinar/Coherent, Laserline, Foba, LPKF
	Water technology	Germany/Austria	BWT, Brita/Ionox, Grünbeck, Antech-Gütling, Wedeco
	Optics/photonics	Jena	Zeiss, Jenoptik, Schott, Analytik Jena und 170 companies/organizations
	Waste sorting/recycling	Germany	Remondis, Saria, Grüner Punkt, Stadler, Unisensor, Hammel, UNTHA, Kahl, Scholz, Cronimet
	Robot valley	Dresden	Wandelbots, ADG Automatisierung, EKF Robotic Systems, Revobotik, Coboworx, Center for Tactile Internet, 5G Lab Germany
	Internet node	Frankfurt	DE-CIX, Interxion, Equinix, Itenos, Keppel, Maincubes
	UVC/LED disinfection	Germany	Heraeus, Osram Opto Semiconductor, Binz, Fraunhofer IOSB
	Electronic interfaces	East Westphalia	Phoenix Contact, Harting, Weidmüller, Wago
	3D printing/additive manufacturing	Germany	EOS, SLM Solutions, Voxeljet, FIT, Concept Laser, and many more

worldwide trade fairs for more than 170 firms. The World Center for Medical Technology Internet portal provides a comprehensive overview of manufacturers and several hundred service providers focused on medical technology.

The Jena Photonics Ecosystem

Jena calls itself "The City of Light." The region is home to more than 170 companies and institutions in the field of optical and photonic technologies such as lasers and laser systems, laser scanning microscopes, light as a tool, optoelectronic components, and optical measurement systems. This ecosystem includes sizeable Hidden Champions like Zeiss, Jenoptik, Schott, but also smaller companies such as Analytik Jena, Laser Imaging Systems, and Optikron. The Jena-based association OptoNet has several hundred members [8].

The Jena ecosystem also includes ten research institutes with 1300 scientists and engineers. The Fraunhofer Society operates the Institute for Applied Optics and Precision Engineering (IOF). The Leibniz Association runs three institutes: the Institute for Photonic Technologies (IPHT), which researches biophotonic methods and technologies; the Institute for Natural Product Research and Infection Biology Hans Knöll Institute (HKI), which researches communication between microorganisms; and the Center for Photonics in Infection Research (LPI). The Helmholtz Association conducts research in high-power lasers and particle acceleration. The Abbe School of Photonics, a public–private partnership of the University of Jena, pursues the mission "to offer the most ambitious and motivated students an educational program in photonics at the highest international level" [9]. At Jena's vocational training schools, more than 200 trainees earn opto-photonics qualifications each year. Specialized service providers such as the engineering company Ferchau Jena and the advertising agency Timespin round out the ecosystem.

Regional Importance of Ecosystems

Regional business ecosystems such as those in Tuttlingen and Jena offer ideal conditions for Hidden Champions, both established companies and start-ups. One important advantage is that complex ecosystems are difficult to imitate anywhere else. This makes them an effective barrier to entry against new competitors who do not have access to comparable support networks.

For their locations and regions, Hidden Champions and their ecosystems are of outstanding importance in terms of jobs, income levels, education, and society at large. This is especially true for smaller cities and towns, and here again most strongly for those in remote regions. The Leibniz Institute for Regional Geography in Leipzig used three case studies to investigate the economic and social relevance of Hidden Champions for small towns and how they shape urban development in their regions [10]. The following Hidden Champions were the subject of the case studies:

- EJOT: global market leader for fastening solutions in construction, with 3,000 employees, based in Bad Berleburg in the Siegerland region (population 20,500)
- Holmer: the global leader for self-propelled sugar beet harvesters, with 400 employees, based in Markt Schierling in the Upper Palatinate (pop. 8,200)
- Kjellberg Finsterwalde: technology and market leader for plasma cutting technology, with 450 employees, based in Finsterwalde in southern Brandenburg (pop. 16,000)

The Leibniz researchers found that the economic situation of small towns with Hidden Champions is significantly better compared with those without Hidden Champions. Hidden Champions have a positive impact on their environment in a variety of ways, through their business activities and through their local and regional initiatives. They are committed to securing skilled workers, to developing young talent, and to supporting educational activities that benefit their own workforce and the region, including commitment in culture, sports, and social affairs. The case studies show that the Hidden Champions themselves create ecosystems which contribute very effectively to Germany's decentralization—a major strength by international standards.

Entrepreneurial Business Ecosystems

As emphasized at the beginning of this chapter, business ecosystems are not fundamentally new. The dividing line between traditional supplier–customer relationships and networks is rather fluid. The following two case studies on Hidden Champion ecosystems, one larger and one smaller, illustrate the high value of these networks when technologies are very complex.

The ASML-Trumpf-Zeiss SMT Ecosystem

Lithography systems for the semiconductor industry are highly complex. The advance of extreme ultraviolet lithography (EUV), which allows further miniaturization of integrated circuits and microchips, has driven this complexity to new heights. The Dutch Hidden Champion ASML is currently the world's only manufacturer of EUV lithography machines. It has more than 80% of all chip manufacturers as customers, as well as a global market share of 65% for lithography systems. The world-class expertise behind these leadership positions is not ASML's alone. The business ecosystem of three Hidden Champions—ASML, Trumpf, and Zeiss SMT—is the basis of the global success. As an integrator, ASML designs the architecture of the overall system. Trumpf lasers, which contain 450,000 parts, provide the EUV light source, while Zeiss SMT provides the optical system. (SMT stands for Semiconductor Manufacturing Technology.) The whole ecosystem shown in Fig. 16.1 is an interwoven structure of three independent companies that, through their very close cooperation, can offer a product that none of the three would be able to make on their own.

ASML sells its lithography systems to foundries and integrated device manufacturers (IDMs). The largest foundries are the Taiwanese companies TSMC and UMC, and Global Foundries from the United States. The leading IDMs are Samsung Electronics and SK Hynix from South Korea, and Intel and

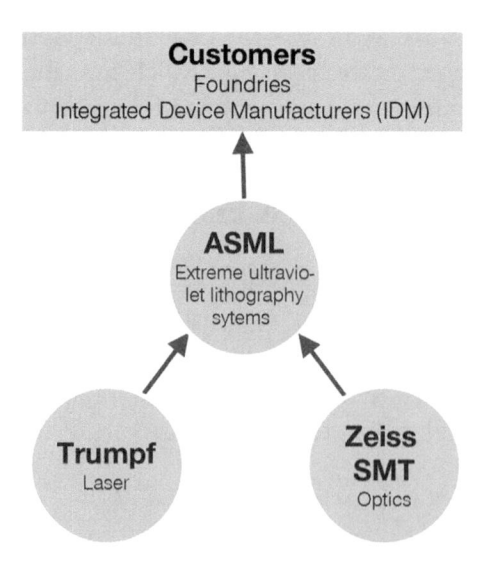

Fig. 16.1 Business ecosystem for extreme ultraviolet lithography (EUV) systems with ASML, Trumpf, and Zeiss SMT

Micron Technology from the USA. Each of these customers invests billions in new chip plants with ASML lithography systems at the core. Both supplier relationships in this ecosystem are exclusive. Trumpf is owned by the Leibinger family, while the parent company of Zeiss SMT is a foundation. ASML owns 24.9% of Zeiss SMT. Peter Leibinger, Trumpf's vice president in charge of research and development, says that the collaboration "feels like one company".[1] The ASML–Trumpf–Zeiss SMT ecosystem is one of the most successful in the world. But even for smaller Hidden Champions, business ecosystems open up great potential that they cannot take advantage of on their own, as the following case illustrates.

The MK Technology Ecosystem

MK Technology is a Hidden Champion which manufactures investment casting systems and special equipment used in extremely complex factory automation processes. A small company such as MK cannot provide all the know-how needed for such highly sophisticated products. Therefore, MK Technology has built a global business ecosystem with partners from China, Germany, Russia, and France. Figure 16.2 shows this ecosystem.

The partners in the ecosystem provide know-how and components on the various competencies that go into investment casting systems: rapid prototyping, fast casting, 3D printing, manufacturing processes, and materials science. Such an ecosystem only works with intensive communication based on trust. Central to this is Michael Kügelen, the CEO of MK. He is the "spider in the web" who has won over the partners and keeps the network alive. It would have been impossible for a company of the size of MK Technology to achieve the kind of world-class know-how within the ecosystem. MK's client list reflects this level of expertise. The best-known and most demanding customer is Elon Musk's rocket company SpaceX. Another important customer is Precision Castparts Corporation (PCC). Owned by Warren Buffett's Berkshire Hathaway, PCC is the global market leader in turbines for jet engines and gas-fired power plants. MK supplies them the world's largest steam autoclave, capable of processing turbine blades up to three meters in size. So, *cum grano salis*, one can say that Warren Buffett and Elon Musk are customers of MK.

---

[1] *Handelsblatt*, September 18, 2019.

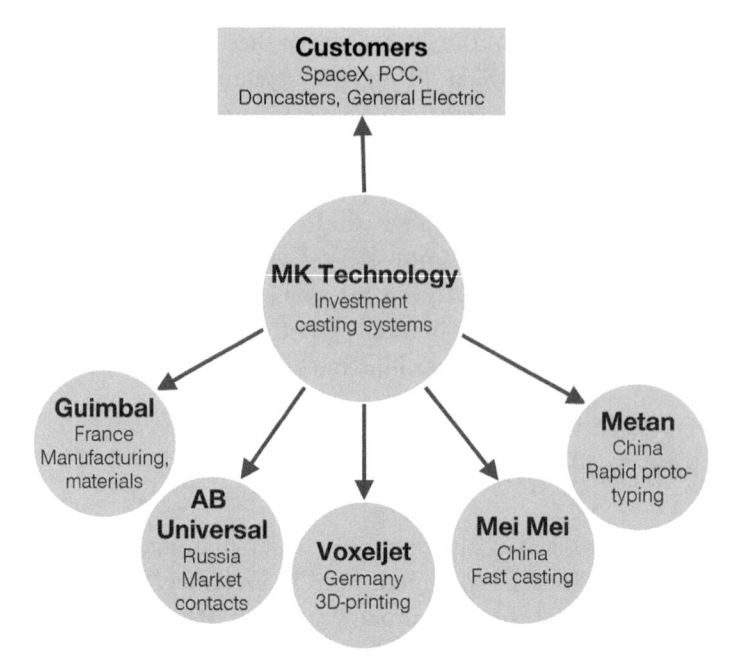

Fig. 16.2 MK Technology's global business ecosystem

On the Future of Business Ecosystems

There is little doubt that business ecosystems will continue to grow in importance. In a McKinsey study of 522 German SMEs, 51% of respondents expect to become more involved in ecosystems in the future [11]. The more complex products become, and the more that know-how from different areas flows into them, the faster the environment and technology will change. That will make it even more important to cooperate with partners in order to expand one's own limited capabilities. Several other factors are driving the move to ecosystems: digitalization, the blurring of boundaries between products and services, and demands for greater agility and resilience [12].[2]

Traditionally, many if not most Hidden Champions did as much as possible on their own and thus had a high degree of vertical integration (more on this in Chap. 22). Such attitudes can become impediments to joining a business ecosystem. Today, one often reads statements such as "firm and industry are no longer relevant units of analysis" or "the value of a firm is no longer found in its own assets, but in a network of relationships" [13]. While I do not

---

[2] We will deal more closely with ecosystems in the chapter on digitalization.

share these extreme views, it is clear that many Hidden Champions must become more open to cooperation within business ecosystems.

References

1. Moore, J. F. (1993). Predators and prey: A new ecology of competition. *Harvard Business Review*, pp. 75–86.
2. Moore, J. F. (1996). *The death of competition: Leadership and strategy in the age of business ecosystems.* New York: HarperBusiness.
3. Crainer, S. (Ed.). (2020). *Ecosystems Inc.—Understanding, Harnessing and Developing Organizational Ecosystems.* Wargrave (UK): Thinkers50.com.
4. Retrieved September 1, 2020, from https://www.celonis.com/de/press/malhar-kamdar-joins-celonis-as-chief-ecosystem-officer.
5. Gummesson, E. (2015). *Total relationship marketing.* London: Routledge.
6. McGrath, R., & McManus, R. (2020). Discovery driven digital transformation. *Harvard Business Review*, 124–133.
7. Dettmer, M. (2008, August 26). Der Siegeszug der Provinz. *Der Spiegel*.
8. Retrieved from http://www.optonet-jena.de.
9. Retrieved from https://www.asp.uni-jena.de/about_us.
10. Görmar, F., Vonnahme, L., & Graffenberger, M. (2020, February 18). *Hidden Champions als Impulsgeber für die Kleinstadtentwicklung.* Leipzig: Leibniz-Institut für Länderkunde.
11. McKinsey & Company. (2020). *How the German Mittelstand is mastering the Covid-19 crisis* (p. 28). Düsseldorf: McKinsey.
12. Cf. Jacobides, M. G. (2019). In the ecosystem economy, What's your strategy? *Harvard Business Review*, 129–137.
13. Hofmann, R. (2020). What if management models ate ecosystem strategies for breakfast? In S. Crainer (Ed.), *Ecosystems Inc. —Understanding, harnessing and developing organizational ecosystems* (p. 91). Wargrave (UK): Thinkers50.com.

17

Digitalization

Digitalization, alongside globalization, is currently the strongest driver of transformation. Hardly anyone will disagree with the statement of Ayla Busch, co-CEO of the vacuum pump Hidden Champion Busch: "Digitalization has the potential to undermine, in a short period of time, previous business models that have evolved over decades."[1]

Attitudes toward digitalization differ widely. Many people still see it as a relatively new development, although it is already a few decades old. Amazon was founded in 1994 and Google followed just three years later. Born in 2007, even the iPhone is already a teenager. On the other hand, the digital penetration of our lives is still in its infancy. Innovations and new apps enter the market almost daily. There is no telling where artificial intelligence, autonomous driving, augmented reality, robotization, brain scanning, and similar technologies will take us.

Radical or Incremental?

Digitalization poses enormous challenges for the Hidden Champions. One question is whether companies should "completely reset," "fundamentally reorganize their business model," "make a radical U-turn," or digitalize their business incrementally?

The incremental approach is probably more appropriate for most Hidden Champions, although the answer depends on the industry, type of product,

---

[1] Personal communication of November 29, 2020.

sales system, and the customer type. Software configuration and implementation should be tailored as closely as possible to a company's requirements. Turning everything upside down all at once might cause major disruptions. Deutsche Bank's chief information officer Bernd Leukert, an SAP veteran, recommends: "Major projects take five to ten years. And in the middle of it, you realize that you're heading in the wrong direction, that the requirements have further evolved. This is where the proverbial 'salami tactic' is called for. Better to develop small, stand-alone applications slice by slice" [1]. Peter Diedrich, head of marketing at Swiss process automation Hidden Champion Endress+Hauser, makes a similar argument: "Due to a lack of interoperability and consistency, the implementation of Industry 4.0 concepts is often complex. To date, 97 percent of data from the field is not used" [2].

But there are other voices. Daniel Wittenstein of the eponymous mechatronic Hidden Champion sees the incremental approach as a potential obstacle to digitalization, because "it could create limitations in terms of scaling digital innovations" [3]. One empirical study identifies high complexity and silo mentality as barriers to digitalization [4].

The situation is different for startups. They can fully exploit the potential of digitalization, because they have the opportunity to design their systems from scratch. Even a completely new business should not underestimate the task of optimally coordinating customer needs and digital infrastructure. That is precisely where many startups fail. The number of digital startups among the Hidden Champions of the German-speaking world is low. In a broad study of digital readiness and dynamic capabilities, Wittenstein compares 116 Hidden Champions with a control group of companies of similar size and structure that are not Hidden Champions and concludes: "Hidden Champions are better prepared for the digital transformation than non-HCs, and firms of similar size, age, and industry characteristics" [3]. The question is whether this comparison with German non-Hidden Champions makes much sense. A comparison of Hidden Champions with digitalization leaders from other countries might be more revealing.

B2C vs. B2B

One needs to distinguish between B2C and B2B markets when looking at the Hidden Champions and digitalization. With a few exceptions such as Skype and Spotify, digital B2C markets are dominated by American and Chinese companies, leaving almost no room for new competitors. An analysis of the internet traffic of 16,000 consumers over a 3-month period measured the so-called Gini coefficient [5]. If one provider accounted for all Internet traffic, the Gini coefficient would be 1. The result for the 16,000 users in the study was 0.988. A very small number of American providers accounted for close to 99% of traffic. So the ship has probably sailed for German providers as far as global penetration of digital consumer markets is concerned. Catching up or even overtaking the Americans or the Chinese in China seems hopeless.

Prospects look much more promising in the industrial sector. Digital industrial markets are generally niche markets with a global sales potential of a few 100 million or a few billion dollars and therefore not attractive for the Internet giants. With sales of $260 billion, it makes little sense for Apple to fight for a market of $500 million. Moreover, industrial processes are far more complex than consumer processes. In an assembly plant, every part has to be in the right place at exactly the right moment, whereas for Amazon it is not really a problem if a delivery arrives an hour or even a day later than planned. The very specialized know-how required for industrial processes is not easily available on the market; it is in the heads of the employees of the companies that are experts in such processes. These conditions create excellent opportunities for Hidden Champions who traditionally operate in niche markets and can use their deep know-how to digitalize their competencies. Their pronounced closeness to the customers, and the resulting in-depth knowledge of customers' value creation processes, are massive competitive advantages in B2B digitalization. The barriers to entry in B2B digitalization are high. This will become clearer when we next take a look at digital products, digital industrial processes, and digital industrial services.

Digital Products

Every owner of an electric car knows that long battery-charging times are a nightmare. Phoenix Contact, a Hidden Champion in the German electronics interface cluster, has developed a battery-charging system called "High Power Charging." It is significantly faster than any other system and can charge electric car batteries in 3–5 min for 100 km of range, more or less the time it takes to refuel for an internal combustion engine.

The Hidden Champion ARRI from Munich used to be the global market leader in professional cinema cameras. Many famous films were recorded with ARRI cameras on conventional 35-millimeter film. Digitalization posed an existential threat to this traditional technology and to ARRI. In cooperation with the Fraunhofer Institute for Integrated Circuits, which also invented the

MP3 system, ARRI developed a digital professional film camera and successfully defended its global market leadership.

BHS Tabletop, the global market leader in premium chinaware for restaurants, has introduced "intelligent tableware." The plates contain a microchip that automatically regulates payment and saves customers from having to wait for the bill.

Ubimax develops software for so-called wearable computing used in intralogistics, in combination with mixed reality glasses such as Google Glass or Hololens from Microsoft. Via a menu displayed in the glasses, the voice-controlled program guides employees through a warehouse while they assemble the items of an order. After Coca-Cola introduced this combination of glasses and the Ubimax software, the error rate fell to almost zero. The acquisition of Ubimax by Teamviewer holds vast potential, because a combination of the Ubimax and Teamviewer systems enables remote access to systems, devices, and machines.

Companies like Waymo, GM Cruise, Argo AI, and Aurora are leaders in the highly promising future market of autonomous cars. All of them are American, but German companies developed a lot of the digital technology incorporated in their systems. No other country has more patents in autonomous driving technology. Around 40% of the sector's 9900 patents registered worldwide in the last decade originated there [6]. The highly specialized competencies required for autonomous driving are ideal niches for Hidden Champions. Munich-based Terraloupe is the global market leader in aerial image data analysis, which is essential for autonomous driving. With the help of artificial intelligence, the software reliably recognizes buildings, signs, etc., from aerial images.

Most users of digital assistants such as Siri (Apple), Alexa (Amazon), or Google Translate do not know what the software is behind them. All these systems use the long short-term memory (LSTM) developed by Professor Jürgen Schmidhuber from the Technical University of Munich. The LSTM software is installed on more than three billion smartphones worldwide. It is by no means Hidden Champions' only contribution to smartphones. When asked how much Germany is involved in the iPhone, Apple CEO Tim Cook replied: "Germany plays in the very top group. The air is pretty thin up there. We have hundreds of suppliers in Germany. The culture of precision here is unique."[2] Apple cites the incredible number of 767 suppliers with German production sites, eight of which are among Apple's 200 largest suppliers. More than 260,000 jobs in Germany are said to be directly or indirectly linked to

---

[2] *Frankfurter Allgemeine Zeitung,* October 2, 2019, p. 26.

the Apple ecosystem [7]. Apple suppliers include Hidden Champions such as Varta (micro batteries), Tesa (adhesives), Wickeder Westfalenstahl (special steel that distributes heat in the iPhone and thus prevents overheating), Manz (high-tech machinery), and Dialog Semiconductor (chips for the iPhone's power supply). Large companies such as Infineon and Henkel are also suppliers to Apple. The glass for the Apple headquarters, including the largest curved piece of glass in the world, also comes from Germany, from the Hidden Champion Seele.

The situation in digitalization mirrors the old situation in the "analog" world. German companies tend to be weak globally in consumer markets, except for cars. German strengths traditionally lie in B2B markets, and this pattern continues with digital products. There is often a massive amount of German technology concealed within the visible end products, which often come from American or Chinese companies.

Digital Industrial Processes

Digitalization has transformed industrial processes even more than products. German Hidden Champions also excel in that area. Customers of Kärcher, the global market leader in high-pressure cleaners, demand a large product variety for a wide range of applications. This makes production and process flexibility a crucial competitive factor. On its latest production line, Kärcher can manufacture 40,000 different product variants in 24 hours. The extremely high level of flexibility allows Kärcher to meet the numerous individual customer requirements accurately and very quickly. This is only possible with fully digitalized processes.

The building materials producer Knauf has reduced its response time from three hours to one when there are unplanned material shortages at large construction sites. Such drastic improvements can only work with a fully digital supply chain. Knauf's customers prize this innovation, because their savings are substantial when construction sites stop work for only one hour instead of three.

RAUH-Hydraulik from Bamberg has adopted the principle of Amazon's Dash Button in its own business. Customers can trigger orders with just one push of the RAUH Reorder Button, which is placed directly on the customer's shelf. This minimizes the ordering process, ensures product availability, and avoids errors in the replenishment process [8].

The flagship combine harvester from Claas, the Lexion 700 model, costs €650,000, a big investment for farmers. In return, they get not only excellent performance, but also quick and flexible digital service. When a hurricane hit

Florida, Claas gave all machines with a 60-kW release a free upgrade to 75-kW battery capacity. This gave the machines a longer operating time and helped mitigate the effects of the hurricane [9].

Customers of Trumpf, the global leader in laser machines for metalworking, need customized tools. In the pre-digital world, customers sent in a drawing which Trumpf used to manufacture the part. That process took four days. Today, customers supply a file online, and the entire production process and subsequent logistics run digitally. The process now takes only four hours. The customer gets the tool much faster, saves on warehousing, and increases its own agility.

At the port of Hamburg, AI-based software increases the productivity of automated block storage by accurately predicting the collection of a container. When containers are placed in storage, it is often unclear when they will be picked up. In some cases, restacking becomes necessary. Using an algorithm based on historical data, the computer calculates the expected storage time of a container in the terminal warehouse. The algorithm also continuously optimizes itself through state-of-the-art machine learning. A second algorithm can predict very accurately whether a container will be loaded onto a truck, rail, or ship.

Customers of Körber, the global market leader in equipment for the tobacco industry and packaging systems for other industries, no longer have to travel to the Körber plant to accept new installations. The process is now digital, as Körber transmits test runs to the customers. All steps in the process are meticulously logged. The process of digitized test runs will probably remain in use even after COVID-19.

MAN Energy Solutions digitally commissioned a fertilizer plant in Uzbekistan during the COVID-19 crisis. This process of remote commissioning is also expected to outlast COVID-19. Zeiss is using virtual reality software developed by the startup Realworld One to train service staff for highly complex electron microscopes. Until now, these employees had to travel from all over the world to the Zeiss headquarters. Now, like in a computer game, they slip into an avatar and learn from their offices.

These examples illustrate that digital processes lead to strong efficiency improvements. These processes take place in the back offices of industry, making them largely invisible to the public. Their importance will continue to grow. Michael Marhofer, CEO of the automation Hidden Champion ifm electronic, says: "By 2030, we expect a further, even more significant shift from components to systems and from hardware to software" [10]. Systems solutions require an ever-increasing degree of digitalization.

Digital Services

Digitalization has spawned numerous new Hidden Champions that offer industrial services using digital methods, but do not manufacture products. Teamviewer, the global market leader in remote screen sharing, facilitates decentralized work and home offices. Its software is installed on more than two billion devices worldwide. Anyone who has problems with a computer can have them resolved, regardless of where they are. The computer user contacts the expert and explains the problem, and the expert fixes the issue from a remote location. This saves hassle, time, and costs. I have benefited from the Teamviewer software many times, whether on vacation or on lecture tour in China. Most of the time, the IT experts solved the problem within a few minutes without leaving their office. In September 2019, Teamviewer went public. Similar to Zoom, the COVID-19 crisis spurred both company growth and stock price. In early 2021, its market capitalization was €9 billion.

One of the impressive phenomena of digitalization is asset-free or asset-light companies such as Uber and Airbnb. Flixmobility, the parent company of Flixbus, is such a purely digital company that does not own a single bus. Instead, it organizes a network. Flixbus now serves 2500 destinations in 30 countries and entered the U.S. market in 2019. Strictly speaking, Flixmobility's business is not passenger transport, which is provided by the bus operators, but the operation of a digital system.

Construction projects are extremely complex and have a tendency to get out of control. The Hidden Champion RIB Software aims to transform construction into one of the most advanced industries in the twenty-first century by means of cloud computing, digital supply chain management, and artificial intelligence. RIB is the global market leader in cloud-based platforms for building and information modeling (BIM) and operates in 25 countries with 2,700 employees.

Many companies have no comprehensive overview of the software programs they use, which can often number in hundreds. Leanix, founded in 2012, solves this problem with enterprise architecture software. CEO André Christ explains this software-as-a-service (SaaS) solution: "Leanix is like Google Maps for the IT landscape in the company. We provide the relevant information about where a company stands in terms of what software is used in what context, and plan the future journey from there" [11]. Leanix has more than 300 international customers, including Volkswagen, Vodafone, Adidas, Santander, Zalando, and Dropbox. Goldman Sachs has invested €80 million in Leanix.

Munich-based Celonis is a pioneer and global market leader in process mining software, which uses artificial intelligence to improve industrial processes. The Celonis system "understands" the real processes, uncovers frictions, and makes suggestions for process automation. Valued at $11 billion, Celonis has been showered with honors and is listed in Forbes' "Cloud 100 companies" [12, 13]. Customers of Celonis include 3M, Airbus, Dell, L'Oréal, Lufthansa, Siemens, and Uber.

For insurance companies, the traditional method of handling motor vehicle claims is labor-intensive, costly, and time-consuming. They have to assess damages, deploy experts, and uncover fraud. The Hidden Champion Control Expert has addressed this problem by using artificial intelligence to automate claims and determine damages. What used to take several weeks now takes just a few hours, thus massively reducing costs and customers' waiting times. Control Expert is already active in 17 countries and processes over ten million claims each year. The database contains more than 50 million cases.

Global supply chains are one of the great achievements of globalization, but they also involve enormous risks. An individual company is only one link in such a chain and can hardly keep track of what happens along the entire chain. This is where the Hidden Champion Riskmethods steps in. Riskmethods uses big data and artificial intelligence to capture and analyze global supply chains. It can detect disruptions 1.5 days faster than before, making early warnings and precautions much easier to deliver and act on.

One of the best, if not the best, translation programs is DeepL.com from Cologne. It offers translations between 24 languages, including Japanese and Chinese. DeepL's neural networks have been trained with over a billion high-quality translated sentences provided by the translation search engine Linguee. The DeepL computer, located in Iceland, can translate a million words in less than a second.

DeepL has been rated clearly superior by professional translators in tests against the translation engines of Google, Microsoft, and Facebook [14]. One comparative study concludes that DeepL's translations "are truly remarkable!" [15] The online portal Tech Crunch says: "Tech giants Google, Microsoft, and Facebook are all applying the lessons of machine learning to translation, but a small company called DeepL has outdone them all and raised the bar for the field" [16].

DeepL.com offers the software in a freemium model. The basic version is free and professional versions cost between $5.99 and $39.99 in monthly subscriptions. Despite DeepL's qualitative superiority, challenges remain. Will this Hidden Champion hold its own against the internet giants in the long term? Or will it be bought by one of them?

Digital Ecosystems

In the context of digitalization, ecosystems are becoming increasingly important. When traditional companies lack competencies they need, many of them attempt to establish an ecosystem with companies that have these competencies, usually startups or research institutes. Figure 17.1 shows such a digital ecosystem of the Hidden Champion Beumer Group. Beumer is active in 70 countries with 4,500 employees and is one of the global market leaders in intralogistics.

The Beumer digital ecosystem includes collaborations with institutes in nearby Dortmund and the Beam Berlin incubator. Its CEO Robert Bach says: "My main task will be to find [business] founders with ideas for the Beumer Group" [17]. EBM Papst, one of the global market leaders for ventilation fans, has founded its own startup in Dortmund called EBM Papst Neo. Together with the local university, two Fraunhofer institutes, and two other startups, EBM Papst Neo is working on innovations for room ventilation. Beumer and EBM Papst are not isolated cases. A recent survey by the German engineering association reported that 71% of companies cooperate with startups. Three out of five companies describe this cooperation as "sustainably successful" [18].

One prerequisite for success is greater openness on the part of the Hidden Champions. Given their traditional secrecy, this requires nothing less than a cultural transformation. Hubertus Breier, the head of technology at sensor Hidden Champion Balluf, says: "We don't set up external startups. While those involve fewer hurdles and risks, know-how and corporate culture remain separated. We prefer internal startups, where employees breathe our

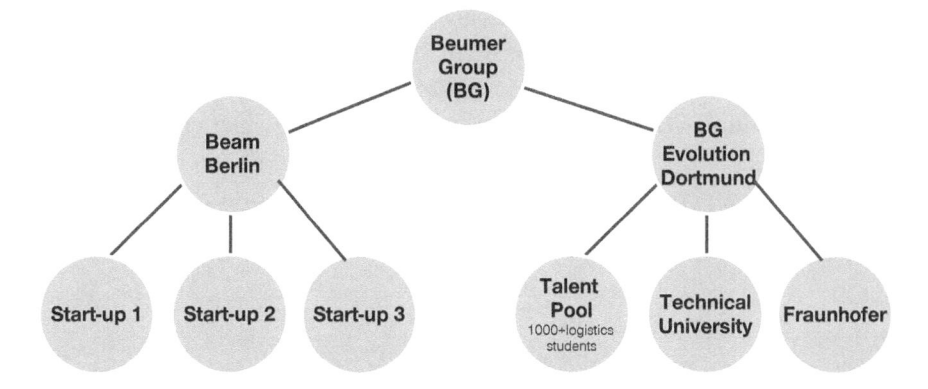

Fig. 17.1 Digital ecosystem of the Beumer Group

resourcefulness and entrepreneurship right away. Our employees become multipliers when co-working with our own startups" [19].

Hidden Champions ultimately want to achieve and retain control over results, which is not always compatible with what startup founders want. This can lead to culture clashes. One alternative is to spin off units to deal with digitalization tasks. The Hidden Champion Mapal, which manufactures precision tools for milling and cutting (C-parts), took that route. The employees of a spin-off called C-Com are developing an electronic platform for the procurement of C-parts. The name Mapal does not appear, and the intention is for C-Com to develop its own digital culture.

Monetization

Providing and selling digital products and services is a first step, but the monetization of digital offerings remains a major challenge, even if this task is mastered.[3] Many Hidden Champions report disappointing results. One empirical study found that "many manufacturers are dissatisfied with the sales performance of these systems" and, especially when it comes to software, "most of them are far from satisfied with their sales performance" [20]. This impression is confirmed in a study by the German engineering association: "Currently, the share of sales for digital platforms and value-added services is only around 0.7 percent of total sales in the European mechanical engineering sector" [21]. Platforms are also falling well short of expectations.

Presumably, there is a multitude of causes behind these disappointing results. Of the platforms mentioned in the study, 60% attribute the results to inadequate business models or a lack of common standards. Some 57% cited a lack of strategic relevance. Another possibility, perhaps more decisive, is that quite a few of the applications offer no real customer benefit. Consequently, there is little willingness to pay for them. That accurately describes more than 90% of the millions of apps in the consumer sector. The same result can occur when a very innovative app addresses previously unsatisfied customer needs, but customers find it difficult to assess. The app offers a benefit, but the customer does not perceive it. In those cases, a freemium model may overcome the initial acceptance barrier.

---

[3] For monetization see Ramanujam, M. & Tacke, G. (2016). *Monetizing Innovation*, Hoboken: Wiley 2016; and VDMA (2020), "Maschinenbau: Nach der digitalen Produktion kommen jetzt die digitalen Mehrwertdienste," VDMA, September 18.

In B2B applications, customers often expect service to be included in the overall offering. This problem is by no means limited to digitalization. It applies equally to traditional services. The question then is whether to continue with the bundled offer that includes the digital component. Peter Diedrich, the marketing manager of Endress+Hauser, offers this advice: "Ideally, digital services are an integral part of the core products and not a separate business" [22]. An alternative is to practice unbundling and offer the digital component at a separate price. In other cases, it may be advisable to outsource the digital service to a third party.

Sales force qualifications represent a major challenge. One study notes that classic "hardware salespeople" are not suited to sell software and digital products. The authors propose a blended sales force of hardware and software experts [20].

Conclusion

Making a general assessment of digitalization among Hidden Champions is difficult. The current list of German Hidden Champions contains only a few digital startups. Only 14% of patents filed by German companies relate to digitalization, compared to 41% in Finland, for example.[4] German Hidden Champions do not play a significant role in the global digital consumer market, but this is not necessarily due to a lack of know-how. Other reasons include the fundamental difficulty of implementing a system or even a platform in global mass markets from a relatively small market such as Germany; barriers to internationalization even within Europe (e.g., regulations, language); an underdeveloped venture capital scene; and a media landscape with only national reach. As a result, Germany is missing out on gigantic opportunities for growth and profit. The really big profits are made in the mass markets by Apple, Google, Facebook, Alibaba, etc., and these profits translate into huge market capitalizations. Apple alone is worth more than the combined value of all 30 corporations in Germany's lead index DAX.

For the Hidden Champions, the situation is more favorable in digital B2B markets. The niche character and the high complexity of these markets fit their competencies. Moreover, Germany's technical universities and research organizations have a strong base in academia and science. Professor Jürgen Schmidhuber of the Technical University of Munich supports this assessment

---

[4] Die Wirtschaft wird von zwei Seiten in die Zange genommen, Frankfurter Allgemeine Zeitung, March 5, 2020, p. V2.

when he says: "Almost all fundamental work on artificial intelligence and deep learning comes from Europeans. Europe is a leader in mechanical engineering and robotics. And it's the combination of robotics and Deep Learning that will reshape the world of production and work in the near future" [23]. Hidden Champions play a key role in translating scientific findings into market success. The administrative frameworks in Germany and in Europe are of crucial importance for the future of digitalization and the competitiveness of the Hidden Champions. The "Automating Society Report" published by the Bertelsmann Foundation and the organization Algorithm Watch provides an up-to-date overview of the situation in Germany and Europe [24].

References

1. Mussler, H., & Schönauer, I.. Hier ist Salamitaktik gefragt. *Frankfurter Allgemeine Zeitung*, p. 25.
2. N.A. (2020). Industrie 4.0 und Dienstleistungsstrategien. Interview, *PT-Magazin für Wirtschaft und Gesellschaft*, 5, pp. 42–43.
3. Wittenstein, D. (2020). Champions of digital transformation? The dynamic capabilities of hidden champions. *Discussion Paper No. 20-065*, ZEW, Mannheim, p. 36.
4. Freimark, A. J., Habel, J., Hülsbömer, S., Schmitz, B., & Teichmann, M. (2018). *Hidden champions—Champions der Digitalen transformation* (p. 14). Berlin: European School of Management and Technology/Hidden Champions Institute.
5. Andree, M., & Thomsen, T. (2020). *Atlas der digitalen Welt*. Frankfurt: Campus 2020, p. 30.
6. Bardt, H. (2019). IW-Kurzbericht. 63, Institut der Deutschen Wirtschaft,. The study covers the years 2010–2019.
7. Retrieved from https://www.tagesspiegel.de/wirtschaft/zulieferfirmen-so-viel-deutschland-steckt-im-iphone/24057266.html#:~:text=Bosch,f%C3%BCr%20das%20iPhone%208%20herstellt. Every year, Apple has to provide a list of its 200 largest suppliers to the United States Securities and Exchange Commission.
8. Retrieved November 2, 2020, from https://rauh-hydraulik.de/Rauh-Reorder-Button%2D%2Dgroup-reorderbutton.
9. Purps-Pardigal, S., & Kehren, H. (2018). *Digitalisieren mit Hirn*. Frankfurt: Campus 2018, p. 195.
10. Retrieved from https://www.smart-production.de/open-automation/news-detailansicht/nsctrl/detail/News/ifm-in-50-jahren-om-produktlieferant-zum-loesungsanbieter-20191114/np/2/.
11. Retrieved July 7, 2020, from https://www.leanix.net/de/unternehmen/pressemeldungen/070720goldman-sachs-fuehrt-80-mio-us-dollar-finanzierungsrunde-fuer-leanix-an.

12. Retrieved November 21, 2019, from https://www.handelsblatt.com/technik/it-internet/process-mining-spezialist-deutsches-start-up-celonis-erreicht-bewertung-von-2-5-milliarden-dollar/25253078.html?ticket=ST-316179-wGRo4VywyvWx69c1Tmfu-ap3.
13. Retrieved September 23, 2020, from https://www.cloudcomputing-insider.de/das-sind-die-innovativsten-private-cloud-firmen-a-965235/.
14. Retrieved May 12, 2020, from https://www.macwelt.de/ratgeber/Google-Translate-vs-DeepL-Uebersetzer-im-Vergleich-10809257.html.
15. Retrieved from https://www.superprof.de/blog/uebersetzung-englisch-deutsch-kostenlos-sofort/.
16. Retrieved August 29, 2017, from https://techcrunch.com/2017/08/29/DeepL-schools-other-online-translators-with-clever-machine-learning/?guccounter=1&guce_referrer=aHR0cHM6Ly93d3cuZ29vZ2xlLmNvbS8&guce_referrer_sig=AQAAAJYDIbfyMTGVR39DjctsBKCn7RoMkJ8ZCuEV2ISmyfgGEqXhl72QTqwePHka8Qwu7IJTSTrq32XTAdYbhBSxn0OIFb1nKE_ouuVHTgjNQg6ytGCJ3ljZZT6GXWbCVkfSd-yKIzd-KXU8gLX5vuc-wejyJo9XmAk_cobgDRwhaXGwj.
17. Retrieved November 1, 2017, from https://www.gruenderszene.de/allgemein/beumer-factory-inkubator.
18. VDMA. (2020). *Gemeinsam stark—Wie die erfolgreiche Zusammenarbeit mit Startups im Maschinen- und Anlagenbau gelingt*. Frankfurt: VDMA.
19. N.A. (2020). Interview with Hubertus Breier, Head of Technology, Balluf GmbH. *Return—Magazin für Transformation und Turnaround*, pp. 22–25, here p. 25.
20. Schmitz, B., Plötner, O., Jarotschkin, V., & Habel, J. (2020). The current frontier in industrial manufacturing: Bringing Software Systems to Market. *The European Business Review*, pp. 26–29.
21. VDMA. (2020). *Maschinenbau: Nach der digitalen Produktion kommen jetzt die digitalen Mehrwertdienste*. Frankfurt: VDMA.
22. N.A. (2020). Industrie 4.0 und Dienstleistungsstrategien. Interview, *PT-Magazin für Wirtschaft und Gesellschaft*, pp. 42–43.
23. Knop, C. (2018, October 4). Interview mit Jürgen Schmidhuber. Auf die Zukunft, Magazin zum Innovationstag, *Frankfurter Allgemeine Zeitung*, pp. 12–14.
24. Retrieved from https://algorithmwatch.org/project/automating-society/.

18

Sustainability

Sustainability has recently gained enormous importance as a driver of transformation [1]. In a survey, 66% of the responding managers saw sustainability as an increasingly important topic that no company can avoid. Only 29% classified sustainability as a mere PR and marketing fad or as a passing trend [2].

In 2020, *The Wall Street Journal* presented its first ranking of the 100 Most Sustainably Managed Companies in the World. They focused on the ability of companies to create long-term shareholder value [3]. Based on specifications from the Sustainability Accounting Standards Board (SASB), the ranking used up to 165 indicators of sustainability and screened a total of 5500 companies. The influential American Business Roundtable, which includes the CEOs of 200 major corporations, has also spoken out in favor of a carbon tax and a massive reduction of emissions [4]. There are even voices postulating that "sustainable is the next digital" [5].

Sustainability is not a fundamentally new issue. Many Hidden Champions have long been active in this field. Harting, a market leader in electronic interfaces, awarded its first in-house environmental prize back in 1989. Hager SE, one of the market leaders in electrical installation systems, introduced an Ethics Charter in 2012. The document addresses all conceivable facets of sustainability and might be seen as a role model [6]. The 39 members of the German "Climate Protection Association" include Hidden Champions such as Harting, Viessmann (heating technology), EBM-Papst (fans), KWS (seeds), Phoenix Contact (connection technology), and Weidmüller (connection technology) [7]. Sustainability has traditionally been closely linked to environmental protection, a view that is increasingly being replaced by a broader perspective including environmental and social aspects as well as corporate governance, abbreviated as ESG (Environmental, Social, Governance).

Sustainability as a Major Transformation

Sustainability has the potential to trigger a transformation as drastic as digitalization. In discussions of what responsible management means, keywords and phrases such as the conflict between economy and ecology, excessive complexity, unintended consequences, risks, obstacles, and staffing problems come up again and again. At the product level, sustainability affects the entire value chain from development to procurement, including production, distribution, marketing, service, and recycling. "CO_2 neutrality must become the goal. All our investment decisions today are based on this principle," says Dr. Franz Josef Konert, CEO of Gelita, the global market leader in gelatin. The necessary transformation requires new competencies, new employees with different qualifications, and targeted training of existing employees. Customers also need to be re-educated to accept new technologies and processes and to agree to pay for more sustainable solutions. The implementation of sustainability is made more difficult by the fact that there is only incomplete data on Life Cycle Assessments (LCAs). Even for electric cars, there is no LCA that includes all impacts from raw material extraction to how to deal with discarded components like batteries.

The Role of Consumers

The widespread tendency to equate sustainability solely with environmental issues is too narrow. Of course, the desire to avoid environmental damage and risks plays a major role, but events such as the diesel scandals of car manufacturers, problems with pesticides, or the involvement of major banks in dubious transactions show that the issue is a larger one. Consumer interest in sustainability is also growing. Consumers not only punish violations through boycotts, but also reward good performance through greater willingness to buy and to pay. Of course, some consumer demands regarding sustainability may be mere lip service without a willingness to pay higher prices. But values are shifting toward more consistent behavior, especially among younger people.

Sustainability will transform from a hygiene factor into one that suppliers can use to differentiate themselves. This transformation brings interesting opportunities for repositioning and upgrading brands. In principle, this is also not new. The Volvo brand has stood for distinctive automotive safety for decades, and the Miele brand has always been associated with exceptional reliability and durability.

Drivers of Sustainability

There are numerous other drivers of sustainability, in addition to consumer demand. Governments are enacting ever more stringent regulations concerning environmental protection, worker protection (e.g., the so-called Supply Chain Act), and corporate governance (such as quotas for female participation in boards). Scandals, particularly in the financial sector, have caused stricter monitoring. A strong push comes from retailers striving to enhance their own sustainability image by demanding sustainable products and processes from their industrial suppliers. For their part, end-product manufacturers are exerting pressure on their own suppliers. For example, producers of personal care products are demanding the replacement of plastic containers with those made from biodegradable materials.

Investors as Drivers

Less obvious but increasingly significant is the influence of investors and finance intermediaries. The *Harvard Business Review* speaks of an "Investor Revolution" and that "Shareholders are Getting Serious about Sustainability" [8]. Respondents in a global study by the French bank BNP Paribas said they plan to invest at least 50% of their assets in businesses that take ESG criteria into account [9]. Blackrock, the world's largest asset manager, is also actively committed to sustainability. German stock exchange Deutsche Börse AG is showing its commitment to sustainability by acquiring Institutional Shareholder Services (ISS), whose recommendations to institutional investors place great emphasis on ESG criteria. Banks pay increasing attention to compliance with ESG criteria when granting loans and reward better ratings with lower interest rates [10]. A good ESG rating is seen as an indicator of resilience and resistance to crises [11]. COVID-19 has further contributed to the growing importance of sustainability.

ESG Ratings

An extensive business ecosystem has developed around the topic of sustainability. Investment funds such as the "Sustainable Hidden Champions Equity Fund" or the "European Sustainable Equity Fund" use sustainability as their primary positioning attribute. Some rating agencies specializing in ESG, such as Sustainalytics, MSCI, ISS-oekom, or Vigeo Eiris, are actually Hidden Champions themselves. General rating agencies like the Berlin-based Scope Group also provide ESG ratings. Deutsche Bank CEO Christian Sewing says: "I personally believe that in five years ESG ratings will become as important as credit ratings."[1]

However, ESG ratings are at an early stage in terms of standardization and comparability. In finance, ratings from different rating agencies have a correlation of 0.99, but the corresponding figure for ESG ratings is only 0.61 [12]. One expert comments: "ESG ratings are controversial in practice. One reason is that ratings from various providers sometimes differ significantly" [13]. A crucial question for investors is whether sustainability pays off. Some observers qualify the statement "sustainability costs returns" as a myth that has long ceased to apply. The Hidden Champion Saria, whose activities range from food additives and animal feed to the disposal of food and animal by-products, says: "We do not regard economy and ecology as opposites. Combining them in the best possible way is a central part of our entrepreneurial activities" [14]. Indeed, empirical research shows that sustainable investments perform better over the long term. A study comparing stocks with high and low sustainability ratings over 18 years concludes: "Stocks of sustainable companies tend to significantly outperform their less sustainable counterparts" [15]. Another study confirms this finding: "From 2014 to 2017, ESG investing outperformed other forms of investment in Europe and North America" [16]. This study also found that stocks with the highest ESG ratings benefited the most.

Sustainability and the Long Term

Sustainability is a result of long-term strategy rather than of short-term measures. Thus, sustainability and long-term orientation are closely related. The Hidden Champions are characterized by a long-term orientation in their leadership. In several surveys, the average tenure of the chief executives was

---

[1] *Frankfurter Allgemeine Zeitung,* September 29, 2020, p. 23.

repeatedly found to be over 20 years,[2] while the average tenure of CEOs in large companies is only about 6 years.[3] Although it cannot be statistically proven, the considerably longer tenure of Hidden Champion CEOs is likely to lead to more sustainable conduct. A CEO with only a few more years in office will be less inclined to make investments that will only bear fruit in ten or twelve years. The fact that the vast majority of Hidden Champions are family businesses and thus not subject to the short-term pressures of capital markets can also be seen as conducive to sustainability.

The sustainability discussion has brought forth completely new ideas, such as the so-called responsible ownership model where assets remain tied to the company, profits are not distributed, and the company cannot be sold. Control lies with people who have long-term ties to the company [17]. Hidden Champions testing this concept include Alnatura, Voss, and Elobau. The concept is similar to the foundation model that some companies like Bosch, Zeiss, and ZF have had for a long time.

Sustainable Products and Processes

Most shirts are made of cotton. One cotton shirt requires an average of 2,700 L of water and 6 m² of cultivated land. A quarter of all pesticides applied in agriculture worldwide is related to cotton production. As the world's population grows, water and land become increasingly scarce while species extinction threatens the very existence of mankind. The Austrian Hidden Champion Lenzing, global market leader for cellulose fibers made from wood, is bucking this trend. Making one shirt of Lycocel requires only 180 L of water, 0.6 m² of land, and no pesticides are used in the forestry certified by the Forest Stewardship Council (FSC). Fashion retailer Zara already sells such shirts. With this innovation and the world's largest pulp mill, Lenzing is securing its ecological lead for years to come.

Golden Compound produces compostable coffee capsules and similar products from sunflower husks that decompose in nature within 100 days without leaving any residue. The sunflower hulls are a waste product from the processing of sunflower seeds, so they do not require extra land for cultivation. They also have massive price advantages over petroleum-based plastics. Golden Compound was awarded the PSI Sustainability Award for this

---

[2] 1995: 20.6 years, 2012: 20 years.
[3] Cf. 6.9 years in https://www.kornferry.com/insights/articles/where-have-all-the-long-tenured-ceos-gone; 6.6 years in https://www.strategyand.pwc.com/de/de/ceo-success.html.

innovation. One can also speak of a business ecosystem. The strategic partner in this is the world's largest sunflower seed processor, Cargill. Other partners in the ecosystem are the Golden Mill from Germany and one of the most modern hulling mills in the world, the First May JSC in Bulgaria.

A foundry is not normally associated with high-tech, innovation, or sustainability. But this is a misperception. Hüttenes-Albertus, a world-leading chemical supplier to foundries, has developed the inorganic binder system, called Cordis, which replaces thousands of tons of oil-based binders. Cordis is superior to existing binders in terms of emissions reduction, turnaround times, manual effort, as well as energy use, and eliminates the need for special equipment to clean up emissions.

Many people are switching to vegan diets. Companies such as the Hidden Champion Taifun-Tofu, the European market leader for tofu, are capitalizing on this trend. Tofu is made from soybeans, which normally could not be grown in Germany. After 10 years of breeding research in cooperation with the Agricultural University of Hohenheim, Taifun developed its own soy variety that is ideally suited to cultivation in the German climate. Now approved for use, this innovation will make it possible to create a local raw material base for tofu.[4]

Sustainability can only be implemented consistently if all those involved in the material cycle work together. The Recyclat Initiative, which is also an ecosystem, brings together the detergent manufacturer Werner & Mertz; the expert for the collection and reuse of sales packages, Der Grüne Punkt; the Austrian packaging Hidden Champion Alpla; the environmental organization NABU; the retailer REWE; and Unisensor Sensorsysteme. Werner & Mertz was a pioneer in ecological household cleaners. Recently, the first ecological shower gel was launched. Sustainability must include the packaging, not just the product. Werner & Mertz makes all of its packages from recycled plastic.

A huge waste of resources comes from the disposal of usable clothing. An obvious solution is the second-hand clothing market. In fact, this market has doubled globally to $28 billion in the last 5 years and is expected to grow to $64 billion in the next five [18]. Globetrotter, a European market leader in outdoor clothing, actively embraces this trend by selling returned and used items from all relevant outdoor brands. Aiko Bode, chief sustainability officer at Globetrotter, says: "The aim is to promote the sustainable and long-term use of existing resources. While in many cases vast quantities of undamaged products are disposed of, we have decided to take a different approach.

---

[4] *Frankfurter Allgemeine Zeitung*, September 3, 2020, p. 20.

Hangtags on the products provide information about their origin, age, and previous repairs. The reuse of high-quality second-hand products does not have a bargain image for us. It is an expression of a conscious, ecologically sustainable lifestyle" [19].

Momox is the European market leader in so-called re-commerce and operates the second-hand online store Ubup for used clothing. Momox employs 1900 people and grew by 61% in 2019. Classic fashion brands such as Tommy Hilfiger, Boss, and Polo Ralph Lauren are doing particularly well. The company is fighting the fast-fashion trend and thus helps to reduce the burden on the environment.

KWS, the global market leader in seeds for sugar beet, silage corn, and hybrid rye, invests 18.5% of its sales in research and development—a percentage that is otherwise found only in pharmaceutical or software companies. Behind this are 2,053 R&D employees, 37% of the workforce. Every year, countless incremental innovations from KWS help improve plant resistance to diseases and pests, foster the efficient use of fertilizers and crop protection products, and increase the stress tolerance of plants to climate-change effects such as drought.

Insulating buildings is one of the most effective methods to reduce energy consumption, but many insulation materials are ecologically problematic. The Hidden Champion Steico, European market leader in wood-fiber insulation materials, consistently focuses on sustainability and recyclability. Steico offers a comprehensive system of natural materials and so-called blow-in insulation for buildings and floors. Steico's systems solution includes training and guidance for tradesmen. Steico has received numerous awards for its contributions to sustainability and also provides proof that sustainability and profitability do not have to be at odds. Steico's net return on sales of 8.9% is excellent for a building materials supplier.

Sonnen GmbH, the global market leader in intelligent battery storage, offers not just a product, but a comprehensive systems solution for power management. In cooperation with the grid operator Tennet and with IBM, Sonnen uses blockchain technology to integrate thousands of batteries into so-called redispatch systems. Sonnen has attracted international attention and received numerous awards, including the $1.5 million Zayed Future Energy Prize. The Massachusetts Institute of Technology named Sonnen one of the world's most innovative companies, along with Amazon, Facebook, and Apple.

A large part of expired or incorrectly packaged food ends up as organic waste. The Hidden Champion Baader, global market leader in fish processing systems, has developed a depackaging solution for recycling food. This machine separates the packaging from the foods, which can then be processed further, e.g., for animal feed.

Terracycle aims to introduce a comprehensive circular economy without waste and is active in 22 countries. The company pursues a radical approach by completely eliminating landfill and incineration solutions. Instead, it directs waste to higher recycling stages. The basis is the classification of waste into five recycling stages: landfill, incineration, recycling, upcycling, and reuse. Upcycling turns plastic bottles into backpacks and cereal bags into shower curtains. Tom Szaky, the founder of Terracycle, is referred to as the "Green Zuckerberg."

Social Sustainability

Uzin Utz, a global full-service provider of flooring systems, focuses its entire product range "on sustainable, low-emission and environmentally friendly products" [20]. Uzin Utz publishes an annual comprehensive sustainability report that addresses all ESG criteria and includes all its subsidiaries. "The strategic goal is to live and increase sustainability in all facets along the value chain, i.e., in product development and manufacturing, in the supply chain, and last but not least with regard to employees" [21].

The Voss Group, a Hidden Champion in automotive fluid line systems with 5,100 employees, provides an exemplary sustainability report that covers not only energy and resource consumption, but also aspects such as compliance, accident rates, occupational safety, age structure, proportions of female employees, and training [22].

Sustainability can also come about indirectly. Visiconsult X-Ray Systems & Solutions is the global market leader in systems for materials inspection with X-rays. Visiconsult systems inspect railroad wheels and aircraft wings. Where is the link to sustainability here? Visiconsult's equipment effectively contributes to making our lives safer or as Professor Thorsten Buzug, head of the Institute for Medical Technology at the University of Lüneburg, explains it: "The non-destructive material testing saves more lives than radiology in the hospital" [23].

Two characteristics of the Hidden Champions are important from the standpoint of social sustainability. First, the extremely low employee turnover rate of 2.7% per year is not only a loyalty indicator, but can be seen as a valid expression of high employee satisfaction. Whenever possible, Hidden Champions avoid laying their employees off. This approach earned them international attention and helped spur Germany's rapid recovery after the

Great Recession of 2008–2010. Second, the Hidden Champions emphasize education activities. They have 50% more of their workforce in apprenticeship programs than the average German company (9% vs. 6%).

The chapter on business ecosystems already acknowledged the contributions of Hidden Champions to the development of their local and regional environments [24]. Hidden Champions are not only taxpayers, but also make many contributions to the sustainability of communities and society in areas such as culture, sports, and social affairs.

Sustainability is not a task that will ever reach a final conclusion. It will push the Hidden Champions to transform their products and processes. In this sense, it resembles innovation, the transformation driver which is the focus of the next chapter.

References

1. Müller-Christ, G. (2020). *Nachhaltiges Management*. Baden-Baden: Nomos.
2. Preußer, J. (2020, September 17). Green Finance kommt. *Frankfurter Allgemeine Zeitung*, Verlagsspezial Mittelstandsfinanzierung, p. V4.
3. Negrin Ochoa, F., Holger, D., Sardon, M., & Lindsay, C. (2020). The 100 most sustainably managed companies in the world. *The Wall Street Journal*.
4. Ip, G. (2019). Business shifts from resistance to action on climate. *The Wall Street Journal*.
5. Retrieved from https://www.linkedin.com/feed/update/urn:li:activity:6719516619292450816/.
6. Retrieved from file:///C:/Users/651/Downloads/EC_DE.pdf.
7. Retrieved 2020, from https://www.klimaschutz-unternehmen.de/startseite/.
8. Eccles, R. C., & Klimenko, S. (2019). The investor revolution—Shareholders are getting serious about sustainability. *Harvard Business Review*, pp. 107–116.
9. BNP Paribas. (2019). *Große Erwartungen an ESG—Was kommt als Nächstes für Asset Owner und Asset Manager*. Paris: BNP Securities Services.
10. Zdrzalek, L. (2020, November 2). Endlich Weltverbesserer. *Wirtschaftswoche*, Special Edition No. 1, pp. 49–50.
11. Serafeim, G. (2020). Social-impact efforts that create real values. *Harvard Business Review*, pp. 38–48.
12. Oliver Hagedorn, O. (2020). Stolperstein ESG-ratings—Lernen Sie die Spreu vom Weizen zu trennen. Avesco Financial Services.
13. Gränitz, M. (2020). Schlechte Noten? *Institutional Money, 4*, 140–144.
14. Retrieved from https://www.saria.com/index.php?id=5246&L=0.
15. Kell, G. (2018, July 11). The remarkable rise of ESG. *Forbes*.

16. Holder, M. (2019, January 22). New research finds that ESG screening boosts stock market performance. *GreenBiz*.
17. Retrieved from https://stiftung-verantwortungseigentum.de/2020.
18. Retrieved from https://www.statista.com/statistics/826162/apparel-resale-market-value-worldwide/.
19. Retrieved September 3, 2020, from https://de.fashionnetwork.com/news/Globetrotter-startet-secondhand-verkauf,1240600.html.
20. Retrieved from https://de.uzin-utz.com/ueber-uns/portrait/
21. Retrieved May 19, 2019, from https://www.uzin.de/detail/news/1558389600-uzin-utz-group-veroeffentlicht-gruppenweiten-nachhaltigkeitsbericht/.
22. Retrieved from https://www.voss.net/de/verantwortung/2020.
23. Benkert, S. (2019, January 3). Sie strahlt bei jeder Prüfung. *Frankfurter Allgemeine Zeitung*, p. 8.
24. Görmar, F., Vonnahme, L., & Graffenberger, M. (2020, February 18). *Hidden Champions als Impulsgeber für die Kleinstadtentwicklung*. Leipzig: Leibniz-Institut für Länderkunde.

19

Innovation

No company becomes a Hidden Champion through imitation, only through innovation. Also, no company remains a Hidden Champion by focusing solely on product innovation. Defending market leadership requires continuous innovation across all stages of the value chain and all aspects of customer benefits. It permeates processes, costs, services, marketing, and human resources.

The innovation activities of the Hidden Champions are clearly well above the industry average. According to an innovation report for SMEs, the innovator rate—i.e., the percentage of companies which introduced at least one innovation in the last three years—has declined for years and recently dropped to only 19% [1]. For SMEs with more than 50 employees, which includes virtually all Hidden Champions, the rate is significantly higher at 49%. According to this study, product and process innovations roughly balance each other out. A study by the Center for European Economic Research qualifies 80% of all Hidden Champions as innovators [2].

Patents

It is difficult to measure innovativeness quantitatively. At the product level, patents are among the most valid and widely available measures of innovative capabilities. Their importance varies greatly across industries, but they are highest in technical areas, where many Hidden Champions are active.

First, we take a look at how individual countries perform in this respect, using the number of European patents per million inhabitants in the period 2010–2019. This is the most international database on patents (Fig. 19.1).

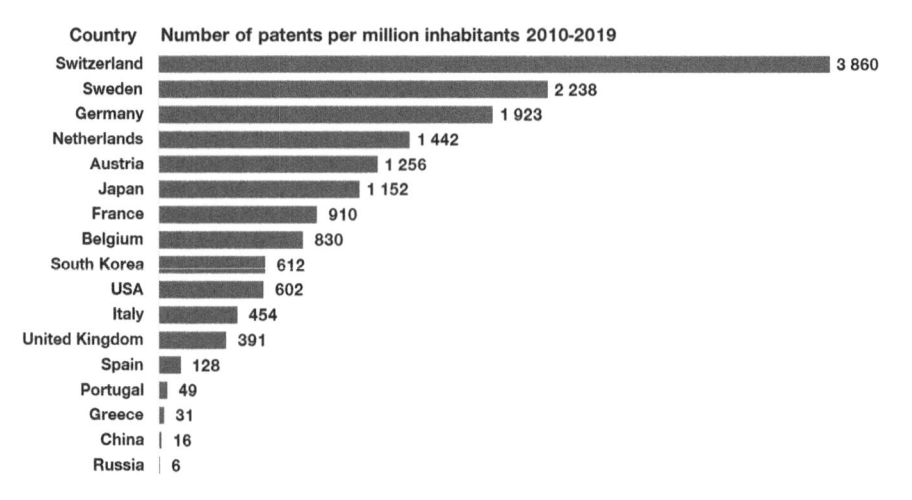

Country	Number of patents per million inhabitants 2010-2019
Switzerland	3 860
Sweden	2 238
Germany	1 923
Netherlands	1 442
Austria	1 256
Japan	1 152
France	910
Belgium	830
South Korea	612
USA	602
Italy	454
United Kingdom	391
Spain	128
Portugal	49
Greece	31
China	16
Russia	6

Fig. 19.1 European patents per million inhabitants by country 2010–2019

Switzerland leads by a wide margin. One reason is that Switzerland has a positive immigration balance of around 18,000 patent-active inventors from 2001 to 2010, while Germany has a negative balance of 7000 in the same period.[1] Switzerland's low taxes attract patent applications and contribute to its top position. Sweden, Germany, the Netherlands, and Austria follow at considerable distance from each other.

The performance of the other European countries, especially those in southern Europe, is noticeably weaker. The innovative capacity of companies in the German-speaking countries and in Northern Europe is one reason for the number and strength of the Hidden Champions located there.

Consistent with the strong performance in European patents is Germany's ranking as number one in the Bloomberg Innovation Index [3]. In this study, Germany's greatest strengths are manufacturing value-added, high-tech density, and patent activity. Switzerland ranked fourth, with particular strengths in R&D intensity and researcher concentration, and Austria was 11th.

World-Class Patents

Not all patents are equal. The Bertelsmann Foundation examined "world-class patents" [4], which are defined as "the 10 percent of all patents that are most significant." The foundation's study is based on an approach developed

---

[1] https://www.wipo.int/edocs/pubdocs/en/wipo_pub_941_2013-section1.pdf. With 184,000, the USA has the highest positive balance. China has the highest negative balance with about −50,000.

by Ernst and Omland, which includes the market coverage, citations in other patent applications, and similar criteria [5]. It looked at a total of 58 future technology fields, including wind power, functional food, Internet of Things (IoT), blockchain, carbon and graphene, drones, and rational drug design.

Wind power is a good case to show the discrepancy between all patents and world-class patents. A total of 40,011 wind power patents had been registered worldwide as of September 2019. Of these, 42% are of Chinese origin, but only 300 of them are considered world-class. The study states "Of China's impressively high number, 16,740 wind power patents are negligible. By comparison, Germany comes in at 958 world-class patents in wind power."[2]

Nevertheless, the study reveals a comparatively weak overall position for Europe and for Germany. The USA remains the undisputed "patent superpower," with East Asia rapidly catching up. Europe occupies the top positions only in wind power and functional food. Germany remains the strongest European patent power, but is gradually falling behind worldwide. In 2010, Germany was among the top three nations with the most world-class patents in 47 of the 58 technology fields. As of 2019, this share included only 22 technology fields, a decline of more than half.

Europe's and Germany's weakness is not research, but commercialization. The USA and China are often faster in turning new ideas into successful products and companies. The study reflects the fact that German and European companies are too weakly represented in the markets of the future. Unfortunately, this even applies to quite a few Hidden Champions. There are very few young companies that are as innovative in the markets of the future as the traditional Hidden Champions have been historically in their more mature markets.

Patents in Germany

The 50 companies with the most patent applications at the German Patent Office include 31 German and 19 foreign companies [6]. Of the German companies, 11 or 35% are Hidden Champions. Four Hidden Champions— Carl Zeiss SMT, Phoenix Contact, Krones, and Voith—account for an impressive number of 1060 patents, which is almost identical to the 1059 patents filed by all German universities and the Fraunhofer Society combined. The patent activity of the Hidden Champions extends far beyond their relative size. This is confirmed by the figures for patents per 1000 employees.

---

[2] Ibid. pp. 9.

Hidden Champions have 31 patents per 1000 employees, while the corresponding figure for large companies is six.

The Gartner Hype Cycle

Before discussing incremental and breakthrough innovations, I would like to briefly introduce a concept that has attracted a lot of attention, the so-called "Hype Cycle" from the market research firm Gartner [7]. This is a graphical representation of the diffusion of innovations. In the classic view, this diffusion follows an S-curve. After a slow and flat start-up phase demand accelerates and grows more strongly, eventually transitioning to saturation. The hype cycle concept postulates that the expectations in the early phase of a technology are exaggerated. This exaggeration superimposes a bell-shaped curve on the longer-term S-curve. Figure 19.2 shows the Gartner Hype Cycle for emerging technologies.

The concept helps to assess the diffusion of innovations more realistically. An innovation in the hype stage can easily be interpreted as a breakthrough, although the longer-term potential may be limited. The Hype Cycle is a useful tool for a sober assessment of innovations.

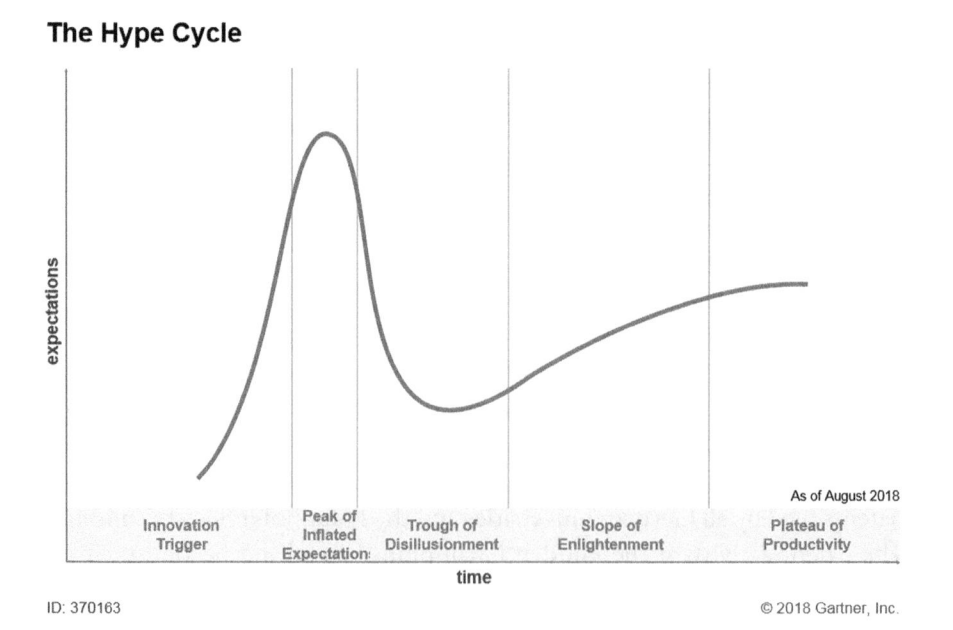

Fig. 19.2 Gartner Hype Cycle for Emerging Technologies [8]

Incremental Innovations

The vast majority of innovations are incremental, meaning they are improvements to existing products. This assessment also applies to the Hidden Champions. Stihl, the global market leader in chainsaws, introduced 42 innovations to its main product in a single year. Hako, a Hidden Champion for professional cleaning machines, aptly describes the culture of incremental innovations with its motto, "A little bit better every day." Such a strategy works well in mature markets, where the focus is on perfecting products rather than on fundamentally new approaches. Ted Levitt put it this way: "Continuous success is mainly a matter of focusing regularly on the right things and pushing through numerous unspectacular, small improvements every day" [9]. A study of 885 family-owned companies listed at European stock exchanges concludes "Permanently working on the smallest improvements is a crucial long-term success factor" [10].

Most Hidden Champion CEOs would agree with these statements. But there are opposing views. The Bertelsmann Innovation Atlas sees the dominance of incremental innovations as "one of the decisive weaknesses of the German innovation landscape" [11]. In a very long-term analysis going back to 1871, Wim Naudé and Paula Nagler come to a similar conclusion. They see "an innovation system locked in incremental innovation" as a cause of the long-term decline in Germany's innovation capability [12].

I do not share this view. I think it is a misperception to assume a need for disruptive innovations in almost all fields. The vast majority of products and services evolve incrementally. However, incremental innovations carry two risks for existing products: the risk of being displaced by a disruptive innovation and the risk of diminishing marginal utility. Approaching a state of perfection means that the innovative effort increases while the additional marginal benefit for customers decreases. Eventually, this process reaches a point where a leap to a new technology becomes inevitable. Missing this point can be a major risk for Hidden Champions.

Breakthrough Innovations

Breakthrough or disruptive innovations are rare, but attract a very high share of media attention. The former CEO of Trumpf once said that they only happen every 15 years. Still, many Hidden Champions have emerged through completely new solutions to problems. That has not changed to this day. Here are some impressive breakthrough innovations.

KSB Additive Manufacturing

The Hidden Champion KSB, one of the global market leaders in pump technology, was the first company worldwide to receive certification for the additive manufacturing of materials and semi-finished products for pressure equipment. Its oil cooler, manufactured by 3D printing, has a cooling capacity per weight that is 3.57 times higher than a conventionally manufactured cooler (65% lighter combined with 25% better performance) [13]. The impact of 3D printing on manufacturing and logistics remains exciting. Amazon has filed a patent on how products can be produced by means of 3D printing inside the trucks that can deliver them immediately.[3]

Volocopter

Volocopter is the world's first electric helicopter. This flying machine is clearly more than a classic electromechanical product. It is an autonomous air cab system, but by no means a futuristic dream. In December 2020, Volocopter signed a contract with Singapore for an air taxi service scheduled to operate by 2023. Negotiations are also underway with Dubai. It is remarkable that Volocopter prevailed against the significantly lower-priced Chinese competitor Ehang. This case shows that even in the most advanced fields, German Hidden Champions are by no means without a chance against their Chinese competitors.

Lilium

No less ambitious than the Volocopter is the project of the Munich-based company Lilium, which is developing a vertical take-off and landing electric aircraft. Its maiden flight took place in 2020. Lilium's focus market will be intercity shuttle flights. In 2021, Lilium went public at the NASDAQ stock exchange in New York.

---

[3] U.S. Patent No. 9,898,776, Washington, DC: U.S. Patent and Trademark Office 2018.

Torqeedo

On Lake Starnberg in the Bavarian Alps, there is a strict restriction on combustion engines for boats. This gave Christoph Ballin and Friedrich Böbel the idea of developing electric motors for boats. They hit upon a real void in the market. Today, Torqeedo is the global market leader for electric outboard motors. In the James Bond film "Spectre," the title character rides in a boat powered by a Torqeedo motor.

Hydrogen Train iLint

The maiden voyage of the world's first hydrogen-powered train took place on September 18, 2018. Since then, this innovative train, named Coradia iLint, has been running regular services between four cities in Northern Germany. The iLint is quiet and emits only steam and water. It was developed at the Competence Center for Regional Trains in Salzgitter for use on non-electrified lines and makes clean, sustainable train operations possible. The range of a tank filling is 1,000 kilometers. In the first two years, the hydrogen was delivered by trucks, but since 2021, the world's first hydrogen refueling station for trains is in operation.

Ottobock Orthobionics

There are groundbreaking innovations at the interface between man and machine. The products of Ottobock, the global market leader in prosthetics and orthotics, detect nerve signals on amputated limbs and translate them into mechanical movements of the prosthetics. This massively improves the quality of life of the users. Ottobock CEO Hans-Georg Näder writes "Ottobock is located at the central interface between man and machine, artificial intelligence, cyborgs, and robotics. At this interface, completely new markets and new business models will emerge for us in the near future. This is what I call 'FUTURING'."[4] A huge challenge is the integration of very different fields of knowledge and research, with medicine and technology gradually merging. Hans-Georg Näder says: "In the future, we'll be sailing on much larger oceans, but first we'll have to discover and map them out." Ottobock is

---

[4] Personal communication, December 7, 2020.

part of an ecosystem, in which the local university offers the only study program in orthobionics worldwide.

Disinfection with UV-C LED

Disinfection is one of the major problems in modern healthcare. In three years of research, the ambulance supplier Binz and the Fraunhofer Institute for Optronics, System Technologies and Image Exploitation have developed a system for disinfecting ambulances and rescue vehicles. This system is considered a "quantum leap in disinfection" [15]. Within a very short time, clean room conditions are established in the ambulance so that even operations could be performed in it. Heraeus and Osram Opto Semiconductor have introduced technologies in which LED light is used for disinfection, including a device that allows consumers to disinfect their environment. Heraeus Noblelight equips buses with UV-C lamps, known as "light swords," which render 99.9% of all viruses harmless [16]. The market for UV-C is expected to quadruple in the next five years.

Va-Q-Tec Thermoboxes

Pharmaceuticals, vaccines, but also electronic devices or works of art have to be transported at constant, often very low temperatures. The first COVID-19 vaccine required temperatures of -70 °C. Va-Q-Tec has invented a completely new technology for thermoboxes that insulates ten times better than Styrofoam and keeps packed goods at a constant temperature for days or weeks without any further energy supply. The company has more than 180 patents. During the COVID-19 epidemic, huge numbers of test kits and vaccine vials requiring extreme low-temperature storage were shipped in Va-Q-Tec boxes. The customer list reads like a Who's Who of the pharmaceutical and biotech industries. The market for frozen foods that must be transported at -18° promises further growth.

Graforce

Organic and inorganic compounds in industrial wastewater, slurry, plastics, or gases hold huge potential as energy sources. Graforce applies a process known as plasmalysis to produce green hydrogen and other valuable industrial gases from these residuals. The production of hydrogen by plasmalysis requires much less energy and is therefore significantly cheaper than the classic electrolysis process. While the cost in conventional processes is €6–8 per kg of hydrogen, it is only €1.50–3.00 in the plasmalysis process.

Magnetically Levitated Train TSB

The magnetically levitated train TSB (Transport System Bögl) was developed by the Hidden Champion Max Bögl and certified by the German Federal Railway Authority (EBA) in the fall of 2020. Bögl was involved in the construction of the Transrapid in Shanghai in 2002, which runs at 450 km/h. After Thyssen and Siemens abandoned the Transrapid project, Bögl took over the development of its own maglev train.

The EBA certification allows this future-oriented transport system to be marketed. Unlike the Transrapid, which was designed for long distances and maximum speeds of 500 km/h, TSB is aimed at short-distance routes and travel speeds of up to 160 km/h. In China, which may have the greatest market opportunities, Bögl is cooperating with Xinzhu, which operates a 3.5 km test track in Chengdu. TSB is "currently the most modern solution for local public transport. The system floats quietly and contact-free on a slim track on elevated, ground-level, or underground rails" [17]. Bögl offers a complete solution from a single source, from planning, to manufacturing, to operations.

Vectoflow

Vectoflow builds flow and dynamic pressure probes with 3D printing. Such additive manufacturing can achieve miniaturization, high precision, flexibility, and customization on an unprecedented scale. Co-founded in 2015 by mechanical engineer Katharina Kreitz, Vectoflow already boasts an impressive customer list including Siemens, Airbus, Tesla, Raytheon, Safran, General Electric, BMW, and Toyota.

Twaice Battery Analytics

Batteries are at the heart of mobility and energy systems. In the near future, they will not only power millions of vehicles but will also serve as a buffer between the generation and the consumption of electric power. At the same time, batteries have all sorts of quirks with respect to charging, lifetime, power output, and similar processes. Identifying these quirks is Twaice's business. This start-up analyzes batteries in terms of every conceivable parameter. Customer benefits are significant in terms of maintenance, charging processes, and replacement.

Combustion Chambers for SpaceX Rockets

Where does Elon Musk buy the machines that make the combustion chambers and other high-stress parts for SpaceX's Mars rockets? From the Hidden Champion MK Technologies! MK produces systems for investment casting, an alternative to 3D printing, which allows the production of extremely complex shapes. MK has supplied SpaceX with several production lines for investment casting, on which the combustion chambers are manufactured. SpaceX is highly satisfied with the results. SpaceX would have needed 1000 large 3D printers to achieve the same output. Other parts of the rockets continue to be manufactured with 3D printers, namely those from the German Hidden Champion EOS, global market leader in this field.

Flying Dogs, Smart Birds, and Chameleons

Festo, the global market leader in pneumatics, repeatedly delivers impressive breakthrough innovations by technically replicating role models from nature. Some of these are demonstration objects that illustrate Festo's technological expertise and technical prowess. The videos with the bionic flying dogs and smart birds are amazing and truly worth watching [18]. Festo technicians have not only succeeded in deciphering bird flight but in technically replicating it. The bionic approach leads to highly practical solutions. One example is the Flex Shape Gripper, which replicates the tongue of a chameleon and can pick up and place small objects of any shape. Again, the video is more than impressive [19]. During my visits to China, I saw for myself that these unusual skills are of practical use in ordinary markets. I asked in dozens of factories whether they are using Festo products and the answer was always "yes."

Quantum Sensor

Hidden Champions are venturing into frontier technologies. Sick, a Hidden Champion in sensors, is cooperating with the laser specialist Trumpf to launch a sensor based on quantum technology. Sick CEO Robert Bauer explains, "The quantum sensor can measure particles one-fifth of a micrometer small, which is 200 times thinner than a human hair" [20]. Potential applications for this futuristic technology are emerging in semiconductor production, the pharmaceutical industry, and the environmental sector.

Innovation Processes

The innovation processes of Hidden Champions have numerous special features. A study by the Center for European Economic Research concludes "Hidden Champions have excellent innovation process management" [21]. Innovation begins with investment in research and development. The R&D intensity, i.e., the ratio of R&D investment to revenue, is at 6% for the Hidden Champions, twice as high as the average for German industrial companies. The 35 publicly traded German companies with the highest R&D intensity achieve 4.8% [22]. For KWS, a Hidden Champion in seed production, the ratio is 18.5%. Note that KWS is not a start-up, but was founded in 1856.

As already mentioned, Hidden Champions have 31 patents per 1000 employees while large companies have only six. The costs per patent differ by a factor of five. For large companies, they are €2.7 million, while for the Hidden Champions the cost per patent is €529,000. This divergence suggests that the innovation processes differ significantly.

According to the Institute of the German Economy, the average patent exploitation rate, i.e., the actual use of patents in products, is only 15% in Germany. Another source quotes only 5–7% [23]. These low rates refer to both large companies and independent inventors [24]. For the Hidden Champions, the rate reaches around 75%, meaning that they use three out of four patents in products. The reasons lie in the Hidden Champions' focus and the closeness to customer. They avoid developing features, products, or services that customers ultimately do not accept.

Innovations are a top priority for Hidden Champions, and top management acts as both an active initiator and an enforcer. Herbert Schein, CEO of Varta, the global market leader for microbatteries, is committed to this mandate: "We need a culture of innovation. For me, one of the most important tasks is to create this culture of innovation. Trust and agility are important. We decide on something and implement it immediately" [25]. This approach can only work when focus and depth come together and the leaders are sufficiently involved in the details to drive innovation effectively. A strategy accepted by everyone involved—as well as smooth collaboration between functions—facilitates and accelerates the innovation process and leads to better results, especially in process innovations. Heads and competencies are more important than budgets for innovation success. "Employees in Hidden Champions are more involved in the innovation process than in other companies, creating an organizational climate that particularly encourages innovation," writes Julian Schenkenhofer [25].

Continuity is essential for achieving constant improvements and ultimately perfection. The customers are a very important source of ideas for the Hidden Champions and are deeply involved in their innovation processes [26]. This requires relationships based on trust. Despite their limited personnel and financial resources, the Hidden Champions prove to be outstanding innovators, not least because they design their innovation processes differently. As a result, their innovativeness is several times higher than that of large companies.

References

1. Kreditanstalt für Wiederaufbau. (2020). *KfW-Innovationsbericht 2019*. Frankfurt.
2. Rammer, C., & Spielkamp, A. (2015). *Hidden Champions—Driven by Innovation, Empirische Befunde auf Basis des Mannheimer Innovationspanels*. Mannheim: ZEW.
3. Retrieved from https://www.bloomberg.com/news/articles/2020-01-18/germany-breaks-korea-s-six-year-streak-as-most-innovative-nation.
4. Breitinger, J. C., Dierks, B., & Rausch, T. (2020). *Weltklassepatente in Zukunftstechnologien—Die Innovationskraft Ostasiens, Nordamerikas und Europas*. Guetersloh: Bertelsmann Stiftung.
5. Ernst, H., & Omland, N. (2010). The patent asset index—A new approach to benchmark patent portfolios. *World Patent Information, 33*, 34–41.
6. Retrieved from https://www.dpma.de/dpma/veroeffentlichungen/statistiken/csv-statistiken/index.html.
7. Retrieved from https://www.gartner.com/smarterwithgartner/5-trends-drive-the-gartner-hype-cycle-for-emerging-technologies-2020/.
8. Blosch, M., & Fenn, J. (2021). Understanding Gartner's hype cycles. Garnter.com, September 23; with permission by Gartner June 24, 2021.
9. Levitt, T. (1988), Editorial. *Harvard Business Review*, p. 9.

10. Conren. (2020). *Studie zu börsengelisteten Familienunternehmen in Europa*. Heidelberg and Zurich, p. 9.
11. Pohl, P., & Kempermann, H. (2019). *Innovative Milieus—Die Innovationsfähigkeit deutscher Unternehmen* (p. 30). Guetersloh: Bertelsmann Stiftung, October.
12. Naudé, W., & Nagler, P. (2021, March 2021). The rise and fall of German innovation. *Discussion Paper 14154*, IZA Institute of Labor Economics, Bonn.
13. Stieler, M., & Munk, A. (2020). Die additive Fertigung bei KSB. *Marketing Review St. Gallen, 60*, 46–53.
14. Retrieved from https://binz-automotive.com/viren-bekaempfung-mit-led-licht-aus-ilmenau/.
15. N.A. (2020, November 7). Ein Lichtschwert gegen Viren. *Frankfurter Allgemeine Zeitung*, p. 28.
16. Retrieved from https://transportsystemboegl.com/gruenes-licht-vom-eisenbahn-bundesamt-fuer-das-tsb/.
17. Retrieved from https://www.festo.com/group/en/cms/13130.htm und https://www.festo.com/group/de/cms/10238.htm.
18. Retrieved from https://www.youtube.com/watch?v=m7l-87r4oOY.
19. Preuß, S. (2021, November 6). *Deutscher Sensor der Superlative*. Frankfurter Allgemeine Zeitung, p. 21.
20. Rammer, C., & Spielkamp, A. (2015). *Hidden champions—Driven by innovation*. Mannheim: ZEW.
21. EY. (2019). *Top 500 F&E: Wer investiert am meisten in Innovationen*. Vienna: EY.
22. Retrieved from https://idw-online.de/de/news445856; and https://uol.de/fileadmin/user_upload/forschung/download/Transfer/Patente/PatFi-PVA-Kap5.pdf.
23. Retrieved from https://www.dpma.de/docs/dpma/veroeffentlichungen/1/dpma-.
24. N.A. (2020, September 1). Ich will überall Innnovationen sehen. Interview with Herbert Schein, *Frankfurter Allgemeine Zeitung*, p. 22.
25. Schenkenhofer, J. (2020). Hidden champions: A review of the literature and future research avenues. *Working Paper Series 06-20*, Lehrstuhl für Management und Organisation, Universität Augsburg, p. 17.
26. Retrieved 2019, from https://www.juliusraabstiftung.at/publikationen/studie-innovation-und-resilienz-bei-familiengefuehrten-kmus/.

Part V

The New Game of Strategy

20

Ambition

How does a company become a Hidden Champion? No Hidden Champion stumbled into global market leadership by chance. They all got there because of the ambitions and goals of the company founders and their successors, driven by the will to be the best in their business, ideally in the global market. The drive to excel fuels strong motivation, regardless of whether the scope is local, national, or global. The legendary founders of established Hidden Champions were driven by this kind of ambition. Does this apply to the younger generation of Hidden Champion leaders and entrepreneurs? The answer is a resounding "yes," as the following quotes show.

Frank Blase, CEO of Hidden Champion Igus, reports: "At 16, we were asked at school what we wanted to achieve in life professionally. I said, 'do something where I am the best in the world'."[1] Today, his company Igus is the global market leader in so-called motion plastics. Nikolas Stihl, chairman of Stihl, the global market leader in chainsaws, says: "Either we're the best, or we don't do it."[2] This statement refers not only to Stihl's classic gasoline-powered products but also applies to the new generation of battery-powered devices. These devices have opened up completely new perspectives for Stihl and required a real transformation of the company. Michael Kügelgen, CEO of investment casting Hidden Champion MK Technologies, states: "We have to build the best machines in the world."[3] Hüttenes-Albertus, one of the leading suppliers for foundries, formulates no less ambitiously: "We have set our

---

[1] Personal communication, October 20, 2020.
[2] *Private Wealth-Magazine*, December 2019, p. 20.
[3] Personal communication, May 23, 2020.

sights on being the most innovative company and the preferred supplier for the foundry industry worldwide" [1].

EWM, one of the global market leaders in the field of welding technology, expresses its ambitions as follows: "Our goal is to be first and best when it comes to technology, quality, and customer benefits" [2]. Herbert Schein, CEO of Varta, global market leader in microbatteries, formulates a similar claim: "We have the will to be number one in every process step" [3]. His majority shareholder, the Austrian investor Michael Tojner, agrees: "We want to become the Apple of battery manufacturing" [4]. These statements highlight the important aspect that every performance feature and every process step opens up new opportunities and fields in which it is possible to succeed and to be the best.

Not only established Hidden Champions compete to be the best. Young Hidden Champions have similar ambitions. The translation service Deepl.com confidently states: "We outperform all other translation systems. The DeepL translator delivers the best translations worldwide. In Europe and America, DeepL is already known as the world's best AI translation provider" [5]. Mackevision, global market leader in computer-generated imagery (CGI), formulates no less ambitiously: "Our claim is to offer solutions and products at the highest level and at the same time to be the absolute number one worldwide" [6]. Perfection is also the goal of Sennheiser, one of the global market leaders in microphones and headphones: "We strive for the perfect sound" [7].

Market Leadership

In many cases, the ambitions of Hidden Champions explicitly relate to market leadership. The claim to be the best in one's market and the achievement of a market-leading position are closely related. Those who are and remain the best have a good chance to become market leaders. The company Sick, one of the global market leaders in sensor technology, says: "Market leadership means becoming the standard of excellence against which others measure themselves. We set the benchmarks worldwide." Max-Ferdinand Krawinkel, head of PWM, the global market leader in electronic price displays at gas stations, puts it this way: "Our goal is to become the market leader in all countries in which we are active."[4] PWM has a market share of about 90% in Germany and is also number one in the US market.

---

[4] *Frankfurter Allgemeine Zeitung*, July 2, 2020, p. 21.

More than one-third of the German Hidden Champions see themselves as the global number one. For most of them, the goal of market leadership transcends having the highest market share. The goal forges their identity. They pursue the more comprehensive claim to be the best in their market, which means to lead all market participants—customers, suppliers, and competitors—in terms of technology, quality, and reputation. Revenue and unit sales are the results and the indicators of the leadership position, but not the primary objectives.

The claim to lead the market is explicitly formulated and communicated early on in the development of these companies, in many cases from the start. The ambition to be the best and to become the market leader is an important driver of employee motivation. Hidden Champions "earn" their market-leading positions and their market shares through superior performance, not through low, margin-ruining prices. They command "good" market shares with high profit margins. The market share mania typical of mass markets where "bad," low-profit market share is acquired through aggressive pricing without regard to profit is alien to the Hidden Champions. Only a market leader who has achieved his position by superior performance will be accepted by the other market participants.

Will

Announcing that one wants to be the best or the market leader is easy. Actually achieving these goals is hard and requires willpower and competence. Willpower is a complex phenomenon that economists and business experts avoid. I am aware of only two management books with the term "will" in the title, and both are by Marvin Bower, the co-founder of McKinsey. After the early death of James McKinsey, Bower shaped this firm according to his ideas and led it to world leadership in strategy consulting. His first book, *The Will to Manage*, was published in 1966, and at the age of 94, he published a second book, *The Will to Lead* [8, 9]. One is reminded of the famous concept "The Will to Power" by Friedrich Nietzsche.[5] The term "will" is otherwise extremely rare in management literature, although will is a crucial element of leadership and management. The corporate culture of McKinsey—as originally

---

[5] "The Will to Power" is not an independent work of Friedrich Nietzsche, but an idea introduced by him in *Die fröhliche Wissenschaft* and the following work *Also sprach Zarathustra* and mentioned at least in passing in all subsequent books.

established by Bower—continues to reflect his influence. Seneca's words come to mind: "Will cannot be learned."

I know hundreds of Hidden Champion entrepreneurs, and almost all of them are characterized by an irrepressible will to be the best in their market and to become the market leader. In his autobiography, Hidden Champion founder Albert Blum speaks of the, "unconditional will to bring innovation to the world" [10]. This will must remain strong for a long time. After all, achieving these ambitious goals is a long-distance race that can take decades.

Competence

Will alone, however, is not sufficient to achieve the noble goal. It is a necessary condition, but not a sufficient one. The necessary competencies are just as important. One must not only want to do it, but also be able to do it.

My encounters with hundreds of Hidden Champion entrepreneurs support the notion that a long process of learning-by-doing, not innate superiority or talent, is the basis of superior performance and market leadership. The typical Hidden Champion entrepreneur is not born with the requisite skills. Only very few of them were the best in their field worldwide or mastered the necessary skills early in their lives. Talent helps, but superior competencies are typically developed through continuous practice over time.

"If you practice one skill for 10,000 hours, you'll have a good chance at becoming an expert at it," is how Malcom Gladwell describes the phenomenon in his bestseller *Outliers—The Story of Success* [11]. The idea that perfection is achieved through sustained practice was already put forward in a 1993 article by Anderson, Krampe, and Tesch-Römer, who explained expert performance as "the end result of individuals' prolonged efforts to improve performance. In most domains of expertise, individuals begin in their childhood a regimen of effortful activities (deliberate practice) designed to optimize improvement. Individual differences, even among elite performers, are closely related to assessed amounts of deliberate practice. Many characteristics once believed to reflect innate talent are actually the result of intense practice extended for a minimum of ten years" [12].

Opportunities

There is another facet that drives up the chance to achieve the ambitious goals to be the best or the market leader. As discussed in Chap. 4, there is a multitude of markets, possibly millions of them. Each of these markets, or more broadly, each market segment, opens up the opportunity to be the best in that segment. Within each of these many markets, every competitive parameter opens yet more chances to be the best at something. In a specific market, you can be the best in product quality or design or price or brand or service, etc. Delivering superior performance in one or a few parameters can create new, separate markets or segments in which a company can be the market leader.

The New Game: Ambition

What is new in the game with respect to ambition? Aiming to be the best in a market is not fundamentally changing, but its importance is likely to increase. The reason is that more and more ambition is penetrating the markets, primarily from Chinese and other Asian competitors, but also from Eastern European and Israel. If you interpret the ratio "own ambition/total ambition in the market" as an indicator of the probability of success, it is clear that the numerator must increase with the denominator if the probability of success is to remain the same. On the other hand, increasing market fragmentation can alleviate the pressure.

If the race for best-in-class and market-leading positions is fought at higher speeds in the future—which seems likely—there is less time to realize ambitions. More agility and faster implementation are necessary in the New Game, within limits to avoid mistakes. Learning through practice takes time. Another change will be the need to recruit more talent internationally to ensure the required level of competencies.

References

1. Retrieved from https://www.ha-group.com/wer-wir-sind/geschichte/.
2. Retrieved from https://products.ewm-group.com/cs/unternehmen/ueber-uns.html.
3. N.A. (2020, September 1). Ich will überall Innovationen sehen. Interview with Herbert Schein, *Frankfurter Allgemeine Zeitung*, p. 22.

4. Seiser, M. (2020, January 20). Wir wollen deutscher Apple im Batteriebau werden," Das Unternehmergespräch, *Frankfurter Allgemeine Zeitung*, p. 21.
5. Retrieved from https://www.deepl.com/de/press.html.
6. Retrieved from https://www.wiwo.de/adv/telekom-digitalisierung/digitour/digitalisierung-im-mittelstand-gute-aussichten-fuer-hidden-champions-in-der-digitalen-welt/23658562.html.
7. Retrieved from https://de-de.sennheiser.com/ueber-sennheiser-auf-einen-blick.
8. Bower, M. (1966). *The will to manage: Corporate success through programmed management*. McGraw-Hill.
9. Bower, M. (1997). *The will to lead: Running a business with a network of leaders*. Harvard Business School Press.
10. Blum, A. (2020). *Von der Werkstatt im Backhaus zum Global Player–Meine Biografie*. Ausdruck-verleihen.de.
11. Gladwell, M. (2008). *Outliers—The story of success*. Little, Brown and Company.
12. Ericsson, K. A., Krampe, R. T., & Tesch-Römer, C. (1993). The role of deliberate practice in the acquisition of expert performance. *Psychological Review*, 363–406, here p. 363.

21

Focus

Only focus leads to world class. Frank Gotthardt, the founder of Compugroup Medical, a Hidden Champion in software for medical practices, succinctly advises: "Focus on what you do best!" This has turned out to be a good idea, as the Compugroup's market capitalization stands at €4.4 billion.[1]

Most Hidden Champions define their markets narrowly and stay true to their focus as they grow. Many of them do not accept the standard industry definition of markets or segments. Instead, they see the definition of their market as a strategic parameter they determine independently. Defining the market and the focus differently from the competition or industry tradition can in itself be an innovation [1].

Some Hidden Champions are ultra-niche players, which means that they operate in tiny markets, but command global market shares of 70–100%. The Hidden Champions Bauer Comp and Sauer are both compressor manufacturers, but leaders in different submarkets. Sauer has a global market share of 75% for compressors for naval vessels, and Bauer Comp has an equally high global market share for breathing air compressors. Such a narrow focus may limit growth, but it also creates high barriers to market entry.

Because of their focus, the fate of Hidden Champions depends on their core markets, for better or worse. At the same time, their customers depend on them as the only providers of a superior product or service. While the dependence on one market increases the market risk, the full concentration of the Hidden Champions' resources makes it hard for other companies to compete, which reduces the competitive risk. It is up to each company to find the

---

[1] January 27, 2021.

right balance between the two types of risks. Once the Hidden Champions have selected a market, they show a strong and long-term commitment to it. Fundamental redefinitions of the market occur as rarely as technology breakthroughs, only about every 10–15 years.

Product Focus

Manfred Bogdahn commits to focus on one product: "We will only do one thing—but we will do it brilliantly!" His company Flexi produces nothing but retractable dog leashes and commands 70% of the world market. Competitors from China and many other countries have tried to imitate Flexi products hundreds of times, without ever succeeding. The total focus on this seemingly simple product is the reason for Flexi's continued success.

Nils Meyer-Pries, CEO of the Fuchs Group, the world's No. 2 in spices, takes a similar view: "Only do what you can do really well, then do it properly and thoroughly. The courage to specialize and to focus on small markets sustains our global development." Franz-Josef Konert, CEO of Gelita, the global market leader for gelatin, formulates unequivocally: "Our focus: production of animal proteins."[2] Gelita's products go to customers in many different industries, but are based on one raw material, so the product focus makes sense.

These statements show that product quality is at the core of the value-to-customer. Product focus can also be found among Hidden Champions in the high-tech sector and not just in traditional industries. Wago, one of the market leaders in electronic connectivity, says: "We focus our thoughts and actions on what we do best: We create the right connections and ensure their reliability in the long term." Jaroslaw Kutylowski, CEO of Deepl.com, was asked in an interview: "Is focus on a single product the recipe for success?" His answer was "Focus is a valid point, and also a vision of the company. I think it's the only way startups can compete against the big companies."[3]

Customer Focus

Hidden Champions that predominantly serve customers from one industry naturally ascribe great importance to customer focus. Uhlmann, the global market leader in packaging systems for the pharmaceutical industry, says "We

---

[2] Gelita Strategy 2020.
[3] https://www.gruenderszene.de/technologie/deepl-ceo-jaroslaw-kutylowski

always had one customer and will only have one customer in the future: the pharmaceutical industry. We only do one thing, but we do it right." Uhlmann could certainly produce systems for food packaging or electronic gadgets, but its priority is to defend its top position in the pharmaceutical industry by focusing fully on that sector.

Customer focus can also be found in digital sectors. The Hidden Champion Nemetschek is the world's leading software vendor for architects, engineers, and the construction industry (AEC), with over six million users in 142 countries. A statement from the company says: "Focus on one thing and be the best in the world. Nemetschek is the only global vendor focused exclusively on the AEC industry."

Focus and Investors

The example of the startup MOWEA, a manufacturer of modular wind turbines based on the Lego principle, shows that focus can play an important role in attracting investors and raising capital: "The possible applications of our turbines are very diverse. But that is not necessarily an advantage when it comes to acquiring investors. They want to see that you have found your niche and are successful in it. So it's better not to meddle in five different areas, but to choose one and really get going there" [2]. Smart investors make sure that startups are focused and do not lose their way. Scarce finances make focus even more important.

Multidimensional Focus

It is not always possible to draw a sharp distinction between product focus and customer focus. Teamviewer, the global market leader in remote screen sharing, incorporates both: "TeamViewer focuses on cloud-based technologies that enable online collaboration and remote support for users worldwide."

Focus can include other dimensions such as technology, processes, or even broader capabilities. Tesla Grohmann Engineering is an example of this. They used to supply specialized systems for microelectronic assembly. For a long time, Intel was their most important customer. After a while, Grohmann started to offer solutions for difficult tasks in the automotive industry, for example assembling door seals. When Elon Musk became aware of Grohmann in the context of battery manufacturing, he was so impressed by their competencies that he bought the company. Most recently, Tesla Grohmann

Engineering has attracted attention as a supplier of manufacturing equipment for COVID-19 vaccines. Tesla Grohmann's focus is not defined by a specific product or customer group. It sees its expertise in solving difficult problems in industrial production. In 2021, Elon Musk dropped the name Grohmann and renamed the company Tesla Automation.

The roots of Rhein-Nadel Automation (RNA) go back to seventeenth-century needle production. If RNA had stuck with this product focus, the company would have disappeared long ago, the fate suffered by seven other needle manufacturers in its region. Instead, RNA underwent a fundamental transformation of focus and is now the global market leader in feeding systems for small parts such as razor blades, roll-on deodorants, or shampoo lids. "We deal with the feeding of small parts. We do it for almost all industries. We create order out of a chaotic mass of parts. Half the parts in a home go through our systems," says Rhine Needle CEO Christopher Pavel [3]. The systems that RNA produces are one of a kind. The focus is on process know-how.

Loss of Focus

Some successful entrepreneurs struggle with focus. Their success in one market can lead them to overestimate their abilities and believe they are similarly competent in other markets. This attitude creates the danger of losing focus and direction. Regardless of how ambitious and competent entrepreneurs are in their accustomed field, it is unlikely that they can become the best in multiple markets. Only one person, Marie Curie, ever won the Nobel Prize in two scientific fields (chemistry and physics).[4] The maxim "cobbler, stick to your last" is difficult for quite a few entrepreneurs to accept. Their success in one market tempts them to prove themselves to the world in other areas. This almost always goes wrong. I have seen dozens of such cases, which out of consideration I will refrain from naming. Anyone who has the ambition to become and—above all—to remain a Hidden Champion is well advised to focus and stay focused on one market.

---

[4] Besides Marie Curie, three other scientists received two Nobel Prizes: Linus Carl Pauling (Chemistry 1954, Peace 1962), John Bardeen (Physics 1956, 1972), and Frederick Sanger (Chemistry 1958, 1980).

The New Game: Focus

Rhein-Nadel Automation (RNA) is an outstanding example for the successful transformation of focus, from the product "needle" to the process "feeding small parts." Every company has to ask itself from time to time whether its focus needs to be readjusted. Traditionally, this used to happen only at longer intervals, but the rapid changes driven by globalization, digitalization, the advance of ecosystems, and sustainability requirements will mean that the New Game will change more often. Increased complexity of business systems and breakthrough innovations may also require a change of focus. Manufacturers of automotive drivetrains, for example, must find a new focus as electromobility advances. Defining market and focus correctly is a difficult task. Hidden Champions have become market leaders by defining their markets and their focus narrowly.

Focus is not diminishing in importance and may even become more decisive. You become world class by sustained concentration, not by spreading your resources thinly. The danger of specializing too much may be smaller than the risk of dissipating one's talents and energies. The specialist often beats the generalist [4].

References

1. Abell, D. F. (1980). *Defining the business. The starting point of strategic planning.* Englewood Cliffes (NJ): Prentice Hall.
2. Kast, G. (2020, August). Windräder für alle. *Vivanty*, p. 63.
3. N.A. (2019, February 11). Die Hälfte der Teile im Haushalt läuft durch unsere Systeme. *Frankfurter Allgemeine Zeitung*, p. 25.
4. Lei, L., & Wu, X. (2020). Thinking like a specialist or a generalist? Evidence from hidden champions in China. *Asian Business Management, 21*, 25–57. https://doi.org/10.1057/s41291-020-00114-2

22

Depth

Depth touches the core and heart of many Hidden Champions. In management, depth usually comes up in connection with terms such as the value chain or integration. In the value chain, depth can be directed toward the customer (downstream) or toward the supplier (upstream). In the same sense, we speak of forward integration or backward integration. One can also use depth to describe knowledge, insight, analysis, or immersive engagement with a problem. The spatial concept of depth fits the Hidden Champions in several respects. In the book *Time and Freedom* [1], the French philosopher Henri Bergson explains that we assign spatial terms to abstract content because only space is accessible to our perception.

Depth of the Value Chain

Hidden Champions often cover several stages in the value chain with a deep range of services in their narrowly defined markets. The depth of value added by the Hidden Champions is 42% of revenue, significantly higher than the industry average. This is even more pronounced for the value added in manufacturing, which reaches 50% for the Hidden Champions versus the industry average of less than 30%.

Some Hidden Champions are fanatical do-it-yourselfers, with a manufacturing value added of 70% or more. Wanzl, the global market leader in shopping carts and airport luggage carts, says: "We have a very deep vertical integration. We produce almost all parts and components ourselves according to self-defined quality standards. With our own electroplating facilities, Wanzl products receive their unsurpassed surface finish."

Vertical integration sometimes extends all the way to the raw materials. Faber-Castell, the global market leader in pencils, grows its own wood for the pencils, operating plantations in Brazil covering an area of 100 square kilometers. When I asked the CEO, the late Anton-Wolfgang Graf von Faber-Castell [2], why he didn't buy the wood on the market, he replied: "My father used to buy the wood. When I took over, I noticed that we weren't getting the same consistent quality every year. Therefore, I decided to grow our own wood."

High-tech Hidden Champions show similar preferences. Herbert Schein, the CEO of Varta, says: "Although I was always advised otherwise, we have kept all stages of the value chain within the company. Today, we design and build the most important machines ourselves, the ones that make the difference. We take care of the tooling, the material finishing, the production, and the packaging" [3]. The statement from sensor technology Hidden Champion Pepperl & Fuchs echoes Schein's statement: "We do everything ourselves, especially in research and development." Hasenkamp, a shipping company specializing in art transport, says: "We don't let anything out of our hands. We take full responsibility. That's what makes us qualitatively superior to large shipping companies that do art transports on the side and outsource a lot." The commitment of many Hidden Champions to do-it-yourself does not seem to have weakened. Most Hidden Champions are very reluctant to outsource core competencies to third-party suppliers.

Non-core Competencies

The do-it-yourself attitude is restricted primarily to core competencies. In contrast, Hidden Champions are more willing to outsource activities related to non-core competencies. Their highest priority is to offer top performance in product features that are important to the customer, such as quality, user-friendliness, or the degree of innovation. They consider this the only way to create and secure competitive advantages. Non-core competencies, on the other hand, are viewed as less important to the customer. Specialized external service providers, especially in areas such as legal or tax advice, design, or advertising, can often perform these tasks better. If outsiders can do a job better, it makes sense to delegate the task.

Uniqueness

The most obvious of depth's many facets is total quality control. A company has a better chance of achieving perfection when it controls all important steps of the value chain than when parts come from many different suppliers. After all, competitors can also buy the same materials on the open market unless one agrees to exclusivity, as ASML, Trumpf, and Zeiss do within the framework of the business ecosystem described in Chap. 16.

Deep value chains are the basis of the uniqueness and superiority of the Hidden Champions' products. Uniqueness and superiority can only be created internally.

Know-How Protection

Another advantage of vertical integration and the secrecy it confers, is effective protection against know-how outflow, copycatting by imitators, and industrial espionage. The Hidden Champions tend to be very secretive in research and development. For some Hidden Champions, depth means that they either develop and build their own machines to manufacture their products, or they modify standard machines for their specific purposes. Max-Ferdinand Krawinkel, CEO of PWM, the world leader in electronic price displays at gas stations, says: "If no one has the same machines, no one can imitate our products and our quality" [4]. Jürgen Nussbaum, a member of the board of Sachtler, the global market leader for professional camera tripods, expressed a similar view: "In some countries, competitors are trying to imitate our products but fail because they don't have the same tools. We make our own machines; they can't be bought on the market."

Depth and Growth

Efforts to deepen the value chain have contributed significantly to the growth of many Hidden Champions. Acquisitions of upstream and downstream suppliers played a major role in this. Krones, now the global market leader in beverage filling lines, started out with labeling machines, a small part of the value chain. Today, Krones offers complete filling lines. Vossloh, global market leader in rail fasteners and switches, became an integrated systems provider for railroad operators through both in-house developments and acquisitions. It offers its customers not only rails, but also maintenance services such as calibration, milling, and high-speed grinding. The story of Wirtgen is similar. It began with road milling machines and is still the global market leader in this field. Over the years, it has acquired Vögele (road pavers), Hamm (steamrollers), Benninghoven (asphalt mixers), and Kleemann (crushing and screening plants for recycling). Today, the Wirtgen Group, now part of John Deere, can cover the entire value chain in road maintenance and construction.

Depth as a Millstone

Depth also has downsides. Among them are higher capital intensity, risks due to uneven utilization of individual capacities along the value chain, and technical reasons. Enercon, one of the market leaders in wind technology, always emphasized its extremely high vertical integration, which even included its own railroad and ships. However, with the crisis in wind energy, its complex value chain turned into a disadvantage. A deeper value chain usually means higher fixed costs. Another example are luxury goods manufacturers who penetrated the retail level by opening their own stores in order to capture trade margin. In times of crisis, though, traffic at their stores dries up and the ongoing fixed costs turn into millstones. I expect that companies will now exercise greater caution with these types of vertical integration.

New Competencies

Digitalization and innovation confront Hidden Champions with difficult challenges. A traditionalist preference for doing everything yourself can be dangerous if a company does not have the necessary competencies or cannot develop them quickly enough.

"It's never a solution to close yourself off," says Hans-Georg Näder, CEO of Ottobock, the world leader in prosthetics and orthotics. In this situation, many Hidden Champions made the correct decision to open up and cooperate with startups and experts within the framework of a business ecosystem. The ecosystem of the Beumer Group described in Chap. 17 exemplifies this.

The Hidden Champion Würth Elektronik, with sales of just under €1 billion and about 8000 employees, practices a similar model by cooperating with seven software startups. It holds minority stakes and acts as mentor to the founders of the startups. Overall, the picture remains mixed. In principle, there is a greater readiness to cooperate, but rather with "neutral" organizations such as universities and institutes than with private startups, who could end up being potential competitors. A research study confirms: "We find Hidden Champions to engage more frequently in cooperation with external partners. The largest difference is found in their cooperation with universities and research institutes. When developing new products, however, Hidden Champions rely more often on their own capacity and are less engaged in joint development" [5].

Technology and Depth

Technological breakthroughs can present both opportunities and threats. In the cases of Krones and Wirtgen, the deepening of the value chain stayed within the companies' mechanical engineering competence. Hidden Champion BEGA, the global market leader for outdoor architectural lighting, took a different route. BEGA historically limited itself to the mechanical parts of the luminaires and bought the electronic components and the light sources from big suppliers such as Osram, Philips, or General Electric. When the LED technology broke up this traditional value chain for the entire lighting industry, BEGA seized the opportunity to become an integrated luminaire manufacturer with a deeper and more sophisticated value chain. It entered into the development and production of its own LED modules. It also supplemented the mechanical processing and assembly plant with a manufacturing plant typical of the semiconductor industry, featuring highly automated machines to manufacture LED modules as well as completely new processes of an electronics manufacturer.

LED technology is not only transforming manufacturing, but also opens up completely new possibilities for product design and sustainability. Such a transformation requires high investments in human and physical capital. That's why every company facing such upheavals must carefully consider whether it can finance and develop the necessary competencies quickly enough in-house. If that is not the case, companies should refrain from deepening their value chains and give preference to outsourcing. A similar transformation of the value chain will become necessary when electric drives replace internal combustion engines. Stihl, the global market leader in chainsaws, went a step further and started its own battery production. With a very deep value chain, Stihl now offers a whole range of battery-powered tools for gardening and landscaping.

The New Game: Depth

A deep value chain is a double-edged sword for Hidden Champions. Traditionally, they consider deep vertical integration as the most important source of uniqueness and competitive superiority. The associated secrecy, especially in R&D, safeguards their know-how. But the advance of new technologies, first and foremost digitalization, forces them to decide whether they can develop the required competencies quickly enough with on-board resources. The more complex the knowledge gets, and the more it departs from previous competencies, the more likely the answer to this question is negative. At that point, it may be wise to follow new rules: open up and find new models of value creation. This often requires greater outsourcing, cooperation with external experts, and recourse to cloud-based services. Agility plays an important role in this high-speed game. Relinquishing some autonomy is not easy for the Hidden Champions, but under the new rules of the game, a transformation in the direction of greater openness is strongly recommended.

References

1. Bergson, H. (1910). *Time and free will*. London/New York: S. Sonnenschein & co., ltd., The Macmillan co.
2. Simon, H. (2013, February 27). Laudatory speech for Anton Wolfgang Graf Faber-Castell at the occasion of the G·E·M Award 2013 of Gesellschaft zur Erforschung des Markenwesens, Berlin, Graf Faber-Castell died in 2017.
3. N.A. (2020, September 1). Ich will überall Innovationen sehen. Interview with Herbert Schein, *Frankfurter Allgemeine Zeitung*, p. 22.
4. Freitag, L., & Schmidt, K. (2019, February 1). Einsame Spitze. *Wirtschaftswoche*, p. 22.
5. Rammer, C., & Spielkamp, A. (2019). The distinct features of hidden champions in Germany: A dynamic capabilities view. *ZEW Discussion Papers, No. 19-012*, ZEW-Leibniz-Zentrum für Europäische Wirtschaftsforschung, Mannheim, Germany.

23

Customers

Closeness-to-customer forms a central element of Hidden Champions' strategies. Their products are often complex and require intensive customer interaction. These requirements are best met by direct sales, which more than three quarters of all Hidden Champions practice.

Closeness-to-customer is second nature to the Hidden Champions, because of their smaller size and the less pronounced division of labor. When necessary, they deploy employees from production or R&D in customer service. Compared with large companies, the percentage of employees with regular customer contact is about five times higher.

In addition, many Hidden Champions favor decentralized structures. Foreign subsidiaries have greater autonomy than they typically would in large companies. Top management places high value on regular, direct customer contact. This has positive side effects, because management gets more and better information on customer issues, and because employees are more motivated.

Martin Kannegiesser, head of the eponymous global market leader for laundry systems, is personally present at the Texcare trade fair, because "the Americans and French who roam the company's stand want to see the boss" [1]. One Hidden Champion CEO told me: "I know and have visited every one of our customers in the world. The direct relationships built through these visits are invaluable." Dr. Wolfgang Willmann and Joachim Pein, founders of Dent-A-Pharm, the global market leader in light-curing composites for dental laboratories, emphasize: "We think it's important that customers can meet us in person. That's why we are present at all the big trade fairs, including Dubai, Sao Paulo, and Singapore."

I once read in a newspaper in the US Midwest about trouble at the paint shop of a local car plant. The hair spray that some workers used contained metal particles which had a tendency to settle on the paint. I cut out the article and sent it to Reinhard Schmidt, then CEO of Dürr AG, global market leader for automotive paint shops. He replied "I know this problem because I've been to this plant. The current paint shop is run by a competitor who can't handle the metal particle problem. We have a solution. I'm optimistic that we'll get the go-ahead next time." This is exemplary closeness-to-customer on the part of top management. Not only does the CEO of a billion-dollar company in Stuttgart, Germany, know exactly what's causing problems at a customer's paint shop somewhere in America, but he has been there in person and has a solution, even though the current plant is from the competition.

"In mid-sized companies, brand and trust-building are always the boss's job," says an article on closeness-to-customer of mid-sized companies [2]. On the one hand, these insights and recommendations are common sense, yet their implementation in practice is anything but simple. Customer relations and closeness-to-customer delineate the greatest differences between mid-sized and large companies, as well as the greatest differences between strong and weak companies. Thanks to their manageable size and flexibility, the Hidden Champions can shape customer relationships in a mutually beneficial way. They are great role models when it comes to closeness-to-customer.

Top Performance

Hidden Champions offer top performance and consistently align their offerings to the needs of their customers. They are always mindful to meet all expectations regarding product quality and service. Their products feature a high-technological sophistication combined with reliability.

Rosen Group, global market leader in pipeline inspection systems, says "We go far beyond current customer requirements by anticipating future market needs." Cerobear, the world's number one in ceramic ball bearings, has a similar claim: "We exceed our customers' expectations and deliver top quality in every respect" [3]. Flexi, the world leader in retractable dog leashes, also makes no compromises when it comes to quality. Its products must pass more than 100 quality tests.

Service

Service is becoming more and more important for the Hidden Champions. Customers increasingly expect comprehensive service packages, training, global presence, and networking. Herrenknecht, global market leader in tunnel boring machines, says "With the experience of thousands of completed projects, we are the only supplier worldwide to support our customers with premium services over the entire project duration, from the initial project idea to dismantling and reconditioning." Festo, the global market leader in pneumatics, has formed a separate training company, Festo Didactic SE, which is now the world's leading provider of technical education.

Some Hidden Champions have transformed from industrial to service companies. Many, especially the younger ones, use network economies and offer services whose benefits increase through global presence. This type of comprehensive service is increasingly expected by customers who operate globally. Setting up a global service network is a major organizational and financial challenge for a mid-sized company.

Systems Integration

A prominent trend in services is systems integration. Systems solutions improve customer benefits and raise the barriers to entry. "Our customers expect systems competence: powerful, simple, unique, reliable," is how Dr. Jochen Schaible, from the Swiss Hidden Champion Hoerbiger, sums it up. The market leader seems predestined to be a systems integrator. However, the transition to systems offerings multiplies the organizational complexity and can jeopardize the focus of the Hidden Champions.

Brand

In their narrow markets, the Hidden Champions have strong brands. Many of them have succeeded in building global brands, while others are still working on it. In order to secure their high market shares or to cover several price segments, some employ multi-brand strategies. Ingredient branding is gaining in importance, because many Hidden Champions are suppliers whose parts disappear in the end product [4].

Price

As a rule, Hidden Champions do not compete on price. In line with the top performance they offer, their prices are often ten to 15% above the market average. However, competitors from emerging markets, especially from China, are catching up in terms of performance and are threatening existing price differentials. In addition, the ultra-low-price segment—which Hidden Champions historically do not serve—is emerging in less-developed countries. Serving customers in this segment requires fundamentally different strategies in terms of product, research and development, production, and marketing. Hidden Champions tend to struggle in the ultra-low-price segment [4]. The Indian low-cost car Tata Nano featured products from nine German suppliers, but their expectations were not fulfilled. Experiments with second brands or the acquisition of low-cost brands have also produced mixed results. Nevertheless, it remains risky to totally neglect the ultra-low-price segment [5].

Focus on Top Customers

To become or remain the market leader, a company should win, permanently satisfy, and retain top customers. Many Hidden Champions therefore focus their efforts on top customers. This has several advantages. Sales to top customers are usually well above average, which reduces transaction costs. Top customers also act as drivers of performance because they demand outstanding quality from their suppliers. Last but not least, serving top customers boosts a company's reputation. Market leaders are typically suppliers to top customers.

Klaus Grohmann, founder of the Hidden Champion that is now Tesla Automation, pointed this out to me. He said that top customers make demands that seem almost impossible to meet. They keep on pressing and are never fully satisfied. But in this way, they constantly drive their suppliers to higher performance. Grohmann has always aimed to be a supplier to the world's top customers in his target industries, regardless of their locations. He said that proving that you satisfy the most demanding customers in the world through a lasting supplier relationship makes it easier to access the rest of the market. Grohmann used to focus on the electronics industry, supplying virtually all the leading companies there. It is one of the few European companies that repeatedly won Intel's Continuous Quality Improvement Award. Ultimately, Elon Musk, who is certainly not known for his low expectations, became aware of Grohmann and was so impressed that he acquired the company.

The input that drives performance improvement does not come from the easy customers. It comes from the unpleasant ones who are never completely satisfied and always demand better performance. Top customers are particularly important innovation partners. One Hidden Champion CEO described these customers as follows: "We don't love them, but we know that they constantly drive us to higher performance and that's why we owe our market leadership to them." Consciously using customers as performance drivers is a very effective strategy. True, it is easier to supply the less demanding customers, but that path does not lead to world class.

A few top customers often account for a high proportion of sales. This is risky, because losing even one customer leaves a void that is difficult to fill, but this risk is usually not one-sided. Even the top customers would have a hard time finding substitutes for high-performance suppliers. In markets with few customers, the strong market position of the Hidden Champions creates mutual dependencies that encourage long-term loyalty. Both sides know that they will continue to depend on each other in the future. One can speak of a symbiosis or of a business ecosystem.

Customers as a Source of Innovation

Customers can be an extremely valuable source of ideas for innovations. I'm reminded of MIT professor Eric von Hippel's lecture and his mantra: "Listen carefully to what your customers want and then respond with new products that meet or exceed their needs" [6, 7]. For many Hidden Champions, joint development with their customers is extremely important. In sectors such as plant engineering or industrial components, practically every new project involves joint development activities. A high level of trust based on long-standing close relationships is indispensable for such close cooperation. This is not only beneficial for the supplier but also for the customers, as the quality of its end products improves and development times shorten. Siltronic, the global market leader for hyperpure silicon wafers, states "In the development of new products we interact closely with our customers right from the start. The close cooperation continues right through to the serial production of the wafers." Swiss Hidden Champion Diametal invites its customers to "knock on the door" at the earliest possible stage of development. Diametal is the technology leader for the highly precise cutting tools used to manufacture gear drives for watches. The early involvement allows Diametal to suggest innovative solutions for the watch's construction, design, or production process. In these cases, Diametal even assumes process responsibility for cycle times and tool life. Givaudan, global market leader in flavors and fragrances, formulates as its vision, "to be our customers' essential partner in developing sustainable fragrance and flavor creations by engaging with our customers in collaborative dialogues during the development, creation, and refinement of their products."[1]

The Austrian Hidden Champion Pöttinger, global number one in hay wagons with a 60% market share, says "We are fully committed to closeness-to-customer and involve our customers in development." Many Pöttinger employees have farms themselves, so in a sense the customer is constantly present [8]. Deutsche Mechatronics, which develops modules or entire assemblies for mechanical engineering, promises its customers, "We'll get your ideas to prototype and series production quickly." A key factor is the integration of development and production, which requires extremely close cooperation between supplier and customer.

Schott is the global market leader for ceramic hotplates with its Ceran brand. Ceran is available in several thousand variants. A Schott R&D team is continuously working on improvements with manufacturers of electric household appliances, of cooking pots, and of cleaning agents, as well as with designers. The history of Ceran is an unbroken chain of innovations to which everyone involved has contributed.

No "No" Without the Boss

Many Hidden Champions use rules and principles specifically geared toward closeness-to-customer and customer satisfaction. Igus, global market leader in motion plastics, has a "No 'no' without the boss" rule. This rule prohibits saying "no" to the customer without the approval of a supervisor. A typical everyday situation illustrates its application: A customer calls and orders an item, combined with a request for an extremely short delivery time that cannot be met by the existing production schedule. The normal reaction of an employee who is taking the order would be to tell the customer that the product cannot be available that quickly: a "no" for the requested delivery time. At Igus, employees are not allowed to give such a negative response. Instead, they must consult their supervisor. The employees are allowed to tell the customer "no" only when the supervisor confirms the negative response.

According to Frank Blase, the managing partner, 80% of the customer requests that employees would have declined can be satisfied by superiors after

---

[1] Givaudan.com, Vision, May 18, 2012.

all. My assumption is that the rule alone creates a greater willingness among employees to solve problems themselves and not to consult their supervisors in the first place. This is how to achieve true customer orientation.

At Arnold AG, a specialist for custom-made metalworks, the company motto is "Not the product, but the customer is the measure of all things." Arnold makes design components, metal sculptures, architectural projects, and spectacular constructions made of metal, which are set up in high-rise buildings, airports, and trade fairs. Every project is unique. That is where uncompromising customer orientation comes in.

Stefan Soiné, managing partner of IREKS, one of the global market leaders in baking ingredients, requires his employees to "focus all their energy on maintaining our customer relationships and feel good about it." Of course, what matters is not whether the corresponding motto sounds good (it does in many companies), but whether the employees really live and practice closeness-to-customer in everyday life.

Employee–Customers

In order to achieve the greatest possible proximity to customers, some Hidden Champions prefer to hire employees from customers' industries. The customer becomes an employee, so to speak. At Rational, the global market leader for hot food preparation in commercial kitchens, 500 of the 2200 employees are trained cooks. They ensure that customer needs are understood and met with precision. Winterhalter, the global market leader for commercial dishwashing systems, employs sales staff with experience in the restaurant and hotel industry. These salespeople are very familiar with their customers' problems and can offer solutions that meet their needs. At IREKS, 500 sales representatives from 30 countries (out of a total of 2900 employees) have backgrounds as master bakers or confectioners and, consequently, a high affinity to their customers.

In-House Customers

Some Hidden Champions have their customers in-house, i.e., they insource the customer relationship. One example is Teepack Spezialmaschinen, the world market leader for tea bag packaging machines with a global market share of more than 50%. Teepack was created as a spin-off of the tea company

Teekanne. Teekanne remains an important customer of Teepack. The in-house experience effectively contributes to continuous improvement.

The situation is similar with the Hidden Champion Bauer, the global market leader for specialized foundation engineering equipment. A division of Bauer also offers the construction services carried out with these machines. The company's homepage states: "Bauer benefits greatly from the interlocking of its business units, and positions itself as an innovative and highly specialized provider of products and services for complex foundation engineering work."

Customers and Digitalization

As the numerous cases in Chap. 17 demonstrate, the customer interface forms a "primary battleground" of digitalization. It affects all customer-related, value-adding activities such as business initiation, sales, offer coordination and submission, project implementation, transaction, service, training, and communication.

Digitalization enables companies to address current and potential customers more precisely, right down to micro-segmentation or the "segment of one." This also applies to the transmission of individualized content. However, because of the Hidden Champions' preference for direct sales, the importance of automated communication is not as great in their markets as in consumer markets [9]. For the typical Hidden Champion, a hybrid model with a case-specific combination of digital and personal communication is more likely to prove optimal.

The high complexity of the products is an argument against the maximum use of digital communication, as the following case illustrates. A company wanted to develop new software for mid-sized companies and to sell it exclusively online. It created a very simple interface with a menu that allowed customers to configure their own solution. However, it turned out that the product was too complex for pure online sales. It required a personal sales team. In addition, it proved necessary to find local cooperation partners to help with the migration to the new system. These acceptance barriers made the original expectations unrealistic because everything cost more and took longer than planned.

On the other hand, the COVID-19 crisis showed that companies could superbly execute some activities that were previously thought impossible to digitize. The CEO of a Hidden Champion in the chemical industry told me that the crisis hardly affected his company, even though neither salespeople nor technicians were able to travel anymore and all office staff worked from home. "Contrary to our fears, sales and the technical coordination with the customers worked smoothly," the CEO said. "This does not mean that we will do without personal customer visits and contacts in the future, but we will certainly travel less and communicate more with our customers digitally. We are, however, keeping an eye on customer retention. We are uncertain how digitalization will affect us in this regard".

Customer loyalty is definitely an important point. You are more likely to become less loyal to a digital contact than to a business partner you meet face to face. Long-term customer retention is an indispensable foundation of the Hidden Champions' success.

The New Game: Customers

Closeness-to-customer is the Hidden Champions' greatest strength and will continue to be extremely important. This will not undergo a fundamental transformation. Despite their growth and increasing size, Hidden Champions should ensure that their closeness-to-customer does not suffer and that they do not fall into the "customer-distance trap" that is so typical for large organizations.

Many Hidden Champion CEOs are aware of this danger and are working to counter it. Due to increasing systems integration, the customer relationship is becoming more complex and places higher demands on employees who have customer contact. Decentralization can be a partial answer, including making certain functions such as training or service independent within the organization. The greatest transformation in customer relationships is coming from digitalization. Numerous customer-related activities can be digitalized. The trick will be to find the optimal combination of digital and personal communication. The Hidden Champions should not confine themselves to digital customer contacts, but will need hybrid systems due to the complexity of their service offerings.

References

1. Ankenbrand, H. (2012, May 20). Der Versöhner. *Frankfurter Allgemeine Sonntagszeitung*, p. 42.
2. Mühlberger, A. (2012, March). Erfolgsmotor Mittelstand. *Sales Business*, pp. 8–11.
3. Retrieved November 2, 2020, from https://www.yumpu.com/de/document/read/21893148/managementhandbuch-cerobear-gmbh. p. 8.

4. Govindarajan, G., & Winter, A. (July/August 2016). Engineering Reverse Innovation. *Harvard Business Review*.
5. Simon, H., & Fassnacht, M. (2019). *Price Management*. New York: Springer Nature.
6. von Hippel, E. (1994). *Free innovation*. Cambridge (Mass.): MIT Press.
7. von Hippel, E. (1994). *The sources of innovation*. Oxford/New York: Oxford University Press.
8. Wiedersich, R. (2010). Österreichs unbekannte Weltmarktführer. *Gewinn*, pp. 70–74.
9. Kopka, U., Little, E., Moulton, J., Schmutzler, R., & Simon, P. (2020). What got us here won't get us there: A new model for the consumer goods industry. Retrieved from https://www.mckinsey.com/~/media/McKinsey/Industries/Consumer%20Packaged%20Goods/Our%20Insights/What%20got%20us%20here%20wont%20get%20us%20there%20A%20new%20model%20for%20the%20consumer%20goods%20industry/What-got-us-here-wont-get-us-there-A-new-model-for-the-consumer-goods-industry-F.pdf.

24

Competition

Competition takes place in the strategic triangle "We—Customer—Competition." In this triangle, a company should offer the customer a benefit that is superior to the competition. In other words, the company should create at least one competitive advantage. A competitive advantage must meet three criteria[1]:

1. It must be important to the customer.
2. It must be perceived by the customer.
3. It must be sustainable and hard to imitate.

This means that a competitive advantage is ultimately determined by the customer's perception, not by the vendor's or supplier's internal view. If the packaging of a product is unimportant to the customer, a company cannot build a competitive advantage on it. If the customer does not perceive the longer lifespan of a product to be valuable, then this feature does not figure in the customer's purchase decision and is not a competitive advantage. A company that lowers prices and sacrifices profit margin in the process will not be able to maintain the lower prices in the long term. The price advantage is not

---

[1] For the concept of competitive advantages cf. Barney, J. B. & Hesterly, W. S. (2014). *Strategic Management and Competitive Advantage*, Harlow: Pearson Education. Backhaus and Voeth speak of "komparativen Konkurrenzvorteil" (comparative competition advantage), cf. Backhaus, K. & Voeth, M. (2014). *Industriegütermarketing*, Munich: Vahlen.

sustainable.[2] Meeting the three criteria of "important—perceived—sustainable" simultaneously is a major challenge, even to Hidden Champions.

Competitive Goals

Hidden Champions often set goals explicitly focused on the competition. Rosen Group, the world leader in pipeline inspection systems, says "Our goal is to be the most competitive supplier in the world." Rosen Group actually achieved this goal by knocking former global market leader, General Electric, out of first place, an outstanding achievement given the extremely high level of technology in pipeline inspection systems.

Hima, the global market leader in automation solutions for functional safety, is also confident about its position vis-à-vis the competition: "The quality of our products, the special knowledge of our employees, our services, and the reputation we enjoy with our customers are unmatched by any other competitor." Hoerbiger, market leader in specialized drive and compressor technology, emphasizes its greater agility: "Our vision is that of a learning, innovative, and globally positioned group that anticipates the needs of markets and customers. That's why we are able to develop the appropriate solutions to problems faster than other market players."

Some statements sound rather provocative. "We don't compare ourselves with the competition, the competition looks at us" says a Hidden Champion from the sensor sector. Another strikes a similar tone: "The competition is not our standard. We set our own standards." One Hidden Champion, a manufacturer of extremely complex machinery, has the motto: "Our profit should always be greater than the revenue of our strongest competitor." Former Fraunhofer President Hans-Jürgen Warnecke praised this attitude: "Once you get caught in the vicious circle of looking to your competitors instead of your own company for solutions to problems, you will forever remain second" [1]. Instead of constantly observing the competition, a company had better focus on its customers.

---

[2] For this and further principles of the management of strategic competitive advantages cf. Simon, H. (2008). *Strategy for Competition*, New Delhi: B. Jain Publishers.

Dynamics of Market Structures

Hidden Champions traditionally operate in oligopolistic markets. Most of them have fewer than 20 relevant competitors worldwide, and often, it is significantly fewer. Teepack, the global market leader for tea bag packaging machines, has only one relevant competitor, the Italian Hidden Champion I.M.A.

Competitors occasionally drop out of the market. After several competitors left the market for automotive paint shops, the global market leader Dürr "has virtually no competition left in the segment of high-quality paint shops for the automotive industry" [2]. Another reason for the low number of competitors is acquisitions, which are often not subject to merger control due to the small market size.

There is also an opposing trend. Market entry by new competitors, especially from China, can increase the number of competing firms. The market for tunneling machines is a telling example. The German Hidden Champion Herrenknecht currently has a global market share of 70%. But there is new competition from China, where 18 companies produce around 1,000 tunnel boring machines a year [3]. The Chinese tunneling market alone accounts for 60% of the world market, and the Chinese machines are not only in use in the home market and emerging countries, but also in Europe, for example on the Paris Metro [4].

Not all 18 Chinese manufacturers will survive, but a consolidation process could give Herrenknecht a hard time. Something similar happened in the concrete pump market when the construction boom in China gave rise to new competitors there. At the end of the consolidation process, the Chinese construction machinery manufacturer Sany took over the former global market leader, Germany's Putzmeister. The former global number two, Germany's Schwing, is now owned by the Chinese construction machinery group XCMG. Mass competition from China poses a serious threat to German Hidden Champions. The most effective strategy for a company to counteract the danger in this New Game is to follow the motto "Germans must become Chinese" by rapidly developing their own activities in China.

Intensity of Competition

The low number of competitors in typical Hidden Champions' markets does not mean that the competition there is not intense. The opposite is true. The Hidden Champions compete against each other intensely. Windmöller & Hölscher, global market leader in paper bag machines, says "The number of competitors is small, but the battle for market share is fierce." In some niche markets, there is cut-throat competition. Harald Schulz, managing director of Sauer, the naval compressor Hidden Champion, recounts: "When I started, there were five competitors in the western world. Now there are only three. We've been steadily taking market share from our competitors" [5]. Sauer has a global market share of more than 50% in compressors for ships. There are two types of competition. Within the group of traditional Hidden Champions, competition is primarily fought via performance characteristics such as product quality, innovativeness, reliability, or service. Price is rarely used as a fighting tool and is actually often a competitive disadvantage. The situation is different when new competitors, especially from China or other Asian countries, enter a market. In the absence of product superiority or equivalence, they deploy price as their main competitive advantage. This resonates with price-sensitive customers, especially in emerging markets.

Soft Competitive Advantages

The Hidden Champions often hold top positions in hard parameters such as product quality, precision, or durability, but it is getting more difficult to maintain the distance to new competitors. At the same time, the importance of soft or intangible competitive parameters is growing. Figure 24.1 shows this development for three soft performance parameters: advice, systems integration, and ease of use.

The concept of the "augmented product" goes back to Ted Levitt [6]. Expanding the range of services beyond the core product plays an increasingly critical role in competition. This includes know-how transfer, digital services, software, information, and training. Systems integration is moving in the same direction. When it comes to sustainability, exceeding minimum standards opens up opportunities to create new competitive advantages. The fact that competitive advantages are shifting toward the augmented product does not mean that core product attributes, such as quality or lifespan, are becoming less important. They remain *conditio sine qua non* ("must" criteria) for

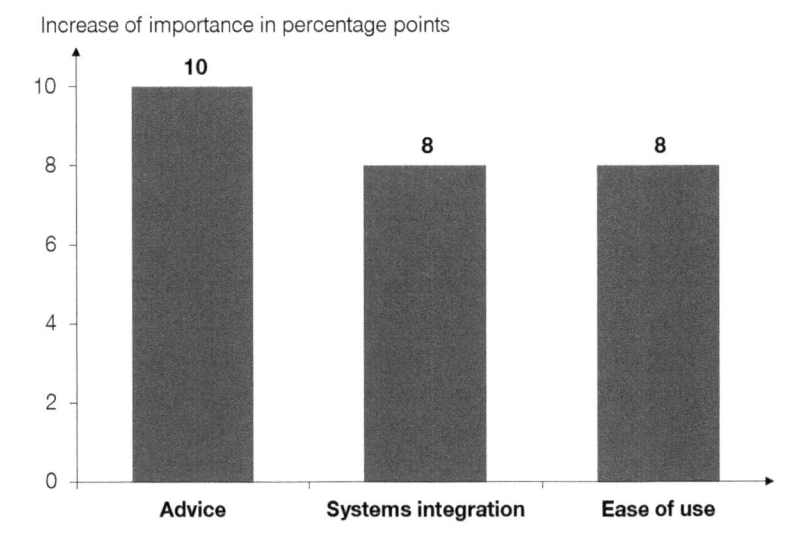

Fig. 24.1 Increased importance of soft competitive parameters

Bar chart "Increase of importance in percentage points": Advice 10, Systems integration 8, Ease of use 8.

customer acceptance. However, intangible parameters offer new opportunities for differentiation. They are often more difficult to imitate than hard features that are embedded in the product and can be re-engineered. Soft advantages can also be more enduring, because they have their roots primarily in employee qualification and motivation. Competitors need more time to reduce know-how deficits among their employees than they need to replicate a product. New intangible competitive advantages in advice, systems integration, ease of use, and sustainability can raise barriers to entry.

Price as a Competitive Disadvantage

Hidden Champions typically have one competitive weakness: price. They predominantly pursue premium strategies and do not compete on price. Nevertheless, there are Hidden Champions that deviate from this strategy. For example, Igus, a leading supplier of motion plastics, offers a price check: "You have a choice: low price or performance for high technical requirements" [7]. A higher price is acceptable if it is counterbalanced by performance-related competitive advantages. The price–performance ratio measures such a balance. The situation for the Hidden Champions is becoming more difficult in two respects: It is increasingly hard to maintain the performance gap, and costs are rising. Therefore, Hidden Champions must constantly work both on the performance side and on the cost and productivity side. Their goal is not to turn costs and prices into strategic competitive advantages, but to prevent themselves from being priced out of the market.

New Pricing Models

The Hidden Champions are pioneers for new business and pricing models. For years, Dürr, the global market leader in paint finishing systems, has been offering car manufacturers the painting of a car at a fixed price. EnviroFalk, a specialist in industrial water treatment, provides equipment free of charge, and customers pay by the cubic meter of purified water. Winterhalter, the global leader in restaurant dishwashing systems, offers a "pay-per-wash" program. "No investment, no risk, no fixed costs, fully flexible, all inclusive," it says on its homepage [8]. Trumpf founded a joint venture with Munich Re, the world's largest reinsurer, to finance laser machines. Customers no longer buy the machines. Instead, they pay a predetermined price for each part in a "pay-per-part" model. This is akin to Michelin's "pay-per-use" model for truck tires. Customers are billed according to miles driven.

On the customer side, such models establish a reliable calculation basis and reduce capital requirements. For the supplier, they provide a predictable cash flow over time and allow the optimal coordination of equipment and consumables. In addition, they can create a competitive advantage because only companies or cooperation partners with strong capital bases can make such offers.

Secondary Brands and LEAs

One reaction to intensified price competition is the introduction of second brands or so-called less expensive alternatives (LEAs). These have achieved mixed results so far. A premium supplier of silent timing chains introduced a cheaper variant under a new brand name. The differences were not primarily in product quality but rather in the accompanying services. It offered the cheaper brand to customers in less demanding segments, with modest success. Customers knew that the second brand came from the well-known manufacturer and demanded the usual comprehensive service, requests that were problematic to reject.

In another case, the second brand strategy worked well. A world market leader in specialty chemicals observed that its unique silicon-based products were losing their competitive edge and coming under increasing attack by Chinese competitors with lower prices. Instead of meeting these threats head on by cutting the prices for its primary brand, the Hidden Champion introduced an LEA under a second brand with a price position around 20% below the main brand. The LEA offered only minimal service, no customization, and was shipped only by the full tank car load. Customers would need to wait between seven and 20 days for delivery, giving the manufacturer flexibility to use free production capacity. After the introduction of the LEA, the company experienced double-digit growth, and sales doubled within the next four years. Cannibalization of the main brand remained limited.

An alternative to building a new secondary brand from scratch is to take over existing low-cost brands. Claas, the market leader in harvesters, acquired the Chunyu brand of its former joint venture partner in China. This approach does not guarantee success. The takeover of the Chinese brand Jouyou caused considerable problems for Grohe, the global market leader in sophisticated sanitary technology.

Competition and Ecosystems

The advance of ecosystems is changing the nature of competition. Traditionally, individual companies have been competing against each other. In the case of business ecosystems like the one of ASML, Trumpf, and Carl Zeiss SMT presented in Chap. 16, competition takes place between teams of companies. This is similarly true for the extended ecosystems of medical technology in Tuttlingen or photonics in Jena. There are two important competitive effects. First, companies in these ecosystems are often competing against each other, which is equivalent to permanent high-performance training, a requirement to reach the top position. Second, the ecosystem supports the competitiveness of the individual firm by providing skilled workers, suppliers, consultants, investors, and other service providers. For certain businesses, the highest level of competitiveness can only be achieved within an appropriate ecosystem [9]. This is just as true for Hidden Champions in German-speaking countries as it is for those in Silicon Valley or Shenzhen.

Lighthouse Projects

Being a market leader creates access to lighthouse projects that signal competitive superiority and, ideally, the "one-and-only" position. Hidden Champions provide countless examples of this communication method, which is cheap and effective.

When prosthetics Hidden Champion Ottobock supports the Paralympics, it gets strong press coverage. Top microphones from Neumann, a Sennheiser subsidiary, are used by Beyoncé, Nena, Sting, Rihanna, and many other celebrities. Lightweight wheels from Carbovision have helped to win numerous Tour de France and world championship races. Putzmeister concrete pumps were deployed on the Burj Khalifa, the world's tallest building, and in the Chernobyl and Fukujima reactor disasters. Sensors from Sick protect the Mona Lisa. Mackevision created the visual effects (VFX) in the popular series "Game of Thrones." The telescopic film cranes of Hidden Champion Technocrane have been used in global cinematic franchises such as "James Bond," "Harry Potter," and "Lord of the Rings." Its inventor won Academy Awards ("Oscars") in 2005.

The products of Cerobear, global market leader in ceramic rolling bearings, are used in space projects. Aco Severin from Büdelsdorf in Schleswig-Holstein, global market leader in drainage technology, has equipped all Olympic Games with sports drainage systems since 1972, with the exception of the boycotted Moscow Games in 1980. Rowa, European market leader for pharmacy dispensing machines, installed its 10,000th system in the Vatican pharmacy. The Viennese Hidden Champion Frequentis, global market leader for safe communication systems in air traffic control, has NASA (National Aeronautics and Space Administration) and EASA (European Union Aviation Safety Agency) as customers.

Even small companies are given a chance to get onto the big stage through lighthouse projects. Hidden Champion Klais built the organs in Beijing's National Theater, in the Petronas Towers Kuala Lumpur, in the World Peace Church in Hiroshima, in Hamburg's Elbphilharmonie, in the Cologne Cathedral, in St. Petersburg's Philharmonic Hall, as well as Asia's largest organ in the Taiwanese city of Koahsiung, and the world's only bamboo organ in the Philippines. Every organ expert in the world knows Klais. The reference list of Gerriets, global market leader in large theater curtains, is almost endless and ranges from La Scala in Milan and the Metropolitan Opera in New York to Israel, Kuwait, China, and Japan. International awards and world records also fit into the pattern. Sennheiser has won technical Oscars and Emmy Awards.

ARRI, the global market leader for professional film cameras, claims 15 technical Oscars. Söring, the global market leader in ultrasound surgery, became world famous in 1989 when it helped surgeons in Malaysia to make the first successful separation of conjoined twins with one liver. Söring also manufactures the world's smallest ultrasound dissector for minimally invasive liver surgery, with an outer diameter of 5.5 mm. In the opposite direction, Voxeljet has the world's largest 3D printer. Even larger are the Herrenknecht machines that helped build the Gotthard Base Tunnel, the longest rail tunnel in the world.

For some products of the Hidden Champions, the name becomes a generic term. The Académie Francaise has recognized "karchériser" as an official verb. It is derived from Kärcher, the global number one in high-pressure cleaners. A recent generic term is the Mennekes plug for electric cars, which was developed by Hidden Champion Mennekes and serves as the European standard plug. It is also used in Tesla cars.

Recognition through lighthouse projects, spectacular achievements, awards, world records, or generic terms convincingly affirms that one ranks as the best or sets the standards. Only the best provider wins these high-profile honors. No one else can use the "No. 1" message. The demonstration of superior performance and the effectiveness of communication form a virtuous circle. One gains access to prestigious lighthouse projects only on the basis of excellent performance. These, in turn, reinforce the communication impact and the perception of competitive superiority. Last but not least, lighthouse projects fill employees with pride and motivation.

The New Game: Competition

What are the changes in competition that require transformation? What has not changed is the fundamental role of competitive advantages, which must remain important, perceived, and enduring. The structure of Hidden Champion markets remains oligopolistic, but more competitors, especially from China, are appearing. This can degenerate into temporary mass competition, which is likely to be followed by consolidation. Hidden Champions must keep a careful eye on the consolidation process, first of all to survive, but also to use it as an opportunity for acquisitions and the purchase of second brands. Hard competitive parameters such as product quality or longevity are not disappearing, but soft parameters are becoming more important. In the latter case, digitalization comes into play. Complex products require more advice, systems integration, ease of use, and sustainability. Heavy investments in employee qualifications are necessary to create and maintain competitive superiority in these areas. Ecosystems play an increasing role for international competitiveness. The Internet increases the effectiveness of lighthouse projects with global reach and thus promotes the desired positioning as the "one-and-only."

References

1. Warnecke, H.-J. (1992). *Die fraktale Fabrik*. Heidelberg/New York: Springer
2. N.A. (2020, July 31). Dürr fast ohne Konkurrenz. *Frankfurter Allgemeine Zeitung*, p. 23.
3. N.A. (2019). Urbanization drives demand for tunneling machines. *China Daily*.
4. Retrieved December 6, 2019, from http://www.xinhuanet.com/english/2019-12/06/c_138611207.htm.
5. Grashoff, J. (2020, November 5). Maschinenbauer unter Druck. *Frankfurter Allgemeine Zeitung*, p. 20.
6. Levitt, T. (1983). *The marketing imagination*. New York: Free Press.
7. Retrieved from https://www.igus.de/info/techup-costdown-chainflex-preischeck.
8. Retrieved November 10, 2020, from http://www.pay-per-wash.biz/de_de/.
9. Bedre-Defolie, Ö. (2020). How do digital ecosystems defend their business. In S. Crainer (Ed.), *Ecosystems Inc.—Understanding, harnessing and developing organizational ecosystems* (pp. 25–29). Wargrave (UK): Thinkers50.com.

25

Organization

"Structure follows strategy" [1].

In other words, the strategy determines the organization, which in turn exerts a strong influence on implementation, the ability to act, flexibility, agility, closeness to customer, and costs. Many Hidden Champions are single-product, single-market companies in which a functional organization works well. Focused businesses allow for simple organizational structures, and one should not underestimate this advantage. The Hidden Champions have a less pronounced division of labor than large corporations. Their employees usually have multifunctional competencies, and the resulting flexibility allows the company to distribute workloads more evenly across employees.

Hidden Champions are thinly staffed at the top and practice "lean leadership." Digitalization enables them to maintain this leanness despite increasing size. The high level of identification among managers and employees means that Hidden Champions get by with comparatively little organization.

Functional Organization

The typical Hidden Champion is focused on one product and one narrow market.[1] Most generate more than 70% of their sales with their main product in their main market. A study by the Center of European Economic Research reports a similar share of 67% [2]. About one-third realize more than 90% in

---

[1] By "one" market, we mean the market for one product or service. In this sense, a product that is sold to the same target group in different countries is "one" market.

their main market, and for more than a quarter, this one market accounts for 100% of sales. The product may well appear in many variants, but these are based on the same technical and production platform. Hidden Champions that fit this description include Brasseler (dental drills), Gottschalk (thumbtacks), Multivac (thermoforming packaging), Bruns-Pflanzen-Export (nursery plants), GfK (market research services), Omicron (tunnel scanning microscopes for nanotechnology), and many others. Almost all single-product, single-market Hidden Champions have a classic functional organization characterized by a clear assignment of responsibilities. The functional focus keeps complexity manageable, which is a major advantage. In mid-sized and smaller companies, the division of functions does not necessarily exist at the highest management level which often consists of only one or two people. In my research, one in five respondents was the sole C-level executive. The full-functional division of labor comes into play at the second management level. The functional organization is a natural form for single-product, single-market companies and indicates simplicity, uncomplicated processes, agility, and organizational clout.

Multifunctionality

In Hidden Champions, particularly in smaller ones, the functional division of labor is less pronounced and less rigid than in larger companies. Work rules and job descriptions are less detailed and sophisticated. Employees are trained to be more broadly deployable and to understand the company's work beyond their own narrow functional requirements. One study found that successful companies practice cross-functional transfers five times more frequently than less successful companies [3].

Rolf Gottschalk, managing partner of the eponymous global market leader for thumbtacks, speaks of his employees as "all-rounders" who can handle a wide variety of tasks. At Maestro Badenia, a leading manufacturer of high-quality acoustic systems, employees must be qualified for all manufacturing tasks. This is an effective way to achieve a balanced workload. It also brings job enrichment and variety in the daily work, which in turn promotes employee motivation, according to Thomas Sauer, Maestro's managing director. Winterhalter explicitly requires its employees to be able to perform multiple functions.

It is not unusual for factory workers of Hidden Champions to help out when there are bottlenecks in the service department. During the COVID-19 crisis, Vitra, the leading manufacturer of design furniture, used office staff in telephone sales. "Some of them discovered they love selling" says Rudolf Pütz, Vitra's managing director. Würth, the global leader in assembly products, has proved repeatedly that such flexibility is not only possible, but also effective during crises. In order to strengthen the sales force during the Great Recession, Würth transferred almost 10% of the staff from office work to field sales.

Foreign Assignments

One specific aspect of multifunctionality is the flexibility and availability of employees for foreign assignments. Broad international deployability is becoming increasingly important in a globalized economy and is a matter of both organization and corporate culture. Many Hidden Champions today have a core of internationally experienced employees who are willing and capable to work anywhere in the world. Even the smallest companies with global operations (such as Klais Orgelbau) constantly rely on a workforce that can be sent to any country in the world and often stay there for months at a time.

Decentralization

The trends and transformations described in earlier chapters affect the organization of Hidden Champions in many ways. When the number of subsidiaries becomes very large, an additional intermediate regional level in the hierarchy is necessary. Regional organizational units such as Asia–Pacific, Americas, or MENA (Middle East North Africa) are standard in large companies and are often adopted by Hidden Champions when they grow beyond a certain size. The substitution of exports by foreign direct investments exerts another strong influence on the organization of the Hidden Champions, as they relocate larger parts of the value chain to foreign sites. This relocation includes not only manufacturing, procurement, and sales, but also research and development and consequently the corresponding management capacities. In other words, more decentralization is inevitable. The typical patriarchal, centrally managed Hidden Champion is transforming into a construct with multiple centers and higher degrees of freedom for regional and local managers. Since such constructs carry the risk of centrifugal forces, it is becoming more important to preserve the cohesion of the whole through a shared corporate culture with company-wide values.

The Wilo Group, global market leader in high-tech pumps, is implementing these ideas to the letter. New headquarters in Chicago for the Americas and in China for the emerging markets will complement the traditional European headquarters in Dortmund, Germany. These three regional headquarters reflect Wilo's expectation that the three regions of the first global league will develop more independently.

CEO Oliver Hermes explains: "We are giving these regional management companies as much autonomy as possible. We are reducing centralization to what is absolutely necessary. The development will also lead to increased regionalization of the value chains in these three economic centers. We are convinced that we are optimally positioned for the future with this structure."

At Simon-Kucher, we have a similar setup with separate management companies in Europe, the USA, and Singapore. The three companies have the same shareholders and, to that extent, aligned interests, but they are legally independent. Operations in other countries are affiliated with these companies.

New Work Organization

Hidden Champions have often been pioneers in introducing new work organizations. Trumpf and Claas have used work-time accounts for years to achieve greater adaptability to changing workloads in boom and bust phases. Good employer–employee relations and the use of digitalization facilitate such innovations. COVID-19 is expected to increase the move toward hybrid models, with working time split between company office and home office. This will result in new requirements for leadership and work organization [4].

I am cautious about making predictions in this regard. My guess is that many Hidden Champion leaders have a preference for office work. But at the same time, Hidden Champion employees are highly motivated and identify with their jobs and companies, which means productivity should not suffer despite less direct control.

Differences between urban and rural locations may also influence the future organization of work. In urban areas, home offices may be more attractive and productive, because commutes tend to be time-consuming and volatile (traffic jams, delays in public transport). Digitalization leads to further changes in work organization. Increasingly digitalized sales and service save travel time and personnel and allow for a greater centralization of tasks. In addition, digital activities can be located outside expensive urban areas or in low-wage countries. It is hard to say whether Hidden Champions differ from other companies on how they capitalize on these opportunities, but as a rule they are faster than large companies in taking advantage of new technologies.

Divisional Organization

Hidden Champions have a harder time maintaining their biggest competitive advantage, closeness to customer, in mature markets with multiple segments differentiated by customer needs. To meet this challenge, many of them are moving toward a divisional organization. The consistency and speed with which the Hidden Champions respond to such market dynamics is amazing. When they switch from a functional to a divisional organization, they follow precisely the same criteria they traditionally use to define their markets, i.e., they gear the new organizational units either to customer segments or to applications.

Austrian Semperit Holding, a specialist for rubber products and the global market leader in several areas, provides an example of a divisional organization. Half of all escalator handrails worldwide come from Semperit, and every second ski and snowboard contain rubber bands made by Semperit. The four divisions Sempermed, Semperflex, Sempertrans, and Semperform shown in Fig. 25.1 focus on different customer segments and their requirements.

Saria is another Hidden Champion organized by division. With 11,000 employees and revenue of €2.6 billion, this group is active at 200 locations in 24 countries. The Saria companies deal with the disposal of food and animal by-products. Figure 25.2 shows its structure.

Saria is organized divisionally to address the different technological demands of heterogeneous target groups. Several group companies are European market leaders, and each of the companies can act as a Hidden Champion in terms of focus, closeness to customer, etc.

Austrian-Swiss Hoerbiger Holding, the global market leader in several areas of drive and compressor technology, shows how specialized the organization can and must become. Hoerbiger Holding employs 6600 people and has sales of €1.22 billion. Hoerbiger has set up a divisional organization to optimally

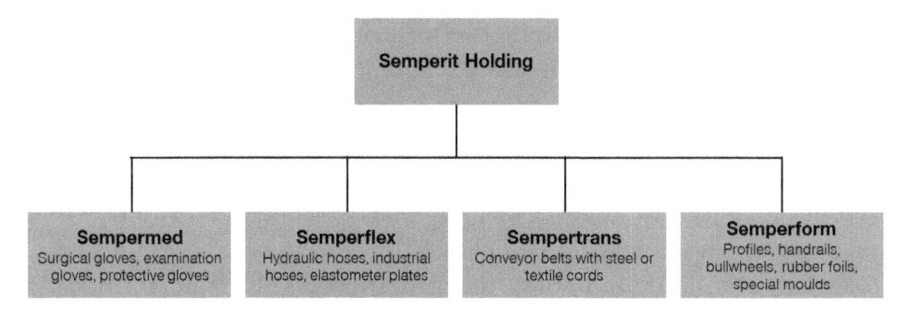

Fig. 25.1 Structure of the Semperit Holding

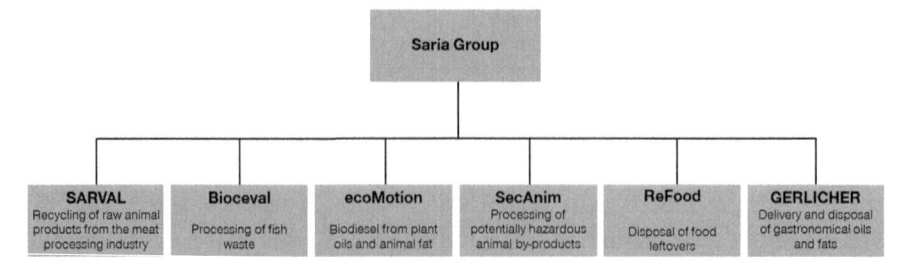

Fig. 25.2 Structure of the Saria Group

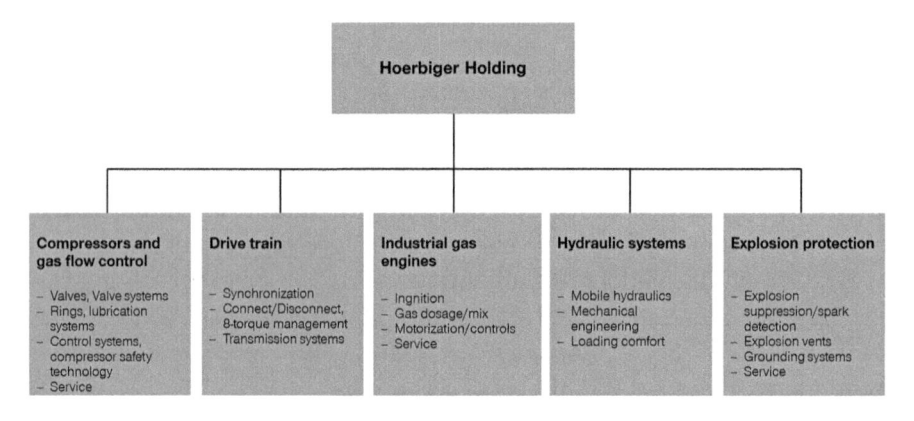

```
                              Saria Group
   ┌────────────┬────────────┬────────────┬────────────┬────────────┐
 SARVAL      Bioceval    ecoMotion    SecAnim       ReFood     GERLICHER
Recycling of  Processing  Biodiesel    Processing   Disposal   Delivery and
raw animal    of fish     from plant   of potentially of food   disposal of
products from waste       oils and     hazardous    leftovers  gastronomical
the meat                  animal fat   animal                  oils and fats
processing                             by-products
industry
```

Fig. 25.3 Structure of the Hoerbiger Holding

```
                           Hoerbiger Holding
   ┌──────────────┬──────────────┬──────────────┬──────────────┬──────────────┐
Compressors and   Drive train    Industrial gas  Hydraulic      Explosion
gas flow control                 engines         systems        protection
- Valves, Valve   - Synchroni-   - Ignition      - Mobile       - Explosion
  systems           zation       - Gas dosage/     hydraulics     suppression/
- Rings,          - Connect/       mix           - Mechanical     spark
  lubrication       Disconnect,  - Motorization/   engineering    detection
  systems           8-torque       controls      - Loading      - Explosion
- Control           management   - Service         comfort        vents
  systems,        - Transmission                               - Grounding
  compressor        systems                                      systems
  safety                                                       - Service
  technology
- Service
```

coordinate the small-parts portfolio and the needs of the different customer groups, as shown in Fig. 25.3.

Numerous Hidden Champions have introduced such target group-oriented organizations in recent years. Examples are Plansee (high-performance materials), IBG (welding technology), and Freudenberg (diversified).

Kern-Liebers, the dominant global market leader in its main product, springs for seat belts, is also pursuing a very pronounced strategy of decentralization. Two out of three automotive seatbelts worldwide are equipped with springs from Kern-Liebers. It also has strong market positions in sinkers for knitting machines, where it offers the world's largest product range and in lancets for medical applications. Overall, the company has 49 subsidiaries divided into 23 organizational units known as "competence centers." They account for a total turnover of €740 million, which means an average of €32 million per competence center. The small size of the decentralized units ensures closeness to customer and agility, the main strengths of a Hidden Champion.

The New Game: Organization

A functional organization will continue to be appropriate for single-product, single-market Hidden Champions. Multifunctional competencies of employees are an important prerequisite for the efficiency of internal work processes.

However, divisional organization structures are gradually penetrating the world of the Hidden Champions, as complexity increases in terms of products or target groups. Having more foreign subsidiaries requires an intermediate management level with a higher degree of autonomy. This development is reinforced by foreign direct investments with a deeper value chain for increased agility and better adaptability to regional conditions. Should the barriers between Europe, USA, and Asia/China continue to grow, companies must delegate more autonomy to regional management companies. In some cases, these units can morph into three relatively independent regional headquarters held together only by a holding company, as practiced by the pump Hidden Champion Wilo. With regard to new forms of work organization, Hidden Champions have proven to be pioneers in the past and can be expected to develop innovative solutions in the future.

References

1. Chandler, A. (1990). *Strategy and structure: Chapters in the history of the American industrial enterprise.* Cambridge (Mass.): MIT Press.
2. Rammer, C., & Spielkamp, A. (2019). The distinct features of hidden champions in Germany: A dynamic capabilities view. *ZEW Discussion Papers, No. 19-012,* ZEW—Leibniz-Zentrum für Europäische Wirtschaftsforschung, Mannheim, Germany.
3. Rommel, G., Brück, F., Diederichs, R., & Kempis, R.-D. (1995). *Simplicity wins.* Boston: Harvard Business School Press.
4. Retrieved from https://hbr.org/2020/10/how-to-manage-a-hybrid-team.

26

Profit and Finance

In the previous chapters, we analyzed aspects of the Hidden Champions strategy such as the ambition to be the best, market leadership, innovation, closeness-to-customer, competitive advantages, and organization. In this chapter, we examine the question of whether and how these strengths are reflected in their profitability.

Finances and profit influence each other. High profits enable self-financing and keep debt low. Low-interest payments generate high returns on equity. Hidden Champions tend to finance themselves primarily from cash flow and have low debt-to-equity ratios. But self-financing can be a constraint that slows down growth, so we will also look at the option of going public, which not many Hidden Champions have chosen so far.

Profit

Profit is the most important and ultimately the decisive measure of entrepreneurial success. What essentially is profit? For me, there is only one true definition. Profit is what the entrepreneur (owner, shareholder) can keep after the company has fulfilled all of its contractual obligations to its employees, suppliers, banks, other creditors, and the various national, state, and local governments that levy taxes [1]. Only profit after taxes is true profit. All other ratios such as EBIT (earnings before interest and taxes) or EBITDA (earnings before interest, taxes, depreciation, and amortization) are not true profit.

To make the following comparisons, I use the net profit margin, which is defined as profit after tax divided by revenue. It is also called net return on sales. From 2003 to 2019, the net return on sales of German companies averaged 3.3%. The 27 large German companies in the 2020 Fortune Global 500 list achieved a median net operating margin of 3.8% in 2019, close to the median margin of 3.7% for the entire Fortune Global 500.[12]

Profit data can only be calculated for a portion of the Hidden Champions, because partnerships and smaller corporations are not required to publish revenue and profit data. The German Hidden Champions for which data are available achieved a net return on sales of 5.8%, while another study found a similar figure of 5.54% [2]. The Hidden Champions thus exceed the long-term German average return by around 70%.

The initial question of this chapter—whether superior market positions actually translate into higher profits—can be affirmed with conviction.

Profit Stars

Among the Hidden Champions, we find profit stars that can keep up with the global profit elite. The Fortune Global 500 list includes 30 companies that achieve a net profit margin of more than 20%, which is extremely high. They include Apple, Alibaba, and Facebook. The best Hidden Champions have no reason to fear comparison with these global profit stars. Table 26.1 lists 25 Hidden Champions that have generated a net profit margin of more than 20%.

What is surprising and revealing about this selection is that these profit stars do not come from just a few sectors where high returns are to be expected, such as pharmaceuticals or luxury goods. They are broadly spread across industries. The list includes the kitchen appliance manufacturer Rational, the electronics companies Puls and Scheubeck Holding (Maschinenfabrik Reinhausen), the software and Internet providers Teamviewer and Scout24, and the chemical company Chemetall.[3]

The Hidden Champions in Table 26.1 prove that it is possible to achieve high returns in different industries, even in Germany, where profits are

---

[1] Cf. *Fortune*, August–September 2020, pp. F1-F22. We use the median to exclude the influence of outliers.

[2] The average of all Fortune Global 500 companies of 5.8% was significantly higher, caused by the extremely high profits of a few companies.

[3] The figures for Chemetall are for the business year 2016. In 2017, the company was acquired by BASF and integrated into the corporate financial statement. The figures for Eppendorf are for 2016. All other figures are for 2017or 2018. For EA Elektro-Automatik, the revenue figures for 2019 and the net profit for 2018 were used.

Table 26.1 Profit stars among the Hidden Champions

Company	Industry	Sales in million Euro	Net profit in million Euro	Net return on sales in percent
Teamviewer	Remote screen sharing	157	61.9	39.4
Dionex Softron	Liquid chromatography	255	98.4	38.6
Blücher	Protective suits	54	19.0	35.2
Chemetall	Surface treatment	188	59.8	31.8
Lohmann Therapiesysteme	Therapy systems	226	69.3	30.7
Kryolan	Professional make-up	25	7.5	30.0
Eppendorf	Laboratory equipment	425	120.9	28.4
Puls	DIN rail power supplies	108	28.9	26.8
Rational	Commercial kitchen equipment	491	129.0	26.3
Pulsion	Medical technology	26	6.7	26.2
A. Lange & Söhne	Luxury watches	114	28.8	25.3
Verder Scientific/Retsch	Sample preparation	73	18.3	25.1
European Energy Exchange	Energy exchange	267	66.0	24.7
RIB Software	Software for construction industry	54	12.7	23.5
Lamy	Writing instruments	112	26.0	23.2
Scout24	Advisory sales	480	110.9	23.1
Buhl-Data-Service	Software	85	19.5	22.9
Evotec	Pharma development	375	84.1	22.4
Weng Fine Art	Art trade	4.4	1.0	22.0
Dr. Falk Pharma	Pharma	324	71.4	22.0
Motel One	Hotel	487	104.0	21.4
C. Josef Lamy	Writing instruments	131	27.5	21.0
Agfa HealthCare	Healthcare software	178	36.9	20.7
Horst Brandstätter Hldg. (Playmobil)	Toys	642	133.0	20.7
Scheubeck Holding (Reinhausen)	Electronics	745	151.0	20.3

generally low. To be a competitor in a particular industry is no excuse for poor profit performance. Ultimately, the profitability depends on the company and its competencies.

Financing

By international standards, the equity base of German companies is weak. This is particularly true of SMEs. Based on a variety of sources, the average debt-to-equity ratio is around 3, which corresponds to an equity ratio of 25% [3]. A study by the Bonn Institute for SME Research states: "German SMEs typically rely on a financing concept with a markedly low equity-ratio. With an equity ratio of approximately 25% over all companies and a 20% average equity ratio among SMEs, these figures lie notably below those of international counterparts, which have an equity ratio of 50% on average" [4].

With a mean equity ratio of 42%, the Hidden Champions differ significantly from the typical SME [5]. A solid equity base is important both to survive in times of crises and to finance expansion in times of growth. Most Hidden Champions weathered the Great Recession of 2008–2010 surprisingly well. Creditreform, Germany's leading credit rating company, reports that the equity base of most Hidden Champions was little affected by the Great Recession, and that on the contrary, the trend toward strengthening equity had "continued in the SME sector despite the Great Recession" [6]. Hopefully the equity strength of the Hidden Champions will prove equally resilient after the COVID-19 crisis.

Initial Public Offering (IPO)

The Hidden Champions' preference for high equity ratios and self-financing from cash flows can restrict growth and rapid expansion. I hear time and again from the founders of start-ups and the leaders of younger Hidden Champions that shortage of capital is a bottleneck for them. In Chap. 15, we learned that Chinese Hidden Champions go public very early. This gives them access to large amounts of equity to invest into growth and into research and development. In Germany, only a few Hidden Champions are listed on a stock exchange. The Avesco Sustainable Hidden Champions Fund counts 145 listed Hidden Champions [7]. The CDAX Index, which contains a total of 413 listed corporations from the Prime and General Standards of the German Stock Exchange (Deutsche Börse), includes only 99 Hidden Champions [5]. Publicly listed companies account for less than 10% of all Hidden Champions, even if we include Hidden Champions listed on regional or foreign stock exchanges.

There is a lot of untapped potential here. A stock market listing could help overcome financing bottlenecks. An IPO could also be a solution to succession problems, but there is a catch. The extreme specialization and small size of many Hidden Champions can stand in the way of fully exploiting their potential on the public capital markets. Many investors do not understand what some of these arcane companies do. Analysts and journalists do not cover them. Some IPOs have ended in disappointment or a withdrawal from the stock market.

Nevertheless, it would be desirable if more owners of Hidden Champions decided to go public rather than to sell to a third party. A public listing would create a stand-alone firm. It would prevent the company from being swallowed by a larger organization and losing its identity. The IPO would also avoid an uncertain future in the hands of a private equity investor who is going to resell the firm after a few years. It is always a pity when a proud Hidden Champion chooses one of these paths instead of going public as an independent entity.

Private Equity

When I started researching Hidden Champions 30 years ago, private equity was virtually non-existent in Germany [8]. Private equity financing emerged in the United States during the 1980s and spread increasingly in Europe from 2000 onwards. A typical feature of private equity is that the investment is held only temporarily. As a rule, an exit takes place after five–seven years. Forms of exit can be an IPO, a sale to a strategic investor, or to another private equity investor.

The exact number of private equity investments in Hidden Champions is hard to determine. My estimate is that over the years, around 12% of Hidden Champions have come into the hands of private equity investors. A considerable proportion of these have been passed on to a second, sometimes even a third PE investor. A recent example is the Hidden Champion Teamviewer, which was taken public by the private equity firm Permira in September 2019. Permira had acquired Teamviewer in 2015 for €870 million and raised €2.2 billion in the IPO by selling around 40% of the shares. Teamviewer's market capitalization reached €8.5 billion.[4]

Opinions are divided on the fit between Hidden Champions and private equity investors. Many owners prefer strategic investors who come from the

---

[4] February 26, 2021.

same industry or who are willing to make a long-term commitment. This highlights the fundamental tension between family businesses with a longer-term focus and private equity investors with a shorter-term focus. The potential for conflict is expressed in the following comment: "Private equity companies usually have an exit strategy with a duration of five years. This clashes with the longer-term horizon of family businesses. The dynastic view in the family business is not compatible with the short-term return expectation of private equity funds" [9]. Private equity plays a significant role in the early stages of a company's development when capital is often the bottleneck and other investors are not available.

Strategic Investors

Strategic investors either come from the same industry or want to buy into an industry through the acquisition. They acquire a company with the intention of holding the stake for the longer term. In recent years, Chinese acquisitions of Hidden Champions have attracted particular public attention. In total, there have been 300 Chinese acquisitions from 2014 to 2020, of which Hidden Champions account for about 15–20% [10]. Examples include KUKA (robotics), Krauss-Maffei (injection molding machines), and Kion (forklift trucks). Chinese acquisitions attract a lot of public attention because they are politically controversial. In contrast, American acquisitions of Hidden Champions are hardly noticed unless they are very large or spectacular cases, such as John Deere's purchase of the Wirtgen Group at a price of €4.4 billion or Tesla's purchase of Grohmann Engineering, now Tesla Automation. In reality, far more Hidden Champions are wholly or partially owned by American companies than by Chinese ones. Exact figures on this are hard to come by, but I estimate that the number of American strategic investments is four to five times higher than those of the Chinese. The interest of strategic investors in the Hidden Champions has been high for years and is likely to increase.

The New Game: Profit and Finance

What will the New Game mean for profit and financing? I think the profitable Hidden Champions will be able to defend their profit levels unless they are in so-called sunset industries (see Chap. 28). The not-so-profitable ones, of which there are quite a few, will have to greatly improve their returns, as will the German economy in general. On average, the equity capitalization of the Hidden Champions is adequate, but there are major differences by industry. Self-financing from cash flow will not be sufficient against the American and particularly the Chinese competition, especially in fast-growing industries. There is a need for greater willingness to go public. Private equity will probably expand its role further. Strategic investors, especially from other countries, will show increasing appetite for Hidden Champions in German-speaking countries.

References

1. Simon, H. (2021). *True profit! No company Ever Went Broke from Turning a Profit*. New York: Springer Nature.
2. Rammer, C., & Spielkamp, A. (2019). The distinct features of hidden champions in Germany: A dynamic capabilities view. *ZEW Discussion Papers, No. 19-012*, ZEW - Leibniz-Zentrum für Europäische Wirtschaftsforschung, Mannheim, Germany.
3. Simon, H. (2020). *Am Gewinn ist noch keine Firma kaputt gegangen*. Campus; as well as Retrieved from https://de.statista.com/statistik/daten/studie/180326/umfrage/fremdkapitalquote-im-maschinenbau-nach-laendern-weltweit/.
4. Schindele, A., & Szczesny, A. (2014). The impact of Basel II on the Debt costs of German SMEs. *Journal of Business Economics*, pp. 197–227, cf. also figures of Institut für Mittelstandsforschung, Bonn 2014.
5. Benz, L., Block, J., & Johann, M. (2020). Börsennotierte hidden champions. *Zeitschrift Führung und Organisation*, pp. 291–295.
6. N.A. (2011). Kriseneffekte beim Eigenkapital–Die Folgen der Rezession für die Kapitalausstattung des Mittelstandes. *Creditreform, Beiträge zur Wirtschaftsforschung*, p. 1.
7. Retrieved from https://www.avesco-shc.de/2020.
8. N.A. (2006, December 14). Studie des Branchenverbandes EVCA—Private Equity im europäischen Vergleich. *Handelsblatt*.
9. N.A. (2006, September 21/22). Familienunternehmen im Zeitalter der Globalisierung. *BDI Forum Familienunternehmen*, Berlin.
10. N.A. (2021, March 5). Chinesen übernehmen seltener. *Frankfurter Allgemeine Zeitung*, p. 20.

27

Employees and Leaders

Ultimately, the success of the Hidden Champions is not rooted in what happens externally. The roots of success lie inside the companies, within the employees and the leaders. What sets these people apart is not one miraculous trait, but rather a multitude of interacting and mutually enhancing characteristics.

Hidden Champions have peculiar and idiosyncratic corporate and leadership cultures that cannot be easily replicated. A saying by Ray Kroc, the founder of McDonald's, describes this phenomenon: "They may copy my style and they may imitate me. But they can't read my mind, and I'll leave them a mile and a half behind." Motivation and qualification are the pillars of employee performance, and the leaders must channel the employees' energies into a direction that serves the company's goal.

Motivation

It is hard to overestimate the importance of soft factors such as corporate culture, employee identification, and motivation for the performance of a company. The cultures of the Hidden Champions do not follow the world of ever-shifting management fads. Instead, they are characterized by conservative values such as long-standing loyalty and strict selection during employee probationary periods.

Hidden Champions have "more work than heads." Leaving employees with no time for useless activities and idleness has proven to be an extremely effective productivity driver. Hidden Champions have a culture of high performance and intolerance for underachievers. A Hidden Champion CEO told me: "I used to work for a large corporation. There, some of the employees read the newspaper during working hours. That would be unthinkable here." Underperformance is noticed more often than in large companies, usually by the team and colleagues, less by managerial supervision, and there is a virtuous circle. The strong competitive position of the Hidden Champions has a stimulating effect on the employees. People prefer working for a respected market leader rather than for a company in decline.

The corporate culture is the basis of high employee motivation. This culture is shaped by the behavior of the entrepreneurs. Here is one truly exemplary case. Busch, a global leader in vacuum pumps, celebrated its 50th anniversary in 2013. To mark the occasion, the entire Busch family visited all 42 locations around the world: "The celebrations for the company's anniversary started early in the year at the Busch sites in the Far East. Following the course of the sun, they reached Busch's headquarters in Maulburg in southern Germany in September, to conclude later in the year at the American sites" [1]. Despite their advanced age, the company founders Karl and Ayhan Busch, as well as the young generation—daughter Ayla, and sons Sami and Kaya Busch—joined the visiting team. All five lead the company as a team of equal managing directors. Busch is probably the only company in the world with five CEOs.

The Hidden Champions see the commitment and motivation of their employees as a major competitive strength, reflected by low sick leave and turnover rates. Their employee turnover rate of around 2.7% per year is about one-third of the German average of 7.3%, which is already low by international standards. Strategically, low employee turnover is more important than low sick leave, because it preserves know-how and customer relationships, reduces costs for training new hires, and makes investments in training and development profitable. The Internet and the global talent shortage render employee loyalty ever more important. Young employees want to gain experience with multiple employers, and social media sites such as LinkedIn are facilitating the contact between companies and potential candidates. These trends create problems for the Hidden Champions. Ayla Busch describes the issue "as a difficult challenge for the Hidden Champions, who depend on the specialization, the loyalty, and the passionate focus of their employees."[1]

---

[1] Personal communication, November 29, 2020.

Qualification

Global competition is increasingly about skills rather than cost alone. The automation of low-skill activities eliminates many of the traditional cost advantages of low-wage countries. Products and processes are becoming more complex and require higher skills. Education is improving in emerging countries such as China and India, and the highly developed countries must invest more in skills to keep up.

The Hidden Champions know that employee qualification and training are necessary conditions for the accumulation of technological knowledge and for high performance. Companies need to focus on professional education and lifelong training. In the German dual system, apprentices work for three days a week in a private company and attend a vocational school run by the government on the remaining two days, thereby receiving a customized combination of practical and theoretical knowledge. At the Hidden Champions, 9% of the workforce is enrolled in these dual programs. The German average is only 6%, which means that Hidden Champions invest 50% more in the training of skilled workers. Kessler & Co, a leading manufacturer of axles, has initiated an innovative revolutionary training model called "High School Plus" (Abitur plus in German). Starting in the eighth grade, high school students can complete a dual training program of four years that concludes with a certificate from the Chamber of Industry and Commerce [2]. Hidden Champions also invest heavily in continuous education. According to one study, they spend 25% more per employee on training than comparable companies [3].[2]

The upgrade in qualifications extends to employees with college and university degrees. Their share has doubled in the last 25 years from well under 10% to more than 24%. With a mean workforce of 2,252, this means that the Hidden Champions employ an average of 540 people with a college or university degree. That is 5% points or 113 employees more than at the comparable companies. One is inclined to describe the Hidden Champions as "research laboratories with production attached." In any case, they are high-qualification organizations. Consistent with this is the finding that wages at the Hidden Champions are 11% higher than at the peer companies.

In emerging markets, achieving high skill levels is one of the biggest challenges for the Hidden Champions. For the most part, local labor markets do not provide workers with the required qualifications. How do the Hidden Champions address this challenge? They become pioneers by transplanting

---

[2] The Hidden Champions spend 600 Euro per year and employee, compared to 470 Euro of the average company.

the German dual training system. They operate their own vocational schools in foreign countries, often in cooperation with other German companies or Chambers of Industry and Commerce.

Talent War

The high-qualification requirements make the recruitment of talented young people indispensable for Hidden Champions. Being "hidden" and the associated low awareness turn out to be a disadvantage in the war for talent. While this may be less evident in the immediate vicinity of the Hidden Champion locations, it is certainly true on a national and even more so on an international scale. Ayla Busch thinks "that Hidden Champions can no longer afford to remain 'hidden' in the labor market."[3] On the other hand, Hidden Champions should not harbor the illusion that they can build up a level of recognition or attractiveness on a national or global scale that is comparable to large corporations and famous brands. Both their limited size and the low visibility of their products preclude this. In terms of recruitment, the rural locations of many Hidden Champions pose a further problem. Young people tend to be drawn to urban areas. A rural exodus has been going on for years in German-speaking countries.

The most sensible response for the Hidden Champions is to focus on recruiting efforts and employer branding near their home bases. There is talent in every region. Nils Meyer-Pries, CEO of the Fuchs Group, the world's No. 2 in spices, speaks of "hidden talents." He rightly says that the aim must be to identify these talents early on and bring them closer to the company. Hidden Champions have a certain level of recognition in their immediate vicinity and often even a high employer attractiveness. Relationships with vocational schools, high schools, and regional universities can build on this. Targeted offers for internships or student research projects bring talented individuals to the company. Brita, the global market leader in point-of-use water filters, maintains intensive relations to the nearby European Business School (EBS) through lectures by managers, student research projects, case studies, and internships. As a result, the number of applications from EBS graduates has increased significantly [4].

In the competition for talent, it is not only the location that counts, but also the brand and the company name. Grohmann Engineering has always had problems attracting engineers to its remote location, but applications

---

[3] Personal communication, November 29, 2020.

have been coming in large numbers since the company became Tesla Automation. Once the young talent joins, the Hidden Champions can use job rotation programs, especially assignments to their foreign subsidiaries, to develop internationally experienced and loyal employees.

With regard to career advancement, one advantage of Hidden Champions is that young people grow into positions of responsibility more quickly than in large companies and are also more often deployed internationally. "Hidden Champions offer employees the best of both worlds: a familiar working atmosphere with a high degree of individual freedom and a dynamic, international environment. Because of this Hidden Champions attract hidden talent," says Nils Meyer-Pries, CEO of the Fuchs Group, a Hidden Champion in spices.

However, I doubt whether this advantage is sufficiently communicated and perceived by the target group. Hidden Champions could also increase their attractiveness by introducing new working models, an eminently important topic for young people. Gelita CEO Dr. Franz Josef Konert points out that there will no longer be one standard career, but many different career and life models. The Hidden Champions could become pioneers in this area, just as they did in work-time flexibility.

Attracting top international talent is an even greater challenge for the Hidden Champions. In this regard, Germany has a serious deficit thanks to the language barrier. In a meeting with the presidents of the four large German research organizations,[4] I reported that after their examinations a large proportion of the 4,000 graduates of the Indian Institute of Technology (IIT) each year go to the USA. One of the presidents objected that his society also receives about 50 applications from IIT graduates. When I asked how many actually come, his answer was "five."

More than 2,000 to America, five to Germany ... that says it all about Germany's attractiveness to these top talents. Even large internationally known German corporations have a lot of catching up to do in this respect. Of course, this is much truer for the Hidden Champions and mid-sized companies in general.

The language barrier plays a key role. Graduates from India can immediately start in English-speaking countries. In other countries, they may have to learn the local language first. Patent attorney Klaus Goeken says: "The battle for the best minds is in full swing, with neither place of birth, social origin, passports, or religious affiliation playing a dominant role." One method of the

---

[4] There are four large research organizations in Germany, Max-Planck (86 institutes, 24,000 employees), Fraunhofer (74 institutes, 28,000 employees), Helmholtz (18 centers, 42,000 employees), and Leibniz (96 research centers, 20,000 employees).

Hidden Champions is to set up branches in cities that are attractive to top talent. In Germany, this is often Berlin. In other countries, it can be the Silicon Valley, Shenzhen, or the Cote d'Azur. For example, Zapier, an Internet company based in Missouri, a state that is less desirable for top applicants, reports that its 250 employees are spread across 17 U.S. states and 17 countries [5]. This is certainly an extreme case, but it points to opportunities and perhaps even a necessity. If top talent is not willing to come to the company, the company must go to the top talent. I learned early on at Simon-Kucher that office locations are often more important in terms of talent acquisition than they are in terms of customer acquisition.

Diversity and Inclusion

Diversity and inclusion, or D&I, is a topic that has gained tremendous attention. It is similar to sustainability and can be seen as one aspect of it. D&I management deals with the diversity and heterogeneity of employees. The focus is on dimensions such as age, gender, ethnicity, sexual orientation, religious beliefs, disability, education, experience, and expertise. D&I aims to take advantage of diversity opportunities and to avoid discrimination, aggression, and subgroup formation.

Yet the topic is by no means new. In 2004, I gave a presentation to the German Council of Deutsche Bank in Frankfurt entitled "Diversity: Opportunities and Challenges for Deutsche Bank." I presented "examples of companies that are working intensively on the subject of diversity management," including Ford, Bayer, Deutsche Telekom, and Commerzbank.

Today, D&I's goals are, in the words of one Hidden Champion's document, "broad, all-encompassing, and far-reaching." Investors are increasingly pushing toward D&I, with the investment firm Blackstone seeking to enforce that every third board member on all majority-owned companies be "diverse" [6]. Hidden Champions face D&I challenges on many fronts. Globalization has created workforces that are "multi" in terms of cultures, nationalities, religions, etc., and require corresponding adjustments. This, too, is not fundamentally new. As early as 1987, during a visit to a German plant in Kuala Lumpur, I was shown prayer rooms for the Muslim employees. In terms of D&I, the Hidden Champions seem to have coped well with globalization so far. With regard to other attributes, such as the participation of women in top management, many Hidden Champions face barriers from traditional, hierarchical-patriarchal corporate cultures, industry habits, and the supply of certain groups is limited. There are simply not enough female mechanical engineers to achieve proportional representation in jobs requiring this qualification. In any case, D&I is an area in which the Hidden Champions will need time to adjust to the rules of the New Game.

The Leaders

The fire that has catapulted their companies into their market-leading positions burns in the leaders of the Hidden Champions. While they are individuals who defy generalization, I nevertheless found certain commonalities. These include an identity of person and mission, a focused determination, fearlessness, perseverance, and the ability to inspire others. For younger leaders, one could add worldliness and higher academic qualifications.

Leadership Continuity

Characteristics such as consistency, continuity, and long-term orientation are typical of Hidden Champions and manifest themselves in lasting market leadership, low turnover, rare structural breaks, and unchanging values. The continuity of a company is based on continuity at the top. Hermut Kormann, former CEO of Voith, says: "The long-term nature of the strategy is a result of the constancy of the strategy bearers and the duration of their tenure" [7]. Viewed in isolation, continuity in itself is neither good nor bad. A long tenure of a weak boss is obviously detrimental. On the other hand, a good business leader who stays at the helm for a long time is a blessing. Surprisingly, the topic of continuity is rarely explored in the management literature. One exception is the book *Built to Last*, which compares the tenures of CEOs of so-called "visionary" companies with those of a control group of less successful firms [8]. In the visionary companies, CEOs achieve an average tenure of 17.4 years, compared with only 11.7 years in the mediocre control group. The average tenure of the Hidden Champions CEOs is 21 years, even higher than in the visionary companies. At large companies, the average tenure of CEOs is 6 years [9]. Hidden Champion CEOs stay at the helm more than three times as long—a strong indication that long-term orientation is taken much more seriously by these companies.

Young CEOs

Long tenures and the corresponding high degree of continuity are only possible if the bosses reach the top position at a relatively young age. The early appointment to a management position is not only of interest from the point of view of continuity and long-term orientation, but also with regard to entrepreneurial energy and dynamism. It is remarkable that many Hidden Champions founders got their companies off the ground at a very young age. Reinhold Würth was 19 when his father died and he had to take over the company, which had one employee at the time and now has 83,000. Reinhard Wirtgen started his company, now the global market leader in road milling machines, at the age of 18. Not much has changed in this regard except that many of the younger founders now have university degrees and are a few years older when they start their companies than the post-war generation. Stefan Vilsmeier founded Brainlab at the age of 22. Ralf Dommermuth started United Internet at the age of 25. Founding entrepreneurs are typically young.

Successive generations of CEOs are also appointed at a relatively young age. Whereas people rarely become CEOs at large companies before they turn 50, the leaders of Hidden Champions sometimes reach the top position in their twenties, often in their thirties and, at the latest, in their early forties. In the case of family CEOs, this early appointment is not surprising. Hans Georg Näder took the helm of the orthobionics specialist Ottobock at the age of 28. Marc Fielmann became CEO of Fielmann AG at the age of 29. Christopher Mennekes replaced his father at the industrial connector of the same name at the age of 32. Hidden Champions also appoint non-family managers to CEOs when they are still young. Robert Friedmann was 38 when he took over the management of Würth. Hartmut Jenner became head of Kärcher at 34. Similar to continuity, there is of course some ambivalence about a CEO's age of arrival. "Younger" means dynamic, energetic, long-term oriented, but also less experienced, possibly prone to mental overload, or a lack of composure. The typical strengths of older managers are their greater experience, more confident leadership, mature personality. It is impossible to make a general statement about what is better for a company.

Female CEOs

Equal opportunity for women is a hot topic in the context of diversity and inclusion. At large companies worldwide, only 5% of CEOs are women. At the 500 largest U.S. companies, the figure is 3.2%.[5] Among the 160 largest publicly traded German companies, the proportion is similar at 3.1% [10].

In contrast, women are more likely to occupy top management positions at Hidden Champions. Some 13.6% of the 500 largest German family-owned companies have a woman on their top management board [11]. Well-known examples of female CEOs of Hidden Champions are Nicola Leibinger-Kammüller at Trumpf and Angelique Renkhoff-Mücke at Warema, the European market leader for sun protection systems. Marie Langer is the CEO of EOS, one of the leading firms in 3D printing. Petra Baader heads the eponymous global market leader in fish processing. Sabine Herold is at the helm of special adhesives Hidden Champion Delo. Nina Patisson heads Albrecht Bäumer GmbH, global market leader in foam cutting machines. Eva van Pelt leads laboratory equipment supplier Eppendorf as co-CEO with Peter Fruhstorfer. Sybill Storz is the chairwoman of endoscopy market leader Karl Storz. Özlem Türeci at BioNTech and Katharina Kreitz at Vectoflow are founders and co-managing directors. Together with her brothers Kaya and Sami, Ayla Busch heads the vacuum pump Hidden Champion Busch. Many women took the helm at Hidden Champions after the death of their husbands and led the companies to new heights. Examples include WIKA (pressure gauges), Kärcher (high-pressure cleaners), Wirtgen (road construction machines), Harting (connection technology), Pilz (industrial safety), Sick (sensors), and Hoerbiger (drive and compressor technology). Unlike the male bosses, the female top executives are almost exclusively members of the owner family.

Internationalization of Management

Hidden Champions often generate 80 or 90% of their sales and employ the majority of their staff, outside their home market. Many of them fill the chief executive positions of their foreign subsidiaries with locals. In terms of these indicators, they are quite international, or even global. However, foreigners are much less frequently represented in the top echelons of the parent company. There are several reasons for this, such as the size and composition of management teams. Around half of the Hidden Champions are run by family

---

[5] Ibidem.

members. In addition, the top management teams are generally very small. Such teams are attuned to each other, and their cooperation is based on common cultural foundations. With such relationships, one cannot expect changes to be very rapid.

Given the global nature of business, one might be inclined to call for a more decisive and rapid internationalization of top management, but there are—as always—two sides of the coin. One should not underestimate the advantages of a small team of managers who share a common culture, a value base, and understand each other blindly. The internationalization of business, employees, and management does not occur simultaneously, but rather with time lags. Sales internationalizes first, followed by employees, then the extended management group. Only at the end, with a delay of quite possibly one or two generations, will the top management positions be filled with people from different cultures and countries.

Nonetheless, this process could be accelerated and intensified. In the U.S., we find dozens of CEOs of Asian descent. Examples include Satya Nadella at Microsoft, Sundar Pichai at Alphabet (Google), Ajaypal Banga at Mastercard, Jen-Hsun Huang at Nvidia, and many others. There are also a few examples in Europe, such as Vasant Narasimhan at Novartis or Sanjay Brahmawar at Software AG, but they are exceptions. Hidden Champions still face a challenging transformation to access the global talent pool for top leadership positions more effectively.

Leadership Styles

Leadership balances the authority of the leaders and the personal responsibility of the team members. If the leadership style leans strongly toward the authority of the leader, we speak of a command system or "authoritarian leadership." Authoritarian leadership can cause demotivation, service by the book, or resignation. If the leader gives too much free rein and does not set clear goals, the result is a lack of coordination and, in the worst case, chaos.

The Hidden Champions, as high-performance organizations, favor a mixed system with clear goal orientation on the one hand, and high employee motivation on the other. Hidden Champion leaders achieve this seemingly contradictory combination by what I call a polarized leadership style, which is a form of mission-oriented leadership. The leadership is authoritarian with respect to the principles, values, and goals of the company, with clear lines of command from the top down and no room for discussion. But when it comes to implementation and execution of specific tasks, the employees and the team have a great deal of latitude. Employees of Hidden Champions usually face fewer rules and regulations than employees in large companies.

This is exemplified in the principles of Wittenstein SE, one of the market leaders in mechatronic drive technology: "Subsidiarity: What can and may be regulated locally (in the sense of decentralized, local) must be regulated there. The phrase 'locally' is to be understood not only geographically (local), but also organizationally (decentralized). Of course, the principle may only be applied within the other guardrails (e.g., other corporate principles, rules of procedure, administrative regulations, competencies). Subsidiarity offers the following advantages: speed, greater proximity to the task, better decisions."

Rational, the global leader in professional cooking systems, has a similar philosophy: "Every employee is encouraged to act as an independent entrepreneur in the company—working with dedication, responsibility and in the interest of the entire company. This approach seems to be on point, as 89% of our employees are proud to be working for Rational" [12].

The typical leadership style among Hidden Champions is authoritarian in the basic values, but participative in the details of execution. This leadership style, known in the military as "mission-oriented leadership system," only works if freedom in execution is matched by adequate competencies and clear responsibility for the results [13]. Reinhold Würth puts it this way: "The greater the success, the greater the degrees of freedom." Decentralization and accountability/responsibility are inseparable. I found this type of leadership in many Hidden Champions.

The New Game: Employees and Leaders

The Hidden Champions are characterized by fundamental strengths that should not be changed: motivation and a high degree of loyalty from the employees, identification with the mission, focused determination, courage, and perseverance, and the ability of leaders to inspire. Low turnover rates must be defended at all costs, as employee retention becomes even more important due to the talent shortage. Ayla Busch offers an interesting observation from China, where high turnover is normal and a serious problem: "After Covid-19, the appreciation and loyalty of the Chinese employees for their employers have increased significantly, especially for German Hidden Champions."

The game has changed when it comes to employee qualifications, talent acquisition, and talent development. Companies must provide higher qualification opportunities more consistently and more rapidly in order to keep up with the accelerated pace of change. This requires greater investments in continuing education. The Hidden Champions also have to catch up in terms of diversity and inclusion. They have to attract more international top talent. Only then can the transition to more internationally staffed and diversified management teams succeed. The promotion of women from outside the family to the highest executive positions needs to increase. However, the lack of female graduates in science and engineering is a serious bottleneck.

The mission-oriented leadership system—with clear specifications of the goals and the basic values, but great scope for execution—is a pronounced strength of the Hidden Champions. This leadership system should be retained at all costs, despite the increasing size of the companies. It requires a high level of qualification and responsibility on the part of the workforce.

References

1. Retrieved from https://impeller.net/magazin/50-jahre-busch-vakuumpumpen-und-systeme/?lang=de.
2. Helmig, L. (2019). *Betrachtungen 2019* (p. 170). Munich: Selbstverlag.
3. Rammer, C., & Spielkamp, A. (2019). The distinct features of hidden champions in Germany: A dynamic capabilities view. *ZEW Discussion Papers, No. 19-012*, ZEW - Leibniz-Zentrum für Europäische Wirtschaftsforschung, Mannheim, Germany.
4. Mattmüller, R., & Rinke, L. (2020). Anziehendes Investment. *Return–Magazin für Transformation und Turnaround, 2*, 58–59.
5. Lazarow, A. (2020). Beyond silicon valley: How start-ups succeed in unlikely places. *Harvard Business Review*, pp. 126–133.
6. N.A. (2020, October 22). Blackstone pushes for diversity. *Wall Street Journal*.
7. Kormann, H. (2006, November 2006). Gibt es so etwas wie typisch mittelständische Strategien? *Diskussionspapier Nr. 54*, Universität Leipzig, Wirtschaftswissenschaftliche Fakultät.
8. Collins, J. C., & Porras, J. I. (1994). *Built to last—Successful habits of visionary companies*. New York: Harper Collins.
9. Retrieved 2020, from https://www.msn.com/de-de/finanzen/top-stories/studie-zeigt-so-wird-man-vorstandschef/ar-BB18UMVV?li=BBqfP3q.
10. Includes companies listed in DAX, MDAX, and SDAX. Retrieved 2020, from https://boerse.ard.de/aktien/zu-wenig-frauen-in-deutschen-fuehrungsetagen100.html.
11. Retrieved December 8, 2020, from https://dienews.net/aktuelles/2020/12/top-500-familienunternehmen-frauenquote-sehr-niedrig/.
12. Retrieved from https://career.rational-online.com/en_au/career/thats_us_1/working_at_rational_2/company_philosophy_1/page_normal_47.php.
13. van Creveld, M. (2007). *Fighting power: German and U.S. Army Performance 1939–1945*. Westport (CT): Greenwood Press.

28

The Future of the Hidden Champions

Rarely has there been an era during which so many disruptive trends occurred simultaneously. The Great Recession of 2008–2010 and the COVID-19 pandemic induced a tremendous expansion of money supply and public debt. Interest rates, migration, demographic disruption, digitalization and automation, climate change, electromobility, and sustainability are challenging established business models and will influence the rules of the New Game. No one can predict today what the long-term effects of COVID-19 will be.

These trends conspire to make forecasting difficult, and the future of the Hidden Champions is no exception. I have been researching them for more than 30 years. When I started, I could not have imagined the progress these companies would make in the ensuing three decades. Many of them are now 20 or 30 times larger in terms of revenue and employment. They have become truly global companies.

Are the Hidden Champions at the end of a spectacular era of growth? Or will their growth trend continue?

A forecast for another 30 years would take us to 2050 and would lack any reliable basis. So I will confine myself to a time horizon of 10–15 years in this chapter. Much remains speculative, though, even for this period.

Nonetheless, rough outlines for the future of the Hidden Champions are emerging. In contrast to the almost exclusively positive outlook at the end of my former books, the outlook in this chapter is a more differentiated and more skeptical one. There are some threatening developments for quite a few Hidden Champions in certain industry sectors. On the other hand, some of the new trends open up tremendous opportunities for those Hidden

Champions who quickly come up with innovative solutions and adapt to the rules of the New Game.

Sunset Industries

Sunset industries include "any industry that holds little promise of future development" [1]. A similar definition states "A sunset industry is an industry in decline, one that has passed its peak or boom periods" [2]. In Germany, mining, steel, and shipbuilding have long been sunset industries. More recent developments, such as electromobility and renewable energies, have extended the sunset industries to fields of German core competencies, where numerous Hidden Champions are active.

In my former surveys, only 1% of Hidden Champions feared slipping into the decline phase of their product life cycle [3]. Today, I estimate this percentage at 5–10%. What will happen to the companies and employees that are primarily involved in combustion engines and transmissions? At Mercedes, around 19,000 people are employed in the development and production of combustion engines. It is not just large companies, but also smaller firms and Hidden Champions whose jobs are in danger. The sales of companies such as Eberspächer (exhaust technology, auxiliary heating, engine management), Mann + Hummel (filters), Elring Klinger (cylinder-head gaskets), or Mahle (pistons) are to a high degree linked to the internal combustion engine. Mahle "is considered a prime example of the threat to an entire industry" [4]. Also affected are engineering firms with a focus on R&D of combustion engines, including FEV with 5,800 employees, EDAG with 8,200 employees, Austrian AVL List with 11,500 employees, and—somewhat less car-dependent—Ferchau Engineering.

While the combustion technology will not disappear abruptly, its decline seems inevitable, regardless of whether the longer-term future lies in electric or hydrogen propulsion. The crucial question is whether the affected Hidden Champions will succeed in generating growth and jobs in new applications and industries and in developing the necessary competencies and marketable innovations. The time aspect is critical. How quickly will markets change? How expensive is it? How long will it take to adapt? Emese Weissenbacher, vice chairwoman of Mann + Hummel, a Hidden Champion in filters, calls the change in the auto industry "too fast and too expensive" [5].

Many of the sunset Hidden Champions have recognized the challenges and are taking action. Stefan Wolf, CEO of ElringKlinger, the global market leader in cylinder-head gaskets, sees battery and fuel cell technology as future fields for his company. ElringKlinger has already developed products for hydrogen fuel cells. Its proton-exchange membrane fuel cell stacks have demonstrated outstanding performance and durability in both bench and field tests. The Ekpo Fuel Cell Technologies joint venture established with the French automotive supplier Plastic Omnium aims to become the global market leader with sales of up to €1 billion by 2030 [6]. ElringKlinger also established a joint venture with Airbus for a hydrogen-powered aircraft that is scheduled to fly in 2035 [7]. Mann + Hummel is also shifting its filtration expertise to filters for batteries, fuel cells, power generation, and air purification.

The impact of the automotive transformation is not limited to component suppliers. It affects the entire value chain. If fewer pistons, crankshafts, and gears are needed, then fewer machines are needed to manufacture these products. It remains to be seen whether the long-term situation will be similar in other sectors, such as the aircraft industry. It cannot be ruled out.

Realistically, one must assume that not all Hidden Champions from sunset industries will be able to manage the change and build a leading position in the new markets. One observer notes: "It's called transformation. In fact, many of Germany's automotive suppliers are in a fight for survival. Studies predict that a quarter of jobs in the industry could be eliminated by 2030" [4]. The number of Hidden Champions in sunset industries will most likely decrease in the coming years. Since quite a few Hidden Champions from German-speaking countries are active in such sectors, the share of German Hidden Champions in the total global number of Hidden Champions is also likely to decline.

Sunrise Industries

The dynamic between sunset and sunrise industries is nothing new and remains healthy as long as sunrise industries appear to replace the declining sectors as creators of jobs and wealth. "A sunrise industry is one that is new or relatively new, is growing fast, and is expected to become important" [8]. The question is to what degree firms in sunrise sectors can compensate for the losses caused by declining Hidden Champions in sunset industries. Will they be able to take over as drivers of growth and creators of jobs? Are there enough current and potential Hidden Champions in sunrise industries? As Table 28.1

Table 28.1 German unicorns

Company	Business	Market capitalization in billion € (3/4/2021)
Delivery Hero	Food delivery	21.7
Zalando	Fashion retailer	21.0
Biontech	Individualized cancer medication	19.0
Curevac	Drugs, vaccines	12.7
Celonis	Process optimization software	11.0
Hello Fresh	Food delivery	10.5
Auto 1	Online used cars	9.2
Teamviewer	Remote control systems	9.0
Scout 24	Digital market platforms	6.4
Trade Republic	Online broker	5.0
N 26	Online banking	2.9
Otto Bock Healthcare	Wearable human bionics	2.9
Rocket Internet	Digital investments	2.6
Flixbus	Long-distance bus network	1.9
NuCom Group	Various online platforms	1.8
Get your guide	Online marketplace	1.5
Motel One	Hotel	1.5
Check 24	Online price comparison	1.5
RIB Software	Construction software	1.4
Mambu	Banking Software	1.4
Personio	HR software	1.4
Xing	Career network	1.3
About You	Fashion retailer	1.0
Omio	Travel comparison	1.0

shows, Germany has a certain number of unicorns, i.e., young companies worth more than €1 billion.[1]

Some of the listed companies have achieved amazing market capitalizations. However, at just over 20, the number of German unicorns is very small compared with China with 203 unicorns and the USA with 195 [9]. In addition, many American and Chinese unicorns have much higher market caps. The world's ten most valuable unicorns have an average market capitalization of $38.7 billion. The online bank N26, the most successful fintech unicorn in Germany, ranks only 19th internationally among unlisted fintechs [10].

While the situation is not hopeless, it does not give cause for great optimism. Germany's (or Europe's) limitation lies less in a lack of innovation than in scaling-up. Hermann Hauser, founder of ARM, the quasi-monopolist in

---

[1] Values researched on October 29, 2020. Values may refer to earlier dates as some companies, e.g., Motel One or Flixbus, may have been affected by Corona.

the design of smartphone chips with a 95% share of the world market, says: "In fact, there are more software engineers in Europe than in America and also more start-ups. Our problem is scaling. We don't lack talent. We lack the money and management expertise to grow these companies quickly" [11]. Nooman Haque, a Silicon Valley venture capitalist, agrees: "Germany has always had an amazing scene to invent new technologies and therapies, but the challenge has been scaling due to a poorer venture capital scene compared to the UK or US" [12].

Europe's leading role in basic research on artificial intelligence is no secret. Professor Jürgen Schmidhuber, who invented the long short-term memory (LSTM), says: "Almost all fundamental work on artificial intelligence and deep learning comes from Europeans" [13]. There are massive deficits when it comes to rapid implementation, and there are very few major market successes. A real transformation would be for German and European startups to scale faster and more strongly in large consumer-oriented digital markets. But the chances of that happening are low as long as only a few German and European Hidden Champions emerge in this sector. Market capitalizations in the higher billion range are unlikely in Europe, above all in consumer markets of digital products with low marginal costs where scaling is the key value driver.

I am more optimistic about the prospects in industrial B2B businesses. These are niche businesses where internationalization does not involve gaining millions of customers in a short time. Many sunrise sectors are actually mature industries undergoing transformation, and in these sectors, the Hidden Champions are already entrenched. Examples include tunneling, renovation or construction of roads and infrastructure, rail systems (classic railroads, but also new technologies such as maglev or hyperloop), energy renovation and insulation of buildings, energy transmission (e.g., super-conducting lines), medical technology, new materials, and many others. Sunrise sectors also include applications in industrial sectors such as automation, robotics, additive manufacturing, and artificial intelligence. Prerequisites for future success in the industrial sunrise sectors are a deep knowledge of customer processes, innovative ideas, and agility—all skills in which the Hidden Champions have proven their excellence and will hopefully continue to do so.

One area where I see great opportunities for the Hidden Champions is sustainability. At the end-product level, the success of sustainable products is driven by government specifications and consumer behavior. The relatively strict specifications in Europe are forcing European companies into a pioneering role. Consumers will accept sustainable products if they are superior in quality and price. Sustainability, as such, is largely determined at the upstream stages of the value chain, in raw material procurement, the manufacturing process, and logistics. Further downstream in the value chain, areas such as recycling, remanufacturing, and the circular economy play a big role. Again, these are fields in which the Hidden Champions have high levels of expertise and thus excellent opportunities for the future.

Preserving Strengths

One question that comes with continuing growth, increasing size, and greater complexity is whether Hidden Champions can maintain their traditional strengths such as focus, closeness-to-customer, agility, and employee loyalty.

Ayla Busch, co-CEO of Busch vacuum pumps, muses: "With success and rapid growth, the question is how to maintain the personal connections with employees and other stakeholders. How do we preserve the positive and trusting culture? How do we align efficient structures and processes without immediately becoming an anonymous large corporation? How do we stay agile and close to the pulse of the customer and the markets? How do we stay down-to-earth and continue to strive for success? These are very difficult questions. Can a company get too big and does it make sense to grow at the expense of agility?"[2] These are the questions that every Hidden Champion and every mid-sized company must ask themselves as they continue to grow. The answers are far from simple, but there is a variety of practical guidelines and New Game rules.

Specialization

There are two key success factors for the future of the Hidden champions. The first is the continued growth of the markets in which they operate. The second success factor is their competitiveness in these markets. I see the high degree of specialization and the depth of expertise as the root of their competitiveness. This extremely specific and deep knowledge makes it difficult for new competitors to enter and succeed in the Hidden Champions' markets. The crucial question is whether they can maintain the lead over the competition in the long term. This depends on R&D investments and on technological saturation. If a technology reaches a saturation point, R&D effectiveness declines, and the competition has a chance to catch up. This can be a danger when a performance increase is overcompensated by a competitor's price

---

[2] Personal communication, November 29, 2020.

advantage. If it is not possible to maintain the old performance gap, lower-cost production must be achieved through relocation or automation. In principle, both options are feasible for the Hidden Champions due to their global presence and technical competencies.

Choice of Location

The choice of location is decisive for the future of the Hidden Champions. Political frameworks play a major role here. In general, every activity should be carried out at the location in the world where the best conditions exist for this activity. This can imply a fundamental transformation, because it means that a company may have to break away from its regional or national roots. This need not induce a conflict. Many Hidden Champions are already both home-grown and global. They demonstrate that these two orientations do not have to be mutually exclusive and can in fact be compatible. The weight of the "global" portion will continue to increase and include more parts of the value chain. In case of an increased "decoupling" of the three large economic zones (USA, China, and the EU), localization could even mean having three headquarters that are not intertwined under company law, as Wilo and Simon-Kucher already practice.

The future of the Hidden Champions will be determined in the first global league: the USA, China, and the EU. China deserves utmost attention, both as a target market and as a source of new competitors. This does not mean that the rest of Asia, Africa, or Latin America is irrelevant, but these regions will not determine who is and remains the global market leader. It goes without saying that a Hidden Champion's leadership in its home market is a necessary condition. From a European perspective, strong market positions in the USA and China are indispensable for market leadership. American and Chinese Hidden Champions must be strong in the other markets of the first global league.

By 2030, those Hidden Champions who assert themselves in all of these markets will be successful. This will depend less on exports than on higher direct investment. So it is obvious where foreign direct investment will have to flow in the next decade. I expect and suggest that the regional distribution of value-added should replace the regional distribution of sales as a measure of internationalization. The transformation of locational structures need not have negative consequences for Germany and Europe. On the one hand, direct investment and thus jobs will move from Germany and Europe to other continents. On the other hand, direct investment and jobs are flowing from the other continents to Europe. Today, American companies employ 4.9 million people in Europe, a third more than in 2000 [14]. China is only just beginning this process. According to the China International Investment Promotion Agency (CIIPA), 7300 new jobs have been created in Germany through Chinese greenfield investments in the last two years.[3] This figure will rise significantly in the coming years. This is one dimension of the coming Chinese century.

Capital

Capital and capital markets are becoming increasingly important for the future of the Hidden Champions. Until recently, the Hidden Champions have been mostly family-owned companies that financed their expansion primarily from their own cash flow. This is a sensible alternative in markets that are gradually and continuously growing. But this "slow" financing acts as a brake on growth and scaling in very fast-growing businesses, where it is mandatory to occupy the leading market position early on in the life cycle.

Chinese Hidden Champions go public much earlier and raise substantial capital, which they invest in growth and innovation. Likewise in the USA, the amount of capital that can be raised for startups and scale-ups through venture capital or IPOs is far greater than in Europe. This is why many European companies prefer a listing in New York. Unless Europe can overcome the capital bottlenecks, many startups will not become Hidden Champions despite their excellent technical competencies. Skepticism is warranted as to whether the European capital markets will catch up and whether many owners of Hidden Champions correctly assess the future importance of the capital market. I am afraid that quite a few either do not comprehend the rules of the capital markets in the New Game or will need too much time to understand them.

Global Citizens

Globalization will change, but it will not stop. The ambition to remain a global market leader is accompanied by the need to become a global citizen. All the New Game rules point into this direction. The shift from exports to

---

[3] Includes investments into factories, R&D centers, sales offices, and service points. E-Mail by China International Investment Promotion Agency, Frankfurt, October 22, 2020.

direct investment means that more workers will be employed outside the home market. The Hidden Champion of the future will not be led by a large number of expatriates deployed to a foreign country, but by top executives from different countries who work together smoothly on the basis of a shared corporate culture.

Digitalization enables and standardizes communication across spatial, national, and cultural boundaries. Sustainability involves overcoming national or racial inequalities and, in terms of climate, can only be achieved globally anyway. In the long run, the leaders of the Hidden Champions and their teams must become global citizens. The ambition to be the best in one's market requires attracting and retaining top talent from around the world. Every top-league club in soccer, basketball, or hockey takes this maxim to heart. Why should that not apply to top companies?

We discussed the strengths and weaknesses of Hidden Champions in terms of recruiting. The recommendation to focus regionally can be applied to foreign locations as well. A focus on regions or selected educational institutions seems advisable. I am not worried about the future of companies that succeed in meeting these requirements. Germany and Europe are becoming more attractive in the global competition for talent. I hope the Hidden Champions are wise enough to continue to pursue prudent policies that enhance their attractiveness.

Money or Fame

Money or fame is a sensitive choice that comes up when succession in a family-owned company cannot be settled internally. The main alternatives are selling the company, launching an IPO, or setting up a foundation. The company can be sold to a strategic investor who holds the shares in perpetuity, or to a private equity company who sells the shares after a few years or takes the company public. Selling is often the quickest option that brings in the most money, but it also means that the company may be headed for an uncertain future in which it passes through several hands and risks losing its independence and identity. In a way, the founder or the following generation will sacrifice their Hidden Champion on the altar of money. I am not mentioning any names, but the following story may explain why I find it deeply regrettable whenever that happens. An inventor and founder had worked his way up from an early age to become the European market leader, employing more than 1,000 people in six factories in Europe, the USA, Brazil, and China. In his autobiography, this entrepreneur writes about the very lucrative sale: "The highest bidder, a northern European group, won the bid. Synergy effects and access to a significant market share were the decisive factors for me: the chance to open up new markets and having sufficient capital available for further growth and innovations! This win-win situation was very reassuring for me, as I now saw my life's work in safe hands." A few years later, the acquirer itself was taken over and the former Hidden Champion was passed on to a Central European group that shut down the original factory six years later. All that remained of the former Hidden Champion's identity was a brand.

Twenty years later, the founder wrote to me that selling his company was the biggest mistake of his life. In his autobiography he says: "Professor Hermann Simon, who counted me among the German Hidden Champions in his book, didn't understand my decision at the time." I did indeed not understand how he could part with his life's work. When I read of the renaming of Grohmann Engineering to Tesla Automation, I tried to put myself in the founder's shoes and replicate his possible emotions. For me, the top priority has always been to keep Simon-Kucher & Partners as an independent company. I would like to encourage Hidden Champion owners to preserve the independence and fame of their "child" in the long term instead of pocketing the quick money.

The New Game

The picture of the future of the Hidden Champions that I have drawn in this chapter is more mixed and skeptical than in my earlier publications. The reason for this is not the COVID-19 pandemic. Instead, there are several long-term determinants which are creating the New Game.

Not all Hidden Champions in sunset industries will manage the required transformations. Quite a few will lose their market leadership status or even go under completely. Moreover, in Germany and Europe there are not as many candidates in sunrise sectors likely to take their place and rise to global market leadership. This is not primarily due to a lack of innovations or start-ups, but rather due to a pronounced weakness in scaling-up. This weakness results from bottlenecks in capital procurement, the fragmentation of European markets, and entrepreneurial deficits. Established Hidden Champions, whose businesses are developing into sunrise markets, have good chances to defend their leading positions and to continue their growth. To achieve this, they must remain highly innovative and play by the rules of the New Game described in this book.

High levels of specialization and deep know-how form effective barriers to entry against new competitors. However, the performance gap must be maintained. If this is impossible, the Hidden Champions must relocate to more cost-effective locations or use cost-cutting automation. The choice of location must be free from traditional preferences and favor sites where the activity in question can best be carried out. The capital market is becoming increasingly important, especially for very R&D-intensive and rapidly growing businesses. Family businesses should consider giving up their skepticism with regard to going public. The new type of globalization demands and encourages that the leaders and their teams become global citizens.

References

1. Retrieved from https://www.collinsdictionary.com/de/worterbuch/englisch/sunset-industry.
2. Retrieved from https://en.wikipedia.org/wiki/Sunset_industry.
3. Simon, H. (2012). *Hidden Champions—Aufbruch nach Globalia* (p. 256). Frankfurt: Campus.
4. Hucko, M. (2020). Kolbenfresser. *Manager-Magazin*, pp. 78–82.
5. Appel, H. (2020, October 20). Und jetzt ausgeliefert? *Frankfurter Allgemeine Zeitung*, p. T1.
6. N.A. (2020, October 30). Deutsch-französische Wasserstoff-Kooperation. *Frankfurter Allgemeine Zeitung*, p. 25.
7. Retrieved from https://boerse.ard.de/aktien/brennstoffzelle-airbus-elringklinger-kooperieren100.html.
8. Retrieved from https://en.wikipedia.org/wiki/Sunrise_industry.
9. Retrieved from https://www.crunchbase.com/hub/united-states-unicorn-startups, https://www.statista.com/statistics/897674/china-unicorn-company-distribution-by-sector/.
10. Retrieved November 6, 2020, from https://www.cbinsights.com/research/fintech-unicorns-q1-20/#:~:text=The%20top%2Dfunded%20fintech%20unicorns,%2Dbased%20Ripple%20(%2410B).
11. N.A. (2020, October 26). Die Übernahme wird scheitern. Interview with Hermann Hauser, *Frankfurter Allgemeine Zeitung*, p. 21.
12. Retrieved from https://scrip.pharmaintelligence.informa.com/SC143289/COVID-19-Vaccine-Results-A-Breakthrough-Moment-For-BioNTech.
13. N.A. (2018, Oktober 4). Interview with Jürgen Schmidhuber, Auf die Zukunft, Magazin zum Innovationstag. *Frankfurter Allgemeine Zeitung*–Beilage, pp. 12–14.
14. Hamilton, D. S., & Quinland, J. P. (2020). *The Transatlantic Economy 2020, Annual Survey of Jobs, Trade and Investment between the United States and Europe* (p. 17). Johns Hopkins University, Paul H. Nitze School for Advanced International Studies.

Printed by Printforce, the Netherlands